# A TIME TO Remember

BETTÉ PRATT

Copyright © 2020 by Betté Pratt.

ISBN    Softcover    978-1-953537-12-6

All Scripture Quoted is taken from the New International Version of the Bible.

All rights reserved. No part of this book may be reproduced or transmitted in any form or by any means, electronic or mechanical, including photocopying, recording, or by any information storage and retrieval system without express written permission from the author, except in the case of brief quotations embodied in critical reviews and certain other non-commercial uses permitted by copyright law.

Printed in the United States of America.

To order additional copies of this book, contact:
**Bookwhip**
1-855-339-3589
https://www.bookwhip.com

# One

The big event in Vansville for January was history. Natt Thomas and Marcy Barnard were married on the last Saturday of the month. As was expected, Marcy's mom tried to disrupt the celebration by whispering, even in the dressing room, that she could cancel the happening and come home. It had happened just that way when Sandy had married Ramon. Of course, Charlie knew his wife and collected her at the door of the dressing room moments later and escorted her away from the lovely bride. However, that didn't keep Marcy from shedding a few tears. Her mom wasn't ready to give up her possessive ways. She wondered if she'd done the same thing when her brother Ed had married Margaret a few months back. Probably not, there was nothing physically wrong with Ed, he didn't have a permanent disability like Sandy did or have a crippling illness as Marcy had contracted.

By now, Marcy had made several friends in Vansville, so while Sandy played for her sister, Nancy and Margaret, Marcy's sister-in-law from Philadelphia were her attendants. Marcy had asked Sandy to be her Maid of Honor, but Sandy elected to support her sister by playing the most wonderful music and also singing several of Marcy and Natt's favorites. Natt asked Ramon to be his Best Man, but his little brother also stood up with him. Except for the bride's mother, it was a lovely wedding. No tears were shed, everyone was happy for the couple.

Ever since Christmas, the couple had been on pins and needles about the weather. They'd had snow on Christmas Day that made for a beautiful setting for the lights in every window and on many small trees and shrubs, but all of January the weather was like a roller coaster, vacillating between snow and ice and fifty degree weather. However, on the last Saturday, for once the weather cooperated. It had been a beautiful day, actually quite pleasant and the town had packed the little church for the happy event. Pastor Roger had fulfilled Marcy's desire to have a service that glorified her Lord.

Because Marcy knew, since she'd suffered with Rheumatic Fever while still in nursing school that she could never be a foreign missionary, as she'd dreamed of being, Natt's family and hers had gone together and sent them to several exotic places abroad, one of them being the wonderful country of India. India was a country she'd had on her list that she'd hoped God would send her for that foreign missionary service. However, God had other plans.

Natt and Marcy had a wonderful time, but Marcy couldn't help but look behind the glitter and expense to see the hungry people, not only for physical food, which was very evident in the many tiny, starving children who were everywhere, but longing to know the real food and water, the Word Who became flesh and Who was also the Living Water. That's what Marcy saw so many times she ached for the people. However, Natt wasn't about to let his bride spoil their time together. Especially when he was very sure they would never come this way again. It had also been a dream of his to spend time overseas as a foreign correspondent, but that had also died a sad death when he'd had to take over running the Thomas Complex for his granddad.

He was glad they had this chance to get away and that, even though Marcy still had some weakness from her illness, which was most evident after a long day of sightseeing, they could go abroad. Still, he reminded her often that they were here to enjoy their honeymoon, she needed to lighten up! For his sake, she had done her best and had really enjoyed herself. She also knew that as things stood, they would never walk this way again.

Only a few weeks before the wedding, the county sent in a road crew and extended a street a block south and parallel to the highway through town. While the crew built the street, a second house was under construction on that extension. Several times the road crew and the construction crew locked horns, but the name 'Thomas' was a highly respected name in the county and the house continued to be built, but the road crew continued to build the street. Brad and Nathan were determined that both would be finished by the time the newlyweds returned from their honeymoon. They were.

They came back to cold and ice. In fact, it was an 'iffy' time as they approached the Atlanta airport. Natives didn't like winter weather much. Until they were in the landing pattern they weren't sure if they could land because of the freezing rain that was falling as they approached. They had scheduled their return for the last day of their honeymoon. They were both scheduled to work the very next day. Marcy didn't know how Natt liked the freezing rain and ice, but they were nothing new to a native of Philadelphia.

Natt took his wife's arm with one hand and pulled the cart with their luggage with the other through the tunnel to the parking garage, settled his wife in the car, then loaded the trunk. He looked out the huge openings of the garage to the big expanse of sparkling asphalt below and also saw the crystals of freezing rain in the air and pulled in a sigh. It was a long way to Vansville. It didn't matter, he'd take it slow and easy, they'd make it.

Natt settled behind the wheel, grinned at his wife and said, "Ready?"

She blew out a breath and said, "I guess. India was so warm…." Still, she wasn't crazy about the donut her new husband did in the Atlanta airport parking lot. As she sucked in air, Natt grinned, he loved to tease his wife. Most of the time she was way too serious.

He shrugged, after the car came to a standstill some distance away from the other cars. "It's warmer here than in Philadelphia."

Marcy nodded. "Mmm, thanks, I needed that."

Chuckling, he whispered, "Always glad to help, Love."

Natt's second cousin, Matt, was to return to his home in Orlando that very afternoon, but it didn't look like he'd get out of Vansville because of the very slick roads. Because he would only be in town for the month, Matt's plans were to stay at Brad and Joyce's house. However, since he'd arrived, he spent many of his off hours with his brother in his cabin. The twins had much more in common than Matt and his older aunt and uncle. Aunt Joyce was so different from Uncle Brad! She talked all the time! Trying to think about all the days in February he'd been in the house with his Aunt Joyce, Matt couldn't remember two minutes strung together when she'd not been talking! Well, maybe between ten and six – in the dark.

The last Sunday of February was no different. To get away from his aunt's constant chatter he'd come over to Eric's cabin for the afternoon. Eric was reviewing his Email and doing a few things on the web, but Matt was restless. Around four o'clock, which was when the newlyweds should have called him, Matt was pacing in the small cabin from one window to another, wishing he was already back in Orlando away from the winter weather. However, life was like that in the foothills of the Appalachians

When Matt had come up for Natt's wedding, prepared to stay to run the store while Natt was gone, he was amazed at the difference in his uncle Brad. Just in the few months, from July until January, the man had lost a lot of ground physically. The family and others in town knew that Brad had had several mini-strokes, but both Brad and Joyce wouldn't accept that fact. Joyce especially, wanted to ignore the obvious signs. Brad, of course, couldn't ignore the changes in his own body nearly as well as Joyce could. However, he wanted to stay in the store as long as he could. He wouldn't admit it out loud, but he probably wanted to stay clear of Joyce.

Both Natt and Matt knew that Brad's time in the store would soon be over, he just couldn't handle eight hours each day. Without telling either Brad or Joyce, Matt had promised Natt to come back permanently when that time came. He had no ties to Orlando, other than it was Florida and usually had decent weather even in the winter. Neither of them wanted to put Brad out of the store, it had been his life for too many years. However, Matt knew that the unhurried pace of Vansville was much better than the constant hype of working in a city geared to entertaining millions of people. He would not miss that part of the job when he left.

Matt's twin brother, Eric lived in Vansville. When the two of them came last July for a visit, Eric had just mustered out of the Marines. He'd been in Afghanistan for two tours and was very glad for the quiet life in Vansville. He had immediately decided that being a hiking guide for DeLord's Hiking Service would be his cup of tea for the foreseeable future. Because of that, he'd immediately rented one of Isabel Isaacson's cabins for the duration. On this dismal Sunday afternoon, he watched his brother pace from his kitchen window to his living room window, as if he could make the temperature rise, the freezing rain stop and the ice melt just by pacing.

Finally, Eric looked up from his laptop screen, shook his head and said, "Brother, will you give it a rest! You've been pacing that carpet for hours! You'll wear a path in my carpet, so Isabel will have to replace the whole thing. Believe it or not, sometime soon, we'll hear from the newlyweds, they'll be back on home soil and you'll be on your way. Mark my word!"

Matt stood still looking out the living room window and sighed, "Have you looked out the window lately, Bro? It's like a skating rink out there! I can't leave until the roads are passable. Who knows when the road crews can get out here to this little place!"

"Oh, they'll make it sometime. You know that's Main Street out there and it's the state highway, they'll have to get some sand and salt on it, eventually."

"Yeah, I know that, but I was supposed to be back in Orlando tomorrow morning and my little car doesn't like icy roads."

Eric shrugged and looked out at his much bigger, safer, four wheeled drive SUV and grinned at his brother. "You sure it's just the car that doesn't like icy roads or could it be you? By the way, you know they won't fire you."

"Thanks, I needed that."

Eric's grin broadened. "Oh, you're welcome, I'm sure!"

Finally, Matt's cell phone rang, it was Natt. They were on the ground in Atlanta and were now on the way to Vansville. Matt could leave any time he wanted. He made another pass by the front window to look at Isabel's parking lot and beyond that to the street. He shook his head Monday morning would be soon enough to tackle the long drive back to Orlando. After all; Vansville, was in the foothills of the Appalachian Mountains and the even closer problem, the road crew still hadn't shown up. Life was like that in a lazy little town. **Vansville** was probably at the end of the county alphabet.

Another month started, March was that changeable month with wind, rain, cold days and frosty nights. However, mid-month, in fact to was on little Jon's birthday, the hiking season started again. There were always a few hardy souls who liked the *early* spring time of year to hike. Hiking in the foothills of the Appalachians was big business in Vansville.

DeLord's Hiking Service started off the season with four guides. Ramon, the veteran and the one who had started the service, only took the shorter hikes and never on Sundays. Even starting in March, the three fulltime guides had only one day off between his hikes, they were that busy. The office phone rang off the hook nearly every day wanting to schedule a hike. Several times as the season moved on Ramon reminisced about how the business had grown in just a few years. Of course he gave all the credit to his lovely wife, Sandy.

Finally, near the end of April the sun decided that spring would make a tentative appearance in Vansville. The rain clouds disappeared, days warmed up a little, trees started leafing out and flowers began blooming in people's yards and window boxes. The hills and mountains around the town burst with color. In some places whole hillsides were covered with Mountain Laurel. Life took on the usual pace for a small town in north Georgia. People took a deep breath of the warmer air and dragged their outdoor furniture out of storage and arranged it on their front porches. One of these days soon they could spend a leisurely evening sitting on their porches, chatting back and forth to neighbors and watching the few cars go by.

For the third week in April, Eric had a teen group from a church in Macon. There were five teens and two youth leaders. The teens were a lively bunch, as most teens are and the leaders were quite young. At first Eric thought the man and woman were a couple, but the young woman soon let him know that she was more interested in him than in the man she knew so well from working with him in the youth program at their church for several years. Eric couldn't understand this, since he was more than five years older than she was. She was pretty enough, but he certainly had no interest in her.

Eric found himself separated from the group several times during the five day hike because Marilyn followed him into the woods or decided that collecting branches when he did was the job she assigned herself instead of working with the two girls from the group who wanted and needed her help. In fact, Jason had called her several times to work with the girls. Reluctantly she'd left Eric and wandered back to wherever the girls were. Even then, she really hadn't helped the girls very much. He'd noticed the girls' attitude and was pleased that they didn't seem to resent the fact that she didn't help them. Perhaps they'd had to learn to do without her help more than just on this hike.

Eric tried for several days to ignore her, but finally Thursday morning, as he stirred up the fire, he couldn't move because she was so close. Still with the stick in his hand, but unable to reach the warmest coals in the pile of ashes, he looked up at the woman holding the metal angle Eric carried with his things that held the large pot to warm water. She was so close her hand with the angle was blocking his view of the coals. Finally, he took a deep breath, moved his rear back onto his heels and looked at her.

Holding the stick only inches from Marilyn's hand, he said, "Marilyn, would you *please* back off so I can at least see the fire! I can't even tell if there's a spark there that I can stir into life or if I must start from scratch, you're so close."

Marilyn also sat back on her heals, of course, that took her arm and the angle out of the way and said, "Oh, I'm sorry, I was just waiting to stick this in the ground when you had the fire going. That water from the pond is so cold and I know how much Jason loves his coffee."

"Yes, I know he does, but there will be no fire at all unless I can see what I'm doing."

"I'm sorry," she whispered.

Jason was helping the boys take down the tents. He looked over his shoulder and saw the problem, so he called, "Marilyn, have you filled the pot with water yet? You know it needs to be filtered before it's put on to heat. I sent Jeremy into the woods to get more wood for Eric, since there isn't too much."

Marilyn cleared her throat. "Um, I sent Nancy to get more water."

"Marilyn," Jason chided, after looking around for both Nancy and Karen. He shook his head and said, "She's still at the pool brushing her teeth. The big pan still sits there beside you, so Nancy isn't getting the water for it. You know you got up when I did and that was before Eric called everyone to get up, so you're all ready for the day and she isn't. Let the poor man stir his fire without you hanging over him!"

Obediently, she murmured, "Yes, Jason."

"Thanks," he said and turned back to the tent work.

Marilyn sighed and finally laid the angle down, picked up the empty pot and headed for the other side of the pool, away from the girls brushing their teeth and washing their faces. "I'm after it, Jason. I didn't realize they weren't ready yet."

As Marilyn left and walked toward the pool, Eric let out a breath and murmured loud enough Jason could hear him, "Thanks, man, much appreciated."

Jason grinned at the other young man. "Hey, I've been rescuing men our age from my sister for a very long time. Ever since she went into junior high she's been like this. I'm hoping one of these days she'll find the right man who'll just eat up all that attention she's so happy to lavish on men so I can stop."

Eric straightened up picked up a large branch Jeremy had brought and said, "Ah, I get the connection now. Much obliged."

"Oh, you're welcome!"

It was finally late Friday afternoon and Eric was extremely glad to see DeLord's parking lot. Marilyn hadn't really left him alone even after Jason had made her back off several times. His group was the only one scheduled to return that day and he had brought his group of hikers back to base an hour or so ago. He'd stood on the parking lot of DeLord's house and waved to all seven as they boarded their church van to head back to Macon. The name of their church was prominently displayed on the side of the van. He was extremely glad that he did not belong or live anywhere close to that church. Eric couldn't believe that he was the first, last and only man Marilyn had treated as she had him.

The kids had told him that tomorrow morning they planned to clean out the van, then in the afternoon the teens would spread out in one of the less privileged areas of their city to visit. On Sunday they'd go pick those people up for Sunday school and church who promised to be ready. He was impressed, truly. Even so, he was glad to slouch into his car. It felt like the first time all week he'd been able to take a full breath and not have to breathe in the same air that Marilyn breathed. What man in his right mind would enjoy that? Marilyn was a pretty young woman, but the way she handled herself gave Eric the willies.

He was so glad to be by himself he decided to drive the few blocks to his home and wait until tomorrow to get his next assignment. His cabin wasn't so far from DeLord's that he couldn't walk over or even drive. He was pretty sure his next hike started on Sunday, from the beginning of the hiking season he'd only had one day off between hikes. He was glad to stay busy, he didn't brood too much that way. Since he'd mustered out of the Marines only a few months ago, he found it was easy to brood about some unpleasant things he'd witnessed overseas. Fortunately, he didn't have PTSD because of the atrocities he'd seen over there, but he did have an occasional nightmare. His commanding officer had assured him that what he had was normal and eventually things would subside.

With a sigh he turned the key in the lock of his cabin that he rented from Isabel Isaacson and took a deep breath. It was good to be home and the quiet was overwhelming and perfect. Five teens on a week long hike and a female youth leader who seemed to want to throw herself at him could frazzle a bachelor's nerves big time, even if they were Christians. Eric wondered if her church didn't have any young men who could take up her time. But then he decided, she saw them all the time they weren't much of a challenge. He was glad her brother had been along, the woman felt like a leech!

The cabin smelled clean, Isabel took care of him so well, perhaps it was Ruth who cleaned the cabins now, but Isabel was still so capable. They kept a calendar of his hiking schedule so they knew when he'd be home and when not. In the early spring and late fall, he turned down the thermostat when he left, but they had it back up when he came home, so right now, the furnace was blowing warm air into the room. In the summer it was the air conditioning. Sighing with pleasure again, he stepped into the comfortable cabin. He was home! Home was where the heart was and his was definitely in this cabin. Tonight he could sleep in his own bed, not on the unforgiving hard ground.

He headed straight for his bathroom, still clutching his huge backpack. Actually, it was only one strap he held. Now that he had it off his back, he was dragging it to the bathroom. Thank goodness for the washer and dryer Isabel had in his cabin, he could come straight home to do laundry and not have to make that stop at Thomas's Laundromat! Sitting in a Laundromat seemed like such a waste of time! It was never busy, he never had to wait for a machine, but he'd rather be home in his cabin. Looking over the clothes briefly and seeing none with outstanding colors, he threw the whole mess into the washer then stripped out of the sweaty clothes he had on and threw them in, too. Anything in his hamper also found its place in the washer. He started it then stepped into the shower to get all the grime of the trail off his body. It felt super to stand in the warm water and let it sluice over his body. He also shampooed his hair, not that there was much of it. His time in the Marines had given him the hair style.

He dressed in clean clothes and headed for the kitchen to heat up one of Alex's frozen dinners. He was no cook, his mom never taught him. She was of the old school, the man supported his family probably worked his knuckles to the bone, while his wife stayed home to cook, clean and take care of the children. He'd never gotten a satisfactory answer from her when he'd asked her what a bachelor did about meals, so most of the time he either made a sandwich or pulled a frozen dinner from his full freezer. Thank goodness for microwaves! They gave the cooking heat for the non-cook that he was.

He detested coffee, so Alex also kept him covered with the special brand of iced tea he preferred. Soon after he'd moved into the cabin, he'd complained to Alex and the man had introduced him to the brand of tea he carried. It came in jugs, Eric now bought it by the gallon so as he waited for the microwave to ding, he pulled the jug from the fridge. He drank water on the trail, so it was good to have his beverage of choice when he reached home. After swallowing a long guzzle; he set the jug on the table and stood in front of the microwave waiting for the ding. His supper, such as it was, would be piping hot and ready to eat. It wasn't a home-cooked meal but it was a fair sight better than the MREs he'd had to eat abroad!

He took the paper tray to the table, found a fork and slid onto the kitchen chair. The comfort of the straight-backed, wooden chair reminded him he wanted to get a camp chair similar to Ramon's that he could take on his hikes. Always sitting on the ground left a lot to be desired. He couldn't be on his feet instantly when he was on the ground. He'd sustained a slight injury in Afghanistan, so he needed a minute to rise to his feet.

He bowed his head and said a blessing over the meal. The aroma was actually tempting. After eating the not-too-taste-worthy meal, he washed it all down with a long guzzle from his gallon jug of tea, threw away the microwaveable tray, rinsed the fork then slid his heavy sweatshirt on and took the jug with his Bible out to his porch. He set the gallon jug and his Bible on the little wicker table, then sat down in the wicker chair beside it to look at the beautiful scene out beyond the houses close by. He decided that this part of Georgia was his cup of tea he'd like to make his permanent home here. Not necessarily in this cabin, however.

He was the only long term renter that Isabel had now. Until Natt's wedding, that young man had been his neighbor. Over the months since he'd come, he and Natt had become much more than cousins. After the hike they'd both gone on, when Natt had become a believer, they'd had many Bible studies together and many times they'd shared problems. After Natt had noticed Marcy and started dating her, their talks had changed. Eric hadn't felt like much of an expert, he'd never had a serious relationship with a woman, but he had been glad to be a sounding board for the younger man. Marcy was an intense young woman and Natt was much more laid back. Those attributes made for a lively romance!

As he sat on the porch, he noticed lights in the cabin next door. There was also another car in the parking lot next to his spot. Probably it was someone staying for the night or the weekend. He didn't care who was there over the short term, he wouldn't go introduce himself. He was only in town on his occasional days off anyway, just because today was Friday didn't mean he needed to be friendly. He wondered briefly when his twin would be coming to town again, but he wouldn't worry. He knew he and Natt had an agreement about the store. Brad's time in the store was nearing its end many in town could see that. He'd had a few mini-strokes since his first major stroke over two years ago. Everyone but Joyce could see the inevitable. Brad not only dozed through the day, but he took an hour nap at home after his lunch.

Vansville was growing. It had been the same for so many years until the clinic went in a year and a half ago. Late last fall the county had sent out a road crew and extended the street behind Isabel's cabins. Isabel knew progress was good, but she surely didn't like the noise the big earth-movers made. Now there were two houses on that extension, Duncan Roads had built the first house, even before the street went in making his gravel driveway very long, but ending at the end of the existing street. When the road crew decided to extend the street, they used Duncan's driveway as their foundation, but had extended the street another three hundred feet passed his house. At the time, that didn't please Duncan either.

Natt's dad and granddad had the second house built for Natt and his new bride. Eric's porch faced that street, but it was a good ways away, probably a good half mile beyond his place. The blocks in Vansville were quite long, everyone had a big backyard. He could easily see the street, because the extension cut into the huge meadow that bordered the town on the east side. The new houses were on the north side of the extension, facing him.

Eric picked up the jug and guzzled a long swallow, then replaced the jug on the table and picked up his Bible that lay next to it. He had his devotions on the trail, but there was nothing like sitting in the quiet of his own home with his Bible where he could read as long as he wanted to then end his time in prayer. He had really learned the true value and power of prayer on the battlefield, not only himself, but those at home whom he knew prayed for him often. He had been in some very tight places several times and he knew he'd been spared because of prayer. He was also very sure he didn't suffer from PTSD like many of his fellow Marines because of the prayers sent to God's throne constantly for him. He had an occasional nightmare or flashback, but nothing like some of his team had. That was something he thanked God for nearly every day because he knew how debilitating those attacks could be.

Some time later, Eric put down his Bible. The light was fading, it would be dusk soon and he hadn't turned on the porch light. He sat with the jug of tea in his hands, but not really drinking, just staring off across the meadow. Both houses on the new street were dark. Duncan was gone leading his own group of hikers and Friday evening was Natt's late night at the store. It was anyone's guess where their wives were, probably at DeLord's house, or maybe those ladies were off seeing some sight. Who would know? Actually, he wasn't really seeing the houses, or even the beautiful hills and mountains behind them or even watching the beautiful sunset that was putting on a display behind those hills and mountains.

Eric's time as a Marine in Afghanistan hung heavily on him in quiet times like this. He'd helped open up a hot spot, but was glad to be stateside finally. Even so, the memories were enough to crowd out the tranquil surroundings of Vansville. He often thought about his good buddy who'd been too close to one of those street bombs and lost his life. That brought to mind the innocent children in that war-torn land. Tom had tried to befriend a tiny child he'd found wandering the street. Many of the children, barely out of toddler age, were forced to become human instruments of war. They were sent to mingle with the American service men, who, because of their American up-bringing, felt the heart-break of these tiny tots were loving and friendly, then by remote control, they would explode. It made him shudder. He'd seen it happen too many times. In fact only seeing it happen one time to his buddy was one too many.

He was glad he didn't have nightmares as some of his team and other service men had, but he also attributed that to prayer. He was very thankful his buddy was a born-again Christian and he would see the young man in heaven some day. He sent a silent prayer for those men and women who were still over there, fighting that abominable war. Remembering some of the atrocities he'd witnessed, it wasn't any wonder those men and women suffered from PTSD, especially those who didn't know the Lord or have prayer support back home.

He raised his eyes then to the sunset and breathed in the fresh, clean air of the little town. The sky was putting on a spectacular display, the clouds were golden some had pink or orange edges. As the sky darkened he saw a golden tail that a high flying plane was leaving as it streaked across the darkening sky. The plane was long past before he heard it. He drank in the magnificent sight. He was at home, in this peaceful land. Vansville was his cup of tea it was helping him heal from the nightmare of war. God was good, all the time.

As Eric sat, looking across the meadow, he became aware of a car driving slowly on the new street. It was rare a different car than what Duncan, Nancy, Marcy or Natt drove on that street. It didn't go anywhere except in front of their houses. By now, it was dark enough that a vehicle should have its lights on, but that car didn't, it was just a dark form moving slowly passed dark houses. The car made slow progress passed the two houses, as if he was looking for someone to be at home, but then much to Eric's surprise, the car kept going, even beyond where the street ended. Eric scowled as the car drove on, thumping over the curb then bouncing across the meadow and finally stopped in the tall grass only a few feet from the small stand of trees. Eric had a strange thought, - it was good it hadn't rained recently, the car would be mired.

Nothing happened, no doors opened, no lights came on, but then the car started moving again, this time it started backing, making a big arc. As Eric continued to watch, the car nearly disappeared into the trees on the far side of the meadow.

By now, it was nearly dark, but what little light was still in the west glinted off the chrome on the front of the car. Eric absently placed his jug on the table, but never took his eyes off the car, watching as the dome light came on. He couldn't see the door or hear it, but it had to be that the driver's door opened then the light went out. He never saw a person the car was too far back into the trees. Only a few minutes later the dome light came on again for a few seconds, then went out again. Seconds later, the car shot out of the trees and nearly before Eric could take another breath the car careened onto the paved street and roared out of sight. Once the car reached the old street, Eric lost sight of it, because there were houses on both sides of the well established part of the street.

Eric sat, puzzled for a few seconds, until the sound of the car faded. Then a thought hit him and he scrambled from the chair, yanked open his front door and tore into his backpack, retrieved his high-power flashlight and his cell phone in seconds and was back out the door. All fatigue he'd felt from coming home from his hike vanished. He never thought to take his car, but set out overland toward those trees. He shivered, wondering what he'd find when he reached the trees. It was dark now, so he had to be careful, but the security light from Isabel's parking lot showed him the way for some time.

When he reached the new street, there was one streetlight that showed the way a little farther beyond the houses. At the end of the paved street, Eric could make out the tire tracks that had flattened out the grass, so he turned on his flashlight and followed them across the meadow. He wondered what he'd find when he reached the trees. The car had been back into the trees far enough he hadn't been able to see the driver or what he did when he got out of the car. The trees and the underbrush were thick enough he hadn't been able to see if a trunk light came on, all he knew was that the car had a trunk, it was not a car with a hatch or a pickup truck. Just after the dome light went out the first time a car went by on the highway, covering any noise – either shutting a door or closing a trunk lid.

Eric moved silently. He didn't want to spook anything or alert anything or anyone that he was coming. In fact, he was so quiet and everything else was too, that the tree toads began screeching and off the other way by the creek that ran through the back part of the meadow, he could hear two bullfrogs croaking out their night sounds. Peaceful sounds, sounds that Vansville was known for. In fact, it would soon be eight o'clock. When the two stores closed, everyone also closed their doors for the night. Maybe the occupants of those houses watched TV for a while, but the doors stayed shut. That's what Vansville did.

He kept his flashlight close, just showing his next step or two until the tire tracks reached the trees. There was no other sound but the woodland birds twittering goodnight and the frogs. As soon as he reached the trees, however, he raised the flashlight and flashed it ahead of him. The car hadn't been very far back in the trees, even the back end.

What he saw made his heart climb into his throat and his stomach turn over he had to swallow hard to keep the last few mouthfuls of tea from coming out fast. In fact, he gulped audibly, trying to keep his stomach settled. It was a sight he was sure he'd remember for a very long time. A young woman lay at the base of a tree. The only cloth she had on was the bound edge of her top around her neck and a few rags attached to it. Her hair was matted and in such disarray that several clumps covered part of her face. As he approached, he realized it was blood from a deep gash on the left side of her head that had matted her hair. The gash had bled enough that some of it had run onto her face. Again he sealed his lips the acid-tasting tea was in the back of his mouth, all too ready to come out. The woman looked worse than some of the terrible atrocities he'd seen overseas!

"Dear God in heaven!" he whispered. "Who could have done this horrible thing?"

As he stood over her he realized that her left arm was obviously broken, the bone of her upper arm had punctured her skin and the wound had bled and run down her arm, but her wrists were bound with duct tape in front of her and another piece of tape covered her mouth! When he arrived beside her he was able to see the terrible bruising and scratches all over her body. It seemed even as he watched that parts of her were still swelling, her face was unrecognizable! It didn't seem like there was an inch that wasn't bruised. Also there was other blood it was obvious the woman had been raped.

Looking at the woman made him shudder, in fact, his whole body was shaking. He couldn't remember seeing this much torture even in Afghanistan! The poor woman, his every instinct urged him to reach out and hold her. The woman was unconscious! No wonder there was only nature noise! He looked more closely, afraid of what he would find, but she was breathing. He pulled in a huge breath, only then realizing he'd been holding it.

A huge shudder slid down his back and tears welled up in his eyes. After swallowing, not only to keep down the bile, but the tears that wanted to fall, he yanked his cell phone from his belt carrier and with trembling fingers jabbed in 911.

Instantly, a male voice with a rather thick southern accent, drawled into his ear, "Yeah? What's your emergency?"

Eric had to swallow again before he said, "I'm… I'm here in Vansville. I live in one of the cabins close to the edge of town, not too far from the new street. I just watched a car go down that street real slow, it didn't have its lights on either, but then it jumped the curb at the end of the street and kept going into the grass and backed even further into the trees. It stayed a few minutes then raced away. I came over to see what was going on and there's a young woman bound and gagged here in the trees. I haven't touched her, I believe she's breathing, but she's definitely unconscious."

His voice much more professional, the man said, "Yeah, we'll get right on that! Like you say, don't touch her, but stay close by if you think it's safe. We'll dispatch officers; in fact, they're headed out the door now."

"I'll stay, I'm not aware of anyone being in the area. In fact, I'll flash my flashlight into the trees when I see the squad cars coming."

"Good idea."

Eric disconnected, looked down at the young woman, his hand trembling and his stomach still churning. Now that his voice didn't need to be steady any longer, the tears slid down his cheeks. He knelt down beside her, raised his hand over her, but didn't touch her and cried out, "God in heaven! Oh, this poor woman! She needs Your help, God help her! Whoever that was in that car, bring him to justice soon!"

Eric knew it was a good half hour drive from Blairsville to Vansville on a good day if you didn't speed. Still, it would take the officers at least twenty minutes to arrive. Just in case someone was watching, he turned off his light and hunkered down not too far away where he could see the woman, but also see the street but not be seen readily. Of course, since it was nearly dark, it wasn't hard to remain hidden. Obviously, whoever dumped off the woman wanted to be rid of her and didn't want to get caught. However whoever it was might want to make trouble for someone who had reported the incident. As he thought about it, it sickened him again and the tears kept coming.

Eric rested his back against another tree and shook his head. In the fading light, he watched as her chest went up and down with each shallow breath. That was her only movement, but she made no sound, she had to be in a coma, surely with all that bruising and the obvious breaks she'd be moaning in pain, if she were conscious. The gash on her head was huge she probably had a bad concussion! Who could do such a thing? He and his brothers were raised to respect girls, then as they grew older that changed to respecting women. In his mind, no woman deserved to be treated as this woman had obviously been treated. It was unconscionable!

It was a good twenty minutes later, but from where he sat, he could see the blue and red flashing lights as two squad cars came into town. Their headlights were also flashing, but they were coming silently, only their lights flashing. He was glad of that, there was no urgency the perp had disappeared. The town's people didn't need to be alerted.

He watched the cars turn from the highway onto the street that connected with the new street, then silently turn and head toward him. As they approached the end of the street, he turned on his flashlight. The first car flicked his headlights, letting him know he'd been seen. Eric flicked off his light and waited. Both cars headed across the meadow, the second car coming abreast of the first and both stopped with their headlights shining into the trees close by. The woman was visible, but the headlights didn't reflect on anything.

The sheriff and several deputies left the cars and even before they reached him, the sheriff said, "What have we here?"

Eric stood up from his post and walked toward the sheriff. There was no need to have his flashlight on, the car headlights gave plenty of light they could easily see him and the woman. "Sheriff, I have no idea who this woman is, but like I told your dispatch, I live in one of those cabins and watched the car that dumped her off. Of course, until he roared out of the trees onto the street, I had no idea he'd left anything. However, when the car disappeared, I came to investigate. I have not touched the woman, but I made the call."

The big man with the impressive collection around his waist approached Eric and the woman and asked, "Has she moved or roused?"

Eric met the officer shaking his head. "No, nothing. This is exactly how I found her. I haven't heard a sound from her."

The sheriff stood silent, watching the woman for several minutes. Then as if he'd been in a trance, he pulled in a deep breath and let it out slowly. He pulled his phone from his belt carrier, but before he hit any buttons, he turned and said, "Deputy Callon, get a blanket from my car to throw over her." It wasn't a terribly cold evening, but there was so little cloth on the woman's body, she needed to be covered.

"Yes, Sir!" He hurried to the trunk of the sheriff's car, popped the trunk and lifted out a blanket, then hurried past the sheriff and Eric and threw the cover over the woman's body. She didn't give any indication she was aware of the activity, not even a groan.

The sheriff kept looking at the woman and listened for several seconds, hit one button on his phone, then waited for an answer. Only seconds later he said, "Need an ambulance here ASAP! Come quietly." As he clicked off, he said to Eric, "You have no idea who this woman is, right? By the way, who are you?"

Still looking down at the woman, Eric said, "I'm Eric Thomas and no, I've never seen this woman before."

"I didn't think you had. You any relation to the Thomas's here in town?"

"Yes, Brad Thomas is my dad's oldest brother."

"Gotcha! Glad to know you." The sheriff held out his hand and he and Eric shook.

It was nearly a half hour later when they watched the approach of the ambulance as it followed the same route as the squad cars. It also came silently, only the lights flashing told its approach. Both sheriff cars still had their lights on, so the ambulance easily followed them across the curb and into the meadow. It also stopped at the treeline, left its headlights and flashing lights on after it stopped. Both doors opened, the man from the passenger seat went to the back of the truck, while the driver approached the sheriff. He pulled something from the pack around his waist then snapped on a pair of latex gloves while he approached the men.

As he adjusted the gloves for a tight fit, he looked from the sheriff toward the trees and said, "So, what have we here, Sheriff?"

"An unconscious female with obvious injuries," the sheriff answered, still watching the woman for any changes.

As the second man came up and laid the stretcher down, the first man said, "We'll get her loaded right up, Sheriff. Got any ID?"

The sheriff looked at Eric who was shaking his head, then said to the paramedic, "Not that we can tell. It looks like what you see is what you get. If you got a blanket in that box of yours, we'll take ours back." He nodded to the still form on the ground and said, "Since you got gloves on, strip off that tape over her mouth. It'll surely help her breathe better she's got some binding her wrists, too. I got an evidence bag here, but I didn't bring any gloves. Maybe we can ID the abductor or maybe not."

The paramedic returned to the ambulance for a blanket, while the driver nodded and proceeded to carefully pull off the tape from the woman's mouth, then took scissors from his waist pouch and cut what was on her arms away. As soon as they were released, the woman's arms started to fall to her sides, but the medical man quickly grabbed the fractured one to keep it from a free fall. Even so, Eric shuddered with the thud of her other arm. Still the woman made no sound or even winced when her arm fell.

The sheriff held out his evidence bag and the man said, "There you go, Sheriff!"

"Right," the sheriff stood silently looking at the woman. Finally, he took a deep breath and sadly shook his head. "This is awful!" he muttered. "This is the worst abuse I've ever seen in our county since I've been in office!"

"That is the truth!" the paramedic exclaimed. "Who would do such a terrible thing to a woman? This is more than abuse!"

They all watched in silence as the ambulance team applied a neck brace, held her fractured arm in place and carefully loaded the woman onto their stretcher, then carried it to the back of the ambulance. As they slammed the doors, the sheriff turned to Eric and opened his mouth, but before a word came out of his mouth, his radio squawked. "Sheriff! A car fire on the highway the other side of Vansville! Thought since you're out there, you'd want to go. Dispatched fire trucks momentarily!"

"Gotcha!" He turned to Eric and said, "Can you come in the office tomorrow to give a statement? I need to get to this other right now." As he turned on his heal he said to the deputy beside him, "This is the most activity we've seen in Vansville in years!"

Eric nodded in agreement, but he said, "Sure, Sheriff, I'll be in early. They're taking the woman to Blairsville Hospital?"

"Yes, that's the plan."

As the sheriff and deputies turned toward their cars, Eric muttered under his breath, "This is Vansville! It's a tiny town! Who would ever think something so horrific could happen in a tiny, peaceful place like this? The major industry in town is a hiking service! For crying out loud, give me a break!"

# Two

Eric realized he still held his phone, so he put it back into the carrier. Then as the night sounds took over, he took one last look at the empty spot. He saw a darker spot on the ground and briefly turned on his flashlight to look. He wished he hadn't, it was blood. He shuddered again, then trudged back across the meadow toward his cabin, but left his flashlight off. He was glad for the street lights to guide his steps. By now, he was shivering, the sun's warmth had left some time ago and the night air was cold. Perhaps that wasn't the only reason he shivered.

He shuddered, the image of the young woman blazed in his mind. "God, be with that young woman! She had nothing! Who could she be? Oh, God, keep her safe!"

After Eric hiked back to his cabin he was exhausted. He stopped long enough to grab his tea and Bible from his porch, where he'd left them. As he opened the door the furnace kicked on, he sighed, glad for the warmth. He put his clean laundry in the dryer and stripped off his clothes, then flopped into his comfortable bed and stared at the ceiling. He pulled the covers up under his chin, hoping to warm up quickly. After several minutes, he put his hands under his head to think for a couple of minutes. He'd seen some awful atrocities in his overseas tour, but the woman he'd just seen in the woods was just as much of an atrocity. As the sheriff had said, he couldn't remember seeing such abuse anywhere he'd ever been.

The furnace was putting warm air into the bedroom, but as a picture of her flashed into his mind, he couldn't help the shiver that went through his body. He really couldn't remember a place on her body that didn't have heavy bruising and scratches. Even on her neck, although he'd seen no strangle marks. Even from the time he'd first seen her until the sheriff came it seemed places, including her face, were swelling. It was obvious she had been raped and in a most painful way! He wondered why she'd been unconscious for so long, but perhaps someone had medicated her. Who knew? He was glad he'd been on his porch and had reacted immediately, but who knew how long she'd been unconscious before she was dropped off. No longer than the car had sat still in the woods, he wondered if she'd been in the trunk! He decided that since he'd only seen one door open and no one had crossed in front of the vehicle that it was a good possibility she'd been in the trunk.

After several minutes he did what he'd done so often overseas, he emptied his mind of horrid things with a prayer for the woman and that the abductor would be caught and punished. A soft bed, rather than the unforgiving ground on a hike he led, was too good to waste. He turned on his side, let out a long sigh and momentarily was sound asleep. He didn't even wake up to use the bathroom. The next time he woke up was Saturday morning with the sun streaming in his window and warming the room. The furnace wasn't even running. He lay in the bed for several more minutes just savoring the day.

Friday evening, Dr. Stan Miles had just walked into the Blairsville Hospital ER to learn his schedule for the weekend when the ambulance pulled up into the bay outside the doors. He watched and waited until the two men quickly unloaded their gurney and brought the still form into the big room. They had radioed ahead and since the ER wasn't too busy, the nurses had a room ready. Dr. Stan followed behind the stretcher and watched as the men transferred the silent person onto the ER table, then one man folded up his gurney and left the small room with it. Stan nearly lost it, the woman was a sight!

The doctor on duty asked, "Who is she and what happened?"

The paramedic said, "We have no idea who she is. The sheriff called us from Vansville. She was in the woods, but terribly abused and raped. We only transported her, didn't start an IV since she doesn't seem to be in any distress. Her vitals are a bit low, but nothing that concerned us. There was absolutely nothing around her, just the rags you see. The sheriff had covered her with his blanket – we removed it and replaced it with ours."

"So what happened?"

"As near as anyone could decide, she was terribly abused, raped, her arm broken and her head bashed. As you can see, there's nothing to identify her. From what I understand a car dropped her off then skedaddled out of sight and was long gone before anyone found her. Who knows when she might have lost consciousness, or maybe she was drugged."

The doctor sighed, "Looks like we've got our work cut out for us for a few hours. She must be in a deep coma, she's not making any noise and she looks like she'd be in a massive amount of pain if she was close to waking up."

"Yes, we both agreed that was the case."

"So we don't know who did this?"

"No, the only people around her when we arrived were the man who found her, the sheriff and three deputies."

"She's in danger!" a nurse standing by exclaimed.

The paramedic nodded. "You said it!"

"Oh, my!" Stan whispered. "Vansville? Really?"

As he was speaking the ER doors opened and a fully armed, uniformed sheriff's deputy entered. "Where's the woman who was just brought in by ambulance?" he asked the receptionist, as he walked up to her desk.

She nodded to her left and said, "They have her in that room over there. She's still in a coma, officer."

He nodded. "I assumed she still was." He turned away and walked to the room. "So this is the victim from Vansville?" he asked.

Dr. Stan still stood outside the room and answered, "Yes, Deputy, is there a problem?"

"Sheriff sent me. Since we don't know who she is or who it was who did this, he felt she needed to be guarded until the perp can be caught. Another thing, we need to keep this out of the papers, nothing should be leaked to any press. Sheriff feels she isn't safe until the perp is caught and put away. Who ever he was obviously thought she'd die before she was found!"

"Ah, good to see you, officer!" the doctor in the room said. "We'll set her fracture first, but then we're about to run some tests to see what's going on with her. Thanks for coming, Deputy it'll make it easier to get on with our work."

"So you're running tests now?"

"Yes and X-rays. There's one obvious fracture, there may be others."

The deputy nodded. "I'm here till my shift changes."

The doctor nodded. "Thanks for coming."

A man hunkered down in the woods a ways from the burning car, but close enough to watch it burn. He'd used the woman's phone that he'd found in her purse to report the fire, then he'd tossed the phone into the blaze. She wouldn't need that phone ever again! He grinned. Tonight he'd done two of his favorite things he'd played with a woman's body, had himself a beautiful plaything and got rid of her when she wasn't of any use. He'd left that little hitch in the road behind then set a fire. Life couldn't get any better than that! He'd missed it for all those eight years he'd been in the slammer, but he was out now! He'd stay out!

The only thing about a car fire, it didn't last too long. But he'd brought the car a good ways from that little town, nobody could connect this car to anything! He'd made sure all the papers, in the car and the woman's purse were burned up. He set the fire in two different places so it'd burn nice and hot and nothing would be left.

He heard some sirens coming from the way he'd come. Ah, fire trucks and a couple of cars! Wow! This was fun! He loved watching those guys rush around, but by now there wasn't much left for them to do. He'd waited long enough before he called. He even loved hearing those sirens, knowing they were coming to take care of something he'd made happen! Life on the outside sure was good!

What he wouldn't do to get his hands on another woman so easily! Maybe in a week or two he'd find another at that convenience store. It was a busy place that was for sure! He chuckled watching the firemen scramble around. Women liked to come to that convenience store, there were a couple of good looking guys who worked there. If he didn't have the job at the med center, he'd see about getting on at that convenience store. After all, he wasn't a bad looker. Thank goodness he'd shed that jumpsuit!

He looked at his watch, as the fire truck left, but the sheriff car stayed and the man ordered a transport. He knew he'd better stay hidden for a good while. He sure didn't want the sheriff to discover him. That prison was the last place he wanted to see the inside of. He'd stay out of there for a good long time, maybe forever! As the sheriff's car and the transport silently left, the man stood up and stretched. He'd come a long ways off the interstate. He needed to catch a ride soon. It was a good thing he'd satisfied his urges today, since he had tomorrow off.

After scrambling some eggs and fixing bacon in the microwave for breakfast, Eric left for the Justice Building in Blairsville, where the Sheriff's Department was located next to the jail. Since he hadn't given any information about the car or the driver, he was sure no one was in the jail related to the woman he'd found. He wondered briefly about the car fire the sheriff had to investigate. Could it have been related to the woman he'd found? Who could tell? It was a few miles away, but it hadn't been that long after the woman had been dropped off. Several miles away could put enough suspicion that it was unrelated. Besides, why would the man who did the deed not want to get as far away from the area as possible? Vansville was a good ways from a major city and even though Main Street was a highway, it wasn't a major artery.

It wasn't hard to find a place to park close to the Justice Building, none of the county offices were open on a Saturday, just the Sheriff's Department and the deputies guarding the jail were on duty in the building. Of course, that whole department took up the entire lower floor of the huge building. If he wasn't mistaken, there was a cage behind the building the official cars would be parked in that lot.

As Eric entered, the man at the desk looked up and asked, "What'll it be?"

Giving the man a pleasant smile, Eric said, "I'm Eric Thomas from Vansville, I'm here to see the sheriff."

"You got an appointment?"

"No, he asked me last night to come in this morning."

"I'll call him."

Eric nodded. "Appreciate that."

Soon the door behind the man at the desk opened and the sheriff motioned Eric in. After they both sat down, the sheriff behind his desk and Eric across the desk in a vinyl chair, the sheriff picked up a file folder from his desk and pulled it in front of him then opened it and found a pen, before he said, "So, can you tell me anything more than you said last night?"

Eric put the tips of his fingers together and rested his chin on them. He pulled in a breath and said, "Not much, Sheriff, except that the vehicle was a car with a trunk, not anything with a hatch or a pickup. I saw a light come on inside the car twice, but never saw a person. The driver's door was away from me. It was also too far away to hear any noise, so I didn't hear if the trunk lid made any noise. When someone left the car it was far enough back in the woods all I saw was a light inside. I don't think he was in the woods longer than five minutes. Of course, I was at my cabin, much too far away to identify the license plate before the car was gone."

The sheriff stroked his chin, still looking at the paper he'd obviously made notes on. "Hmm, the car we found burned up was a compact with a trunk, but there was nothing salvageable and no one was around. The license plate was in the trunk, the paint burned off. It had to have been purposely set on fire and then abandoned. The glove box was open and there were a few charred papers too far gone to see anything on them."

"Wow!" Eric exclaimed. "Could this vehicle be connected in some way? You say no one was around when you got there?"

The sheriff nodded. "That's right. It looked like the fire had been set inside, since the seats were burned as much as they could be only the springs were left. It's possible that was the vehicle used to bring the woman to the woods there. Even the flammable articles in the trunk had burned, so we were unable to find anything there. Even the paint was scorched off the tire iron. That gash on her head looked like it could have been inflicted by a tire iron, but it had been burned clean. The caller who reported the fire didn't identify himself; just gave the location. It was an obscure part of the road, too. It was next to an open field, there were no houses in sight. Perhaps whoever discovered the fire was still at a farmhouse from making the call. I actually stayed a few minutes hoping someone would return."

Eric shook his head then ran his hand through his short hair. "Sounds like the perfect crime, unless the woman can identify him."

The sheriff made a face and leaned back in his office chair. "That's the other thing. I've kept tabs on her at the hospital. One of my deputies is there, but according to him and the hospital staff, she hasn't come out of the coma yet."

Eric was shocked that the woman was still in a coma, he exclaimed, "They've run tests and everything? Set her arm? Man, that's hard to believe!"

"Yes. Surprising, she didn't have any damaged organs, nothing internal was damaged. From the way she looked, that surprised me. She was raped and there was some damage there, there was a lot of blood. She did have a severe concussion that was quite obvious because of the blow to her head that drew blood and damaged her skull. It looked like that blow was with something very heavy, possibly a tire iron or something else just as solid. As I say, if it was the tire iron we can't tell. The fire in the trunk burned anything on the iron off.

"They did a battery of blood work, but it came back inconclusive, the tech wasn't sure if there were drugs in her system, perhaps an illegal substance. We even dusted for fingerprints on what she had on. We were surprised, there were none. Of course, there were only rags, a few short pieces of material was all. The perp must have thought about what he was doing and worn gloves." He shook his head. "No, I don't think so, she had too many scratches. Perhaps he'd used some of the cloth he'd ripped from her clothes to wipe off any fingerprints, we couldn't tell about that. Of course, the tire iron had been through the fire, so there was no paint, blood or fingerprints on it. Another thing, we have no way of knowing when that tape was applied."

Eric still had his fingertips together and held his chin on them, then shook his head. "Yes, I wondered about that, too. Seems like overkill."

The sheriff nodded. "Yes, I agree. Of course, the perp may have applied the tape right away while she was still conscious. After all, he wouldn't want her calling attention to anything happening in the car. At least that's my take on the tape."

Eric nodded. "Yes, I guess that's a real possibility. It makes me shudder to think what happened to her! I mean, I didn't see a place that hadn't been bruised or scratched or bloody, not one place! So can I go see her?"

The big man shrugged. "I don't see any harm in it. You'll have to ID yourself with the deputy at her door, that's all. He's been given strict instructions to let no one in to see her without ID. The staff is calling her

Jane Doe until we can get something from her, but of course, you won't be any help in that department, either." The sheriff pulled in another breath. "By the way, can you tell me a little about yourself?"

Eric shrugged. "Not much to tell, Sheriff. I'm a single man and all of my family except my aunt and uncle live elsewhere. I mustered out of the Marines less than a year ago. I'd been deployed to Afghanistan for two tours. Right now I'm employed by DeLord's Hiking Service as a hiking guide." He grinned. "End of story."

The sheriff nodded. "Thanks for coming in, Mr. Thomas. We'll see you around."

Eric put his hands on the armrests of the uncomfortable chair and said, "Well, if there's nothing else, I guess I'll go to the hospital and make a visit. I really wish I could have been more help, but who knew until he was long gone?"

"Not a problem. By the way, you saved that young woman's life. It was cool enough and she was exposed enough she could have never woken up! And she's still unconscious...."

Eric shuddered. "Yes, I'm aware of that, Sheriff."

Only a few minutes later, Eric parked in the hospital parking garage and walked inside, up to the information desk. When he stopped in front of the desk the woman asked if she could help him and he said, "A woman was brought in by ambulance last evening. I believe they're calling her Jane Doe, unless she's woken up and told her name. I just came from the sheriff's office and he said I could come see her."

The pink lady scrolled through several pages on her computer, then looked up and smiled. "No, she's still Jane Doe. You know her?"

"No, I never saw her before finding her in the woods last evening. I was the one who called the sheriff about her."

The woman nodded. "She's on fourth floor, room four twelve, but there's a deputy at her door. You'll have to speak with him."

"Yes, I'm aware of that. Thanks."

"Not a problem."

When Eric walked onto the ward, he looked down both wings. He easily saw the deputy in the hall, so he walked toward the room. When he saw the man approaching, the deputy stood and rested his hand on his revolver, but he asked, "You have business here?"

Eric raised his hands and said, "Deputy, I just left the sheriff who said I could visit. I was the one who called in about finding this woman in the woods close to where I live. I don't know this woman I was only hoping to speak with her."

"Sure, go on in. Can't be too careful, you know."

"That's true, thanks." *Actually, I'm hoping to see her cleaned up! I think I'd have nightmares about seeing her with all that blood. And that place on the ground...*

Eric walked around the deputy, pushed on the closed door and walked into the silent private room. The light over the bed was shining toward the ceiling, but was subdued and the blinds in the window were nearly closed, so the room was quiet and restful. Even though the sun was shining outside, the room was dim. Probably a much different scene from what the woman last remembered. Eric stood at the foot of the bed for several minutes. A sheet and light blanket covered everything but her head. All the blood was gone from her face and her hair now lay in clean waves around her face. Some had been shaved because of the huge dressing on her scalp. Other than that, she could have been lying in the woods she looked the same as she had there.

He shuddered. There were no bandages on her face, but her eyes were nearly swollen shut with dark bruises around them. In fact, every bit of skin he could see was discolored. Her arms were covered by the hospital blanket, but he was sure there was a cast on one arm. When he'd discovered her, a jagged edge of the bone in her upper left arm was protruding through the skin. The question he'd asked several times since he'd discovered her came to his mind: *How could anyone do this? How could anyone mistreat a woman so badly?* Not only treat someone so horribly, but then throw them in the woods! If he hadn't seen the car and gone to investigate, she'd have died of exposure! The night had been chilly and she had only rags on. Eric shivered just thinking about finding her – nearly naked – with a cool breeze blowing.

The deputy hadn't followed him in the room, so he was alone with her. He felt such compassion that he walked up beside the bed on the side without the IV. He touched her shoulder, laying his hand down on top of the blanket, she didn't even flinch. After another moment of silently looking at her, he whispered, "Father, God, this woman had been abused so badly! Perhaps her body has shut down because it is in so much pain. Perhaps it's the concussion that's keeping her in a coma. Bring whoever did this to justice soon. Touch this woman's body and heal her. Not only physically, Lord, but in every way. If this was an abusive husband, oh, God how horrible! Wake her up soon, perhaps she can identify who did this to her. This criminal needs to be brought to justice soon! I pray in Your Son's Name, amen."

He stepped back and shrugged. He didn't know her, she couldn't talk to him. He turned and left the room. He smiled at the deputy who was seated again and said, "Thanks."

"Hey, no problem. You didn't wake her up, did you?"

"Nope, she didn't even move."

The deputy shrugged. "Can only hope."

"You're right. Have a good day."

"Oh, I'm sure it'll be more boring than anything."

"I agree with you there."

Eric left Blairsville, but the young woman wouldn't leave his thoughts. The bruises were getting darker and the flesh of her face was so swollen you could hardly see any features. He left the city and went back to Vansville, but instead of stopping at his cabin, he went on to DeLord's house. It was the base of operations for the hiking service, so he could get his information for his hike going out tomorrow, but it was also the home of Ramon and Sandy DeLord. Ramon might not be home, but Sandy was an inspiration and he needed that desperately right now. Because he'd been the only one to bring back a group yesterday, the parking lot had the same number of cars, so he parked in his spot.

Since it was a comfortable April day, Sandy had the windows open and had heard the car drive up. Through the window, Eric heard, "Come on in, Eric! You know the door's open."

He did, knowing that Sandy was in the office, her little son toddling close to her knees. She looked up and with a smile, asked, "What's on your mind, Eric? You're not going out until tomorrow afternoon. Do you need your itinerary already?"

Eric slouched into the comfortable chair next to Sandy's desk and shook his head. "Eventually, Sandy, but the reason I came has nothing to do with hiking. Have you got a minute to listen to my tale? Believe me; this is really weighing me down. It almost feels like it did when I witnessed such awful stuff overseas!"

Sandy scowled something very unusual for her, and said, "Sure, what is it? Actually, you look really stressed out and I've never seen you like that!"

"I know. What happened last night is really bothering me. I mean, it was really awful, something I could have easily done without!"

Sandy's expressive face changed numerous times while Eric told her the story from start to finish. Finally, she said, "Eric, how awful!" She held out her hands to him and said, "Come on, let's pray for her!" He grasped her hands and she said, "Father in heaven, we come to You for this young woman that Eric found last night. Oh, God, this is so terrible! It doesn't look like it'll get solved easily, either. Heavenly Father, keep this woman safe, put Your loving arms around her, heal her physically, but more important heal her soul and spirit. And Lord God, if she doesn't know You, bring her to Yourself. And Father, please help the law officers find who did this fast! In Your Son's matchless Name, amen."

Tears hanging in Eric's eyes, he squeezed Sandy's hands and whispered, "Thank you. I really needed that."

Sandy looked up at the clock that hung over the door into the rest of the house and said, "Ramon'll be home soon, why don't you wait and have dinner with us? You look like you don't need to be alone right now."

"Sandy, I don't want to put you out!"

Scowling at the young man, she said, "You have a love affair with Alex's TV dinners?"

Chuckling, Eric said, "Sandy, when you put it that way, I'll stay."

"Good."

It was less than a half hour later when a group of people came on the parking lot. Eric turned just enough to see the group with their huge backpacks struggle onto the asphalt. Since it hadn't rained while they were gone, they weren't all muddy. Eric was sure they were glad of that. Soon car doors and trunk lids thumped, then engines roared and soon the office door opened. Right at that moment, Eric wanted to be invisible when Ramon said, "Sweetheart, what a sight for my weary eyes you are!" His backpack hit the floor and his arms circled his beloved wife's shoulders.

After a very long kiss, he looked up long enough to catch up the tiny boy who was latched onto his leg. "How's Daddy's big boy?"

A huge grin covered the toddler's face and his baby voice said, "Daddy!" The little boy laid his head down on his daddy's shoulder and patted his whiskered cheek. "Daddy," he whispered again. Eric nearly lost it. This was what he really wanted. Eric wanted his own family, a wife who loved him unconditionally and that he loved with his whole being. He wanted children that would smile at him, as if he was their whole world and who would call him, "Dada!" He sighed would God give him that pleasure? He was thirty years old, he wasn't old, but so far, no young woman had captured his interest, not ever. As he thought about it, he knew he wasn't really fussy, just wanting the woman God had for him. He wouldn't mind a pretty woman, but she must share his faith, he hoped she wasn't ugly. If they could love each other with all their hearts he wouldn't complain.

"So, you're here?" Ramon turned to his friend and asked.

His question pulled Eric from his musing. "Yep, got invited for supper with you guys. Hope you don't mind?"

"Good, tag along, Man!" Ramon grinned at his friend and colleague.

Sandy grinned. "He decided he didn't have a love affair with Alex's dinners."

Ramon slapped Eric on the back. "Never learned to cook?"

"You got that right. Mom wasn't into teaching us boys how. Said it was woman's department. You know, that's something else she didn't teach us was how to snag a woman. I never could figure that out! She said cooking was woman's work, but she left us in the dark about how a man went about finding that woman."

As they left the office, Ramon said, "Believe me, it's usually the woman who snags you."

They left the office and Sandy said, "Go on in the living room, Eric. I'll get supper started in a few minutes. Ramon always takes a shower as soon as he gets home, but we'll eat soon after that. Make yourself comfortable."

"Thanks, Sandy. I know you have some hiking magazines there to look through."

She laughed. "Yup, we have plenty of those!"

Eric followed the little family until they turned into the master bedroom, then Eric went on into the large living room and sank onto the comfortable couch. He picked up one of the colorful magazines, but didn't open it. Instead, he laid his head back on the top of the couch and closed his eyes. The scene in the woods flashed into his mind, as he'd first laid eyes on the young woman. He shuddered, just as he had last night. He'd never seen a woman so badly abused, not here in America! Today in the hospital room, even with the subdued light, it wasn't hard to see her swollen and bruised face. He wondered how long it took swelling to go down and bruises to fade. She'd been raped…. Eric groaned. Would she get pregnant? He shook his head and quickly opened his eyes and opened the magazine. That was another whole can of worms he didn't want to open and examine.

He heard the shower running, but to his amazement, he heard Ramon's rich bass voice and a lovely alto voice singing in harmony. They were singing a hymn. Without even thinking about it, Eric joined in, not that he harmonized very well, but he loved the hymn they sang. The words blessed his soul. These two people were amazing!

A nurse pulled a computer on a small rolling stand behind her, but walked around the deputy and into the quiet room. It was nearly time for shift change and she must enter readings into the chart. She stopped close enough to view the entire woman lying in the bed, but also close enough to see any expression on her face. The nurse made a face all she could see on the woman's face were bruises and extreme swelling. It was impossible to see any features. Of course, the gash on her head was covered with gauze, but it was still oozing and she'd had to change the dressing. A shiver went down the young nurse's back, the victim's head seemed like it was dented! Even with the dressing on it.

It made her wonder if it would always be deformed. If she were conscious she'd be in excruciating pain. How could she not be? So far, they only gave her minimal pain medicine, because they wanted her to come out of her coma, but when she woke up, the nurse knew she'd be in agony. What a horrid experience!

After taking her visual assessment, she looked down at the bag hanging on the rail, entered her findings into her computer, then emptied the bag and replaced it. After striping off her gloves, she looked at the bag hanging on a pole at the head of the bed and entered that reading. The IV would need a new bag soon after shift change. She took a step closer to read the reading on the wall from the blood pressure machine and the oxygen meter. Comparing them with the last readings, everything had improved.

However, before she could shake down the thermometer to put in the woman's mouth, a groan came from her lips and the nurse nearly hyperventilated. She gently touched the young woman's face and whispered, "Are you waking up?" The woman didn't move, or respond, but another groan left her lips.

The nurse stood silently beside the bed watching and looking at the woman's face. She shook her head the poor woman was in terrible shape! When she came to the floor she'd had nothing with her, only the hospital gown the ER had put on her. Where were her clothes? Her purse? Had they been lost? Left at the scene? Surely the ambulance personnel wouldn't have left anything personal behind! They were a very conscientious bunch.

When nothing else happened with the woman, the nurse pushed the button on the control and when someone answered, she said, "This woman's groaned twice since I've been in here, but she doesn't answer when I speak to her."

"Dr. Simon's here, he's on his way."

"Okay, I'll wait."

Moments later, the charge nurse and the doctor walked in the room. The doctor had his mouth open to speak, but another groan left the patient's mouth. "You've tried to wake her?"

Angela nodded. "When she moaned the first time I touched her face and asked if she was waking up, but she didn't move or respond."

Dr. Simon shook his head. "I guess we aren't any closer to a solution then."

"Seems not," the charge nurse sighed. The charge nurse turned to Angela, "Be sure you record the time she groaned and that it's been more than once."

"Right. So we're just waiting for her to respond?" Angela asked, incredulous, thinking about all the places on the woman's body that were injured.

Dr. Simon shrugged. "I guess that's the bottom line, really. None of the tests showed any particular problems. We'll do another battery of blood work to see if it comes back clean, we couldn't be sure at first. She does have a severe concussion, so we need her to fully wake up. They set and casted her arm in the ER before they sent her up. The X-rays didn't show anything else damaged, so yes, we're waiting for her to wake up."

"What'll happen to her when she wakes up?"

"Well, hopefully, she can tell us who she is and where she's from. Perhaps she'll be able to ID the man who did this, too. When we know, we'll call whomever and send her home so her family doctor can take her from there. I'm sure her family doctor is much more acquainted with her than we could ever be."

"And if she doesn't? What if she doesn't remember all those things? She didn't come up here with anything," the young nurse whispered.

"Don't know, we'll cross that bridge when we come to it," Dr. Simon said, with another shrug. "Other than the terrible bruising, scratches, swelling and the bad concussion, nothing seems to be life-threatening, so I expect her to wake up eventually." He looked at the quiet patient again. "Try to speak to her again."

"Hi, girl, I'm Angela, your nurse here at the Blairsville Hospital, can you wake up for me?" Angela stroked the patient's face, but not even a groan came from her. Dr. Simon shook his head, but kept watching the silent woman. After several minutes he left the bedside.

From the doorway, Dr. Simon said, "I guess we never left square one."

Angela gave him a sad smile. "Yeah, I guess so."

The three staff members left the room and Angela pulled her computer out behind her and closed the door. "Wish she'd wake up," she murmured.

"Yes, don't we all," her charge nurse answered. As they reached the desk, the meal trucks came on the ward from the back elevator. The silence of the ward was shattered.

The shift changed and the same team leader who'd been on when the young woman was admitted sat in report. When the day charge nurse's report finally reached the room where their mystery woman lay, she said, "Our Jane Doe has groaned several times but hasn't responded to anything, any kind of stimulus. Angela touched her several times and spoke to her when she groaned, but she never acknowledged it."

Marg scowled, she'd been there when Jane had been admitted. "So none of the tests showed anything unusual in her blood, nothing on X-ray either?"

"They're still not convinced about some of the blood tests. It's been more than eighteen hours since she's been on this floor and nothing. Dr. Simon was very interested in that, so he'll do more blood work tomorrow he said. There's a deputy sitting at her door and we're afraid to post anything to go over the airwaves or in the paper in case someone's after her. If they meant to leave her to die and she was rescued, if the wrong person found out…"

"Oh, my! That is something to think about, isn't it?" the team leader whose patient she'd be gasped. "Wow! Glad the deputy's there!"

"Dr. Simon says we must wait for her to wake up, then ask her those questions and send her home." Fear showed in her eyes as she looked at the night charge nurse. "Angela asked what happens if she has amnesia, what'll we do? He had no answer."

"Amnesia, yes, that's a possibility."

A CNA asked, "Didn't she come from Vansville?"

Allison shook her head and said, "That's where she was found, that's where the car left her, but we have no reason to believe that's where she's from or where she was going. From everything anybody knows, she wasn't a resident and the sheriff hasn't gotten any calls about a missing person anywhere around here. Vansville's just a widening in the road. Whoever dropped her there probably thought his tracks were covered."

"Yeah, remember, a car was found later all burned up. It could have been her car or the car the kidnapper had and wanted to get rid of any evidence."

"This is scary!" the CNA exclaimed. "I thought little towns were supposed to be really safe places to live!"

"You're right, it is! And from what I've heard about Vansville, not much goes on there, but you can never be sure what somebody can do! She had one visitor this morning, he was the man that found her in the woods and called in about finding her. I could tell he was military, but you can't hold that against a guy. He seemed like a nice guy, but he didn't ask questions, not that we could have given him any answers."

"So he wouldn't know anything, would he?"

The charge nurse shook her head. "No more than you or me. He may know more than we do, who knows?"

"We'll do our best to keep her safe. How long's the deputy staying?"

"We don't know. One came with her from the ER, had all that high power stuff around his middle and now there's a new man down there, same way, so I guess at least for your shift she's being guarded. Try to convince him we need those guys. We sure can't spare anybody to keep an eye on that room like they can."

The night charge nurse shrugged. "We'll do our best. It gets a bit quiet around here at two o'clock in the morning, you know."

Allison closed her computer, then turned and grinned at Marg. "Yeah, I remember doing this shift when I first came here. We'll see you girls in the morning. Don't let the hooligans and the hobgoblins get you tonight."

"Oh, we'll send them all down to ER if they show up here. They're good with those things. They ship 'em right out the door!"

"Yeah, so I've heard."

"Hey, guys, have a good evening! Don't let Jane Doe keep you from a good night's sleep. She'll probably be here in the morning."

"I'm sure that's true."

It was about two in the morning when the team leader walked in the young woman's room. She hadn't slept too well during the day, for some reason her air conditioning hadn't cooled her apartment, so she needed some activity to wake her up. She stopped in the break room for a cup of coffee, then walked around the relaxing deputy into the room and walked up to the quiet body in the bed. Tina stood and looked at her for a while. There wasn't a place on her that she could see that wasn't bruised or scratched!

Remembering what the day nurse had said, Jane Doe had come on the ward with nothing. Usually ER sent clothes or a purse, but there was nothing. They had casted her arm, but the cast had a window in it. They'd shaved almost one whole side of her head so they could make a huge dressing stick. The patient was still covered from her chin down, but somehow, with all the swelling, her mouth had fallen open and her respirations were much louder. Tina wondered if she should put some ice chips in her mouth, surely it was much dryer now that she had it open.

Tina shook the pitcher, but only water sloshed in it. She took the pitcher to the treatment room, dumped out the water and filled it with crushed ice. With a spoon in hand, she returned to the room. She dipped the spoon in the ice chips, brought out two and placed the spoon on the patient's lip. Much to Tina's surprise, the woman's whole body jerked and her mouth let out a loud groan. However, she didn't open her eyes or even close her mouth.

With shaking hands, Tina put the cover on the pitcher, left the spoon and hurried up to the desk. "Marg, Jane Doe has her mouth open, so I got some ice chips. The cold spoon on her lip made her jerk and she groaned, but nothing else changed."

"I'm not sure ice chips are a good idea, Tina, if she's not awake, she could aspirate and then we'd be in a world of hurt."

Tina nodded and made a face. "Yes, I won't try it again. I was kind of concerned that her mouth was drying out."

Marg shrugged. "I'm not sure what to tell you on that. Could use some swabs. I know we have some in the treatment room."

"Right, I'll get some swabs right away." Tina looked at her friend. "Marg, what'll happen to that young woman? Nothing came to the floor with her, I know because I was the one who helped the guy get her into the bed. There was no bag with her, nothing! There were bruises everywhere! I didn't see one place that wasn't bruised or have scratches on it."

Marg answered, "Nothing did come with her. I read the notes from downstairs, nothing came to the hospital, just a rag around her neck – like the edge of a T-shirt or something. They quizzed the ambulance people about that, too. According to them, they were the first to touch her and there was nothing. There were only rags on her body! What'll happen to her? Who knows! All we know for sure is what we can see. We're in the dark until she wakes up. We can only hope that'll be soon, but once she does, I'm sure she'll be in lots of pain. We're hoping she'll give us some information."

"Oh, for sure!"

*It's dark, I hurt, oh, I hurt all over! I've never hurt so badly! Where am I?*

About five o'clock, Tina made rounds to all her patients. Handed out wash pans to those who were awake, threw covers over those who weren't. She went back in Jane Doe's room and immediately saw that she had moved. The call light for four-twelve went on immediately and one of the CNA's answered. Tina said, excitedly, "Jane's moved! I talked to her and she squirmed in the bed, but her eyes are so swollen she can't open them. She didn't respond to what I said, but she has moved."

From her seat a bit farther away from the intercom, Marg said, "Keep an eye on her, Tina, but when Dr. Simon comes on we'll have him take a look. Dr. Ramoz doesn't know her, so he won't be much help."

"Yes, I'll do that."

At about six-thirty both Dr. Ramoz and Dr. Simon came on the ward. Dr. Simon stopped at the desk and asked, "Has our patient responded yet?"

Marg looked up and said, "Tina saw her move, Doctor, but she hasn't responded to anything we've said to her."

Dr. Simon sighed, "I guess we're still waiting on square one."

"Seems so, Doctor."

"It's been what? Twenty-four hours?"

"Longer than that, Doc, she was brought in Friday evening."

"Yeah, that's right. We'll go see her."

The two men walked down the hall and Marg caught up pulling the chart computer in case the doctors gave orders. The deputy watched the little parade, but said nothing. The three staff entered the room and Marg saw that the patient's right arm rested on the pillow over her head. Her head was turned into her arm. By now the bruising was very dark and the swelling was so bad that her face looked like a beach ball with a point on it where a nose would be. The woman had to be in incredible pain. Was she comatose because of pain or the concussion? Who knew? According to the doctor and new blood test results those were the only reasons for her comatose state. Marg was glad she hadn't eaten breakfast yet, the patient looked that bad.

Dr. Simon watched for several minutes and finally said, "Let's do some more blood work. It can't hurt to get something to make comparisons." He walked up the left side of the bed, pulled back the cover and looked at the cast on her arm. "Better make sure that pillow stays under this, keep her arm elevated. It looks like her fingers are swollen. It might be from the break or it could be from bruising."

This was the first Dr. Ramoz had seen the young woman. He gasped as he looked more closely. "These bruises are incredible! There isn't a natural skin color anywhere! And her face! You can't see any of her features!"

"I know," Dr. Simon said, simply.

Dr. Ramoz shook his head and laid a hand on her good arm. "This criminal must be caught! Why would *anybody* hurt a woman so badly!" That was the question that everyone in the room had been asking since Jane came in.

# Three

Marg typed in the order for the blood work. Simultaneously the lab received notice and a tech would be up shortly to take the blood for testing. There was always an extra pillow in the room, so as soon as she finished writing the order, she readjusted the one already under her arm and pulled the pillow from the stand next to the bed. She moved next to Dr. Simon, lifted the young woman's arm and placed the pillow on the bed. Neither the activity nor the voices brought any visible response from the woman.

*Those voices, who are they? Where am I? Why can't I open my eyes? What's wrong with me? Oh, I hurt, everything hurts!* Jane groaned.

Early Monday morning, before shift change, the night nurse aids were handing out wash pans and the medicine nurse pushed a cart down the hall. The deputy outside of room four-twelve felt his phone buzz in his waist carrier. He pulled the phone out and saw it was the sheriff. The ward was still quiet, so the man whispered, "Yeah, Sheriff."

"Deputy, no one will be relieving you this morning, so when it's time for you to go off, tell the staff. Tell them I'm sorry, but we just can't spare the manpower."

He looked at the closed door and said, "Will do, Sheriff. You think she's safe? She hasn't woke up yet, so we don't know anything."

Sheriff Winslow let out a big sigh. "Don't know, Germain. I've seriously debated that most of the weekend. Seems if someone was still close by after her, there'd been some inquiry around town over the weekend and as far as we know, there's been none. We'll have to hope for the best. Besides, she is there on the ward, it's not like she's alone at home. They did put her close to the desk, right?"

"Yes, there's no patient room between her and them. Okay, I'll let them know."

"Good, but I'm sorry."

"Yeah, I'll tell 'em that too."

"Thanks." The phone went dead.

The young man watched the staff getting ready for the change of shift. Soon different people started coming through the door onto the ward. These people looked rested and chipper after a good night's sleep. He glanced at his watch it was time for him to head on home. He could use a good sleep. Protecting someone who was in a coma, in a hospital bed, in a private room through the night, was a bit boring. They'd been instructed to turn off their radios so he hadn't heard any of the police activity during his shift. He was ready to go home.

He walked up to the desk and leaned on it. The charge nurse looked up and he said, "I just got a call from Sheriff, he said to tell you nobody would relieve me this morning."

The night charge nurse sighed, "Thanks for telling me, Deputy. I'll let the day staff know. I was surprised, actually, that you guys were posted all weekend, but we thank you. Who knows if she's safe or not!"

Flirtatiously, the deputy grinned at the nurse. "Hey, that's our major job is protecting the citizens of our fair county."

"Yup, I know that." She looked into the deputy's eyes and asked, "Have any ideas who she is or where she's from? Nothing came with her from ER, I wondered if anything was lost and has turned up." She made a face and added, "Although, I know the EMT's are very conscientious, they wouldn't leave anything behind."

The deputy shook his head, leaning heavily on the desk. "Not a clue. I didn't go on the call, but I heard she was nearly naked, unconscious and sprawled under a tree. All of us have looked at her she doesn't look familiar to anyone. She could have been passing through. We haven't dared put her face in the paper for fear whoever did this to her is still out there and will finish her off if he knows she's still alive."

"Yeah, I heard that. But if he dropped her off in a town… Well, I'd think he meant for her to die, you know?"

"Yeah, I'm with you on that. Well, guess I'm out of here. You folks have a good day. When she wakes up give my regards to Jane Doe."

The charge nurse sighed again, "Since I'm sure you're off to dreamland, I'll be among those catching some Zzzzz pretty soon, too."

"Hey, one of my breed! Have a good one."

"Yeah, thanks again for the protection."

"Absolutely! Not a problem." The young man grinned and winked at the pretty nurse. She wasn't above a little flirting, she winked back at him. She sighed and watched him swagger off the ward, then turned back to her charting. She hated the mystery surrounding Jane Doe. Remembering what she'd seen, it made her shudder to think what kind of monster did this to her. They'd had abuse victims on the ward before, but this was over the top!

*Oh, I hurt! I hurt so badly! What is that noise? Where am I? I…I can't open my eyes!*

Monday morning at eight o'clock, the Vansville Clinic opened after being closed on Sunday. Nancy and Marcy always walked together to the clinic, since they were neighbors and lived so close to the clinic they could walk across the grass to the back door. They loved walking together and they could share lots of things on the short walk. In fact, they had a lot in common besides being neighbors.

Of course, they were first, so Marcy opened the door and Nancy flipped on the lights. Inside, Marcy hurried to her station to set up her tray for blood work, while Nancy went to the front door to open it for the other staff that came from Blairsville. Of course, she didn't expect Dr. Stan any time early, he never did that. However, only moments later, she'd only made it to her supply closet to check the list for things needed in the exam rooms, when the front door whooshed open and Dr. Stan walked in. Nancy nearly swooned. She couldn't believe Stan would show up on time, let alone early! He looked like a man on a mission it was Monday, for heaven's sake! If anything, Doctor Stan Miles arrived even later on Monday mornings!

"Stan! You're here early!" she exclaimed, whirling around enough to see both him and the clock on the wall. She didn't make it a secret when she looked at the clock she even pointed to it and said, "Stan, it's not even eight o'clock yet!"

He didn't acknowledge her outburst, instead he said, "Did you hear about what happened in this fair town on Friday – Friday evening?"

Nancy frowned. "Something happened here on Friday that you know about and I don't? Remember, we're talking about the booming metropolis of Vansville, here. Were we still at the clinic when this happened?"

Nancy and Stan talked loudly enough that Marcy heard them and came from the lab. "Something happened here in Vansville on Friday?" She looked at Nancy and asked, "Weren't we here all day and in the evening too?"

"Friday." Nancy scowled. What could have happened in the little burg they called home on a Friday? "Wait a minute! No, after work we all met at Sandy's place and went with Raylyn to a quilt show right from work, remember? We grabbed something down the road and weren't home until after Natt was home from the store."

"Oh, yes, I remember now."

Stan looked from Nancy to Marcy and asked, "So you didn't hear about the woman dropped off in the woods Friday night?"

"In what woods Friday night?" Nancy echoed. "There're woods all around Vansville. We're talking Vansville, Stan! This little place?"

"It was Eric Thomas who reported it, so I guess it was some woods close to where he lives, where is that?"

Agitated, Marcy crowded close beside Nancy. Still holding a packaged syringe in her hand, she blurted out, "There's some woods close to our houses, actually right over there! There are woods on the other side of the parking lot and Eric lives in one of those cabins just behind the clinic. What happened there?"

"Seems a car drove down that new street all the way to those woods and dropped off an unconscious woman under some tree. Looked like she was tortured, I mean, awful! Her arm was fractured and she had such a bad concussion from a bash on her head, she's still in a coma. I saw her there in the ER when they brought her in. She was a horrible sight!"

"Here in Vansville!" Marcy gasped. She pointed her thumb over her shoulder. "You… you mean in those woods close to our houses? You mean somebody tortured her back in those woods? Oh, my!"

"Well, no, not tortured in those woods. She got dumped off there. Eric saw the car do some weird stuff then peeled out of there. He found the woman and called the sheriff after it left. Whoever it was was long gone."

"Oh, my! Oh, my!"

"She's still in Blairsville Hospital?"

"Yes, she had no ID, hardly any clothing, nothing, so Dr. Simon says we must keep her until she wakes up. Of course, he'll send her home when that happens, but we can't send her anywhere until she's awake and can tell us where she's from."

"Did anybody catch who did it?"

"No, the sheriff said Eric didn't think to investigate until the car peeled out of there. I guess it's a good ways, so he had no way of getting a license number or anything. He said the houses on that street were dark."

Nancy gasped, "Well, yeah, that's where Marcy and I live and we were gone! She's not safe! Oh, my! Whoever could come back to the hospital and finish her off, couldn't they? Is somebody guarding her or something?"

"Yes, that's true. There's been a sheriff's deputy outside the door until this morning. The sheriff can't spare anyone any longer."

"Wow! Goodness, those woods are only a few yards from our houses, Marcy!"

Marcy nodded at Nancy, but she said, "We must pray for her!"

"You think that'll help?" Stan scoffed.

Marcy looked shrewdly at Stan and nodded, emphatically. By his actions and many words she was sure the man wasn't a Believer. "Absolutely, Stan! At this point, that's the only thing that can help her! If she's still in a coma and nobody saw who did it, only God saw! But He's all powerful and all knowing, so it's in His hands!"

Stan wasn't about to argue, he knew Marcy was Sandy DeLord's sister. Sandy had tried to convert him when she was pregnant two years ago. He hadn't bought it, but he wouldn't let her sister brow-beat him into anything, either. By now, other staff had arrived and it was about time for the clinic to be open officially. Those who lived in Blairsville asked about the woman, wanting to know where something like that could happen in this little town. They'd heard about Jane Doe on the hospital grapevine.

Stan left the staff and headed for his office. He needed a lab coat before he could be officially on duty. "Hey! I'll be in my office until you need me!"

"That's fine, we'll call you," Nancy called after him. Stan walked in his office and closed the door behind him. Let the gossipmongers talk, he had things to do. Not the least was to add up statistics about the clinic, did they need a full time doctor?

Since no patients were breaking down the door for early morning treatment, Nancy went back to the supply closet and took the list from Saturday to fill the needs in the different treatment rooms. She pulled the door nearly closed behind her, then stood facing the shelves and murmured, "Father, God, put Your hedge of protection around this young woman there in Blairsville Hospital. We have no idea who she is or where she's from. Lord, You know all things, keep her safe, heal her, I pray, amen."

Marcy also went back to the lab and prayed for the young woman.

Melody walked into room four-twelve. She had been off the weekend, but she was surprised to see how little Jane Doe had changed from what she'd read in her entry notes. She had been moved and obviously been bathed, she had a fresh gown on. Her face was still terribly swollen, so much so her eyes were tight shut. She couldn't see her eyelashes. The bruising on her face and neck was very dark. The dressing on her head needed changing, but there was no blood or any discoloration on the white gauze. Her hair was clean. The covers were up to her neck, covering her arms. The woman's right arm was under the blanket, but Melody had no way of knowing if she had moved herself or if someone on duty during the last two days had moved her. All Melody could do was shake her head, how could anyone do this?

Of course, Melody had taken nurse's training in Atlanta, she'd seen many women brought in who had been abused. Working at a city hospital, it was a given she'd see quite a few cases of abuse over the years. Women and children. However, she had to admit, it had been a long time, maybe never, since she'd seen someone abused this badly.

The nurse walked up to the side of the bed and laid her hand on the woman's shoulder. Much to her surprise, the woman moved, shrugging a bit under the pressure of Melody's hand. She glanced at the woman's face, wondering if her hand registered and her facial expression had changed. Softly, she whispered, "Are you waking up? Can you open your eyes?"

In response, the woman groaned, maybe there was some eye movement under the lids.

A few minutes later the charge nurse walked in and closed the door. Allison looked at Jane Doe and asked, "Melody, is there anything? It's been two and a half days she's been here!"

Melody put her hand back on the patient's shoulder, but nothing happened this time. "A minute ago I put my hand on her shoulder and she kind of shrugged. I asked if she was waking up and she groaned. Maybe her eyes moved under her lids, I can't be sure."

The two nurses stood quietly looking at the young woman for several minutes. Melody's hand was still on her shoulder, but Allison shook her head. Still looking at Jane intently, Allison said, "She couldn't open her eyes if she wanted to! She still has so much bruising and swelling, it almost looks like her skin's stretched!" She mouthed the words, *What kind of monster would do this to another human being!*

In response, Melody shrugged, but she asked, "Could I put some ice on her eyes? Perhaps that would take down the swelling some."

"Can't hurt, it's for sure she can't open her eyes, even if she wanted to until some of that swelling is gone. You know, it's amazing, she must have had some terrible trauma, but nothing showed fractures but her arm! The swelling still hasn't gone down much at all."

"I'll get a CNA on that right away!"

"Okay, put a note in her chart."

"I'll do that."

There was a male CNA working his shift on a male medical ward in the huge teaching hospital in Atlanta Monday morning. He'd missed a day of work, but he'd told his supervisor he'd been sick. He'd had a hard time getting back to Atlanta. Drivers were leery about picking up a hitchhiker off a country road and nobody picked up a hitchhiker on the interstate. It felt good to be back! Especially now that all his urges had been met – at least for a while.

Eric was back on a trail. It was something he enjoyed very much. When he'd mustered out of the Marines he'd wondered what to do with his life. God hadn't painted anything spectacular in the clouds and nothing had come to mind until his brother had mentioned he was going to see their uncle in Vansville over the Fourth of July. Matt had agreed to help man the store so their younger cousin could go on a hike. Eric hadn't seen his uncle in years, so he'd agreed to go with his twin. They had both remembered that their uncle Brad had told them that the hiking service in Vansville had expanded over the last few years and it was like a light burst on in Eric's brain. That was something he'd like to do, at least for a while.

For this time in his life he was perfectly content to lead groups of hikers in God's great and beautiful out-of-doors in his home country of good old USA! Leading hikes in the foothills of the Appalachians was totally different from the deserts of Afghanistan. The only sounds on a trail were happy hikers and nature sounds, not terrified screams and gun fire. Those he would happily do without, actually for the rest of his life!

It was another church youth group and the trail led to the plateau where the spring fed high pool was. For late April, the sun had warmed the water enough that a few of the more hardy hikers had braved putting their feet in that water for a few minutes, but no one had put on a swimsuit and jumped in, it was just too cold. Even Eric decided he wasn't part of the polar bear club. The water was great for drinking, very refreshing and tasted delicious, no ice was needed.

Mornings started early, dawn came before the hikers had to get up to get on the trail. Eric was used to rising early and usually he had his private devotions in the morning. This morning, he climbed up on the rock under which the spring gurgled into the pool. He had decided when he first hiked this trail that this place was his most favorite spot. It was so peaceful he could hear the soft gurgling of the water, but also the birds twittering as they woke to greet the day. He looked off to the east and saw the first rays of the sun fan out on the horizon. It was a magnificent display of God's handiwork, but mostly it was ignored. No one else saw it except Eric. It would be a perfect day for hiking. He plunged his hands in the icy water, then splashed his face and was wide awake.

He'd weathered those rainy days in March and the first days of April, but now it was time for flowers and flowering trees and shrubs. He would enjoy every minute he was out in God's marvelous world! In fact there was a beautiful smell in the air. He was sure that off in the woods close by Mountain Laurels were blooming. Last year at this time he was still overseas, but getting ready to come home, that was nothing like this! There certainly weren't any Mountain Laurels in the dry, barren desert, more like grenades and roadside bombs.

Before he opened his Bible, still with his eyes open, he said a silent prayer. There was so much to thank God for, so much beauty around him. The peacefulness right where he sat was enough to make his lips praise. God had been so good when he was overseas, he'd been in some horrendous places, but God had kept him safe and brought him back to this beautiful, peaceful land. How could he do less than praise Him for His goodness, His faithfulness, His love? He couldn't, the words of praise filled his heart and his mouth.

The pool he sat beside, God had put it there, He'd supplied the spring that fed the pool. Until only recently only the wild creatures knew about the pool, but God had supplied it for them, just because He loved them. Now he and his fellow guides knew about it and brought their hikers to enjoy it. God was good!

Jane Doe was never far from his thoughts, so Eric ended his prayer, "Lord, has that young woman woken up yet? Are the deputies still guarding her? What will happen to her when she's released? Oh, Lord, what _will_ happen to her? Was she trying to get away from an abusive husband, but he learned about it and came after her? Did someone find her and abuse her? Whatever happened to her is just too terrible to think about! What was done to her was every bit as bad as atrocities of war I've seen! Keep her safe, I pray. In Jesus' Name, amen."

Eric read a while, but then his watch beeped. He closed his Bible and scrambled off the huge rock. It was time to get the sleepyheads out of the sack and on the trail for the day. He smiled, sometimes he wished he'd been into military music, he could play Reveille and get the troops out of their tents. He'd heard about Duncan and Nancy's hike with the lazy man and how they'd rousted him from his tent, once even dumping cold water over his face. The cold water from this pond would surely have done the job! He chuckled and wondered if someone had played a horn right outside his tent if he'd responded. Finally, they were all out of the tents for another day. No one had complained or needed extra 'encouragement' to get a move on.

While they ate breakfast the sun let them know it was almost May. It would be a hot day. They'd set up camp by a stream tonight it wasn't as cold as this pond, perhaps some of the braver souls would want to splash in it to cool off. Eric thought he'd be one of those. He was pretty sure some of the older boys would follow his lead and jump in. As he watched the group at lunch time, he was almost sure at least one of the girls would also take the plunge. He knew the type some females wouldn't let any male outdo them. Sometimes that was good, he had respect for a woman who lived up to her potential, but some women just did what they did to prove something, usually to themselves.

After cleanup, everyone shouldered his pack and Eric set off. All that was left on the meadow was some matted grass that would rise after a while. Every group knew never to leave anything at a campsite. Maybe they didn't see any wildlife while they were at their stop, but after they left, animals would investigate. They'd eat whatever was left, sometimes that wasn't something that was good for them.

As they set off across the high meadow, the female youth leader started out beside him. "So, that pool is spring fed? It sure is cold!"

"Yes, my colleague found it two years ago, first on his computer then discovered it when he brought a group of hikers this way. The spring is under the biggest rock next to the pool. If you're quiet, you can hear it gurgling underneath. That's also why it's so cold." He grinned. "So far this year nobody's gone swimming in it."

Gloria shivered. "Yeah, I stuck my hand in it when I filtered some water last night, it was frigid and took forever to warm what we needed for dishes. I thought the fire might go out before it was hot enough. So you do this all the time?"

"You mean lead hikes?" Gloria nodded. "Yes, as of right now it's what I feel God wants me to do with my time. Perhaps down the road I'll find something else. As of now, I'm perfectly content to live in Isabel's cabin. I discovered the cabins last year when I first came to town. My landlady's a Christian and takes excellent care of me. I love her to death."

"That's great!"

"Yeah, I agree."

One of the boys moved up beside Eric and said, "Hey, Eric, Larry told us to bring a swimsuit along. Can we swim in somethin' sometime?"

"Sure! I won't stop you." He grinned at the teen and pointed his thumb over his shoulder. "You could have taken a dunk in that pool when we camped last night." He chuckled at the look on the teen's face. "There's no sign saying there's no swimming."

The boy shivered. "I stuck my hand in there, Man! It was frigid, like from a freezer! No way I'd have jumped into that place."

"Maybe tonight. We'll camp by a stream tonight. Maybe that won't be quite so cold. In fact, if it gets much warmer today it'll feel good."

Gloria shivered and said, "Maybe splash your face, Jason."

"Ah, come on, Gloria, don't be a spoilsport!"

"Believe me, I'm only thinking about what your mom would say. Don't you think she'd want you well and not have to take you to your doctor?"

Jason made a face. "Gloria, I'm a big boy now! She pretty much lets me take care of myself. I don't get sick!"

Eric didn't say anything. Oh, to be young and foolish again!

As Gloria moved back to walk with the girls in their group, Eric breathed a sigh of relief. At least she wasn't like the leader in the last group who wouldn't leave him alone. This lady didn't interest him, either, but at least she didn't throw herself at him! Jason kept walking beside him and said, "You really like leading hikes?"

Eric grinned at the teen. "Yeah, as a matter of fact I do. I love being out in God's great out-of-doors, it's good for the soul."

"Yeah, in summertime I could see it, but all the time? No way!"

"Hey, I don't do it in the wintertime. Our hikes only go through part of October. Still, I don't plan to do this until I die, you know."

"Well, yeah, maybe that's okay. So you get all winter off?"

"Oh, I kept busy. I'm the only single guide here in town, so I worked on opening up some more trails to expand where we take people."

"Sounds good."

Eric nodded. "It was fun. We have a program that shows the area in color and lays out the mountains, valleys, trails and streams. You get to walk the trails while you're sitting in your cabin. In the wintertime that's the best way to do it."

"Mmm, I get it."

Jane Doe had a bag of ice resting across her eyes when Dr. Ramoz made his rounds later on in the day. Of course, Allison was in the room with the computer, ready to write orders. The doctor looked at Jane and said to Allison, "Why the icepack?"

Allison swallowed a retort, *was the man dense or something?* and said, "Doctor, even if she woke up she couldn't open her eyes for all the swelling. It's a bit hard to tell if she's awake when she can't open her eyes." She really tried to say the words without sarcasm.

The doctor shrugged. "Guess that's right. Sure wish she'd wake up! We need to know who she is and what we can do for her. The Sheriff's Department hopes she can ID whoever did this to her. We can't know anything until she can tell us."

Allison shrugged. "I guess, as Dr. Simon said, we're still at square one."

"That's about the size of it." The doctor looked at Jane and said, "You've tried?"

"To wake her up? Sure, every time someone comes in. So far, no go."

"That is a shame! Whoever did this is still out there!"

Allison nodded. "We all know that! In fact, it doesn't help us feel too safe. I mean, suppose he is in Blairsville? The guy has to be a monster!"

"No, I imagine not. Well, yeah, to do stuff that made her look like this, he had to be a monster!" He shrugged and took a step toward the door. "Keep up the good work, Allison. I'm off for a few days."

*Who are they talking about? Who is that? Oh, I hurt so bad.*

A few minutes after rounds Melody came in Jane's room with a new bag of ice. She took the melted one away and was about to put the new bag in its place when she looked at the young woman's face and saw tiny slits between her eye lids. Her face was still so swollen she couldn't open them any more. Melody gasped, "Are… are you awake?"

The young woman groaned, but couldn't seem to make any words come out. It was understandable, her lips were swollen twice their normal size.

Melody quickly pushed the call button. When a voice answered, she exclaimed, "I think we have someone who's awake in here!"

Dr. Ramoz had left the floor, but Allison rushed into the room. Melody still held the bag of ice in her hand, but she grinned at Allison and said, "I guess it was good we thought to put some ice on her eyes. The swelling's gone down some, see, she's looking at us!"

Allison put her hand on the woman's shoulder. Slowly what they could see of her eyes moved toward where the hand was. "Hi, we're Allison and Melody, nurses here on the ward where they brought you. You're in Blairsville Hospital. Can you tell us anything?"

The young woman couldn't seem to open her mouth, but a groan worked its way from her throat. She moved her head barely from side to side, but said nothing. Allison smiled at her and gently patted her shoulder. "That's all right, you rest. We're glad you woke up, maybe things will start coming to you and as the swelling goes down, it'll get easier to remember. Do you hurt?" The woman moved slightly and groaned again. "I'll take that as a 'yes'. Melody'll check and find out what you can have for pain, we'll get you something right away." What little bit of her eyes the nurses could see disappeared, the lids closed and the woman drifted off. "The poor thing!" Allison whispered.

Melody put the ice over the woman's eyes, but both women stood and looked at the young woman for several silent minutes. Melody left first and went to find out what she could have for pain. Allison went back to the desk and called Dr. Ramoz on his beeper. When he answered, she said, "The ice over Jane's eyes paid off, Doctor, Melody saw her eyes open, but she can't speak. She did understand when I asked if she hurt. She nodded just a little, so Melody's getting something for her."

"She can't talk?"

"Didn't seem like she could open her mouth. All she did was groan. But really, her eyes were only slits. We had to look really closely to see that they were open."

Acting a bit agitated, Dr. Ramoz exclaimed, "I need to check that out! I'll have another look at her X-rays. I'm sure Dr. Simon ordered pictures of every part, surely she doesn't have a broken jaw or something!"

"Oh, man!" Allison exclaimed. "Maybe it's just the swelling."

"We can hope so."

Allison hung up and shook her head. "That poor woman," she murmured. "I just cannot imagine anyone treating another human being so dreadfully!"

"I know," Melody agreed. "Have you seen the rest of her? It's not only her face and arms, but her whole body is one huge bruise! She has lots of scratches, too, but they all look like fingernail scratches and aren't too deep."

"She was raped, too," Allison whispered.

Tears sprang to Melody's eyes. "How horrible! That's an atrocity!"

When Melody went back in the room with the pain medicine, Jane was asleep again. The nurse didn't have to prepare her for a needle stick, she put the medicine in her IV tubing and Jane slept on. Melody stood and watched the young woman for several minutes. In fact, she pulled down the blanket so she could watch her through her hospital gown. It appeared that since she was no longer in a coma, Jane's breathing was a bit labored perhaps her ribs had also been injured. Melody was a compassionate nurse, she felt tears scratching the back of her eyes, this woman had to be suffering terrible pain to have such bruising all over her body! If only she would wake up and be able to talk to them!

Perhaps she'd be able to tell them something. The most pressing was to know who had done this to her. She hoped Jane wasn't suffering from amnesia, without any ID only her words and what she remembered could help them. The monster who had done this to her needed to be caught and prosecuted! How could anyone catch him if she couldn't identify him? Another thought sobered her even more. Since nobody had seen him, he was still out there! Were they safe when they arrived in the mornings or left in the evenings? The thought made her shiver.

She was glad she didn't know any men who treated their wives or girlfriends like this, but she knew it happened and frequently. She knew that in big cities some men took pleasure in torturing women and girls, just for the sport of it! She'd read all the books in her classes and knew all the theories about abuse, but ultimately, men were responsible for their own actions, they let their anger get the upper hand. She shook her head. Women could be brutal just as much as men. Look at all the child abuse cases and a lot of those were caused by women. Some of those cases were women taking it out on the children because of what the man did to her.

Some time later, Jane woke up to the silence of her room. There was a weight on her eyes, so she didn't try to open them. However, what she was most aware of was the pain she experienced all over her body. There was nowhere that she didn't hurt, in fact, it felt like a sledgehammer had made a dent in her head she had a terrible headache. Not only on the outside of her body, but also inside she hurt, too. She felt the heavy object on her left arm and finally determined it was something that covered her entire arm on both sides of her elbow, but inside it, in her arm, was pain. Her headache seemed to take in her whole head. Her throat was sore, almost felt raw and very, very dry. She also felt other things she wasn't sure what they all were. She finally remembered someone telling her she was in a hospital. As much as she hurt, she was glad she was someplace as safe as a hospital. How had she gotten there? What hospital was it? She knew someone had told her, but she couldn't remember, the pain blotted everything out.

Before she fell back to sleep she heard a door open. It sounded close by. Immediately her heart rate sped up, she wasn't sure why. She felt like her whole body was ready for a flight pattern, only she couldn't. The weight on her eyes and the heavy object on her arm seemed to magnify and pin her body to whatever she was lying on. However, only a second later, someone lifted the weight from her eyes. She opened them as wide as she could and stared at the strange woman. A cold chill spread down her spine as they looked at each other. Who was this woman? Did she know her? Was she lost?

Melody immediately saw the blue of her eyes peeking through the swelling and smiled at her. "Hi, I'm Melody, your nurse here at the hospital. You're finally awake and you can see a bit. I'm sure you hurt all over, you have some terrible bruises. Can you tell me your name?"

Melody could see the fear in her eyes replaced with confusion, as the young woman remained quiet for several seconds. Her right arm moved under the cover and Melody had the feeling that her patient wanted to grab her hand. "I... I don't know!" she whispered, very slowly, her swollen lips hardly moving. "Where am I? What... Why?"

"This is Blairsville Hospital in Blairsville, Georgia. Does that ring a bell?"

"No... no, no!" She looked into Melody's eyes. "Water?"

"Of course! Here's a full jug, but you can't reach it!" Melody picked up the jug and gave the woman a drink through a straw. Moving the rolling table, she said, "I'll pull the table closer, could you reach it yourself?"

Jane lifted her right arm, but only a few inches from the bed it fell back as she groaned. "No... I can't. Hurts"

"Doctor says your left arm's the only thing broken, but everything's bruised."

"How?"

"How did you get bruised?" Jane nodded. "You don't remember?" Jane shook her head. "Somebody must have beaten you up. You have bruises all over your body. Your arm was broken and someone clobbered you on the head. A man who lives in a little town not far from here found you in some woods behind his house. He saw a car that had dumped you off in those woods. He called the sheriff. You don't remember being beat up?"

"No." Jane was quiet for a few seconds, obviously trying to put it all together. Melody stayed quiet, watching the different expressions coming and going on Jane's face. "Miss..." she finally said, "I... I don't remember anything!" Tears slid down her cheeks. She slid her right arm slowly along the bed until it rested close to her head. "My head, it hurts, but... but it feels like an empty space! Why?"

Melody stroked her right arm, wanting to be reassuring, but also feeling her heart sink. "The doctors are calling it amnesia, Honey. Dr. Simon says he's pretty sure it's something temporary. Maybe it'll clear up before you leave the hospital. At least we're hoping that's what'll happen. It's okay, though, you'll remember soon enough, I'm sure. We've been calling you Jane, since your purse never made it in here with you, but as soon as you remember your name, we'll be sure and call you your real name."

"I... I guess that's okay," Jane said hesitantly, but brought her right arm down and pushed her hand under the top sheet. A minute later she shook her head and whispered, "I can't even remember my own name!" Both of Jane's hands were under the sheet, but Melody could see them twisting together. This news was really bothering her.

Still stroking her arm gently, Melody realized that Jane was becoming a bit agitated, probably because she couldn't remember anything. She continued to stroke her arm and said, "I know, but don't try to rush anything, it'll come when your mind is ready. This isn't something that's unique, the doctors call it amnesia."

"I hope it goes away soon," Jane whispered.

"Yes, Honey, we all do."

When the shift changed Allison told the night shift, "Jane woke up finally. With help, she ate a soft meal for supper. Of course, her left arm's in the cast, but she doesn't have much strength in her right arm, she can't lift it but a few inches off the bed without pain, so she'll need help. She seems to be very thirsty, so check on her often."

"Okay," Marg said, "so who is she? Where's she from?"

"She can't tell us."

"She can't tell us!" a young CNA said. "Why?"

"The doctors think she's suffering from amnesia, at least that's what Dr. Simon put in his notes he thinks it's the concussion that's causing it for right now."

"Has Dr. Ramoz or Dr. Simon decided what we do with her?" Marg asked.

"Do with her?" the CNA asked. "What do you mean, do with her? She's in that bed, she's all banged up her eyes are swollen nearly shut. She hasn't talked, what do you mean, do with her?" The CNA's words were belligerent.

"Yeah," Marg answered, defensively. "I think y'all heard me, it's a legitimate question. Now that's she's woken up, what'll happen?"

Allison answered, "They'll talk about it before Dr. Ramoz goes off. He wasn't too talkative about it. Actually, I don't see how they can do anything right away, she's so sore she can hardly move! She still has so much swelling, she barely can open her eyes or her mouth. Even that soft diet took her a long time to swallow. She needs pain medicine now that she woke up. Since she's so weak and in so much pain she needs help with everything. I doubt she could get up to the bathroom. She's barely able to open her mouth wide enough for a spoon to give her the soft diet."

"That poor woman!" a compassionate CNA exclaimed.

"That's my feeling exactly!"

"Is somebody going to tell her she was raped," Marg asked.

The CNA gasped, "She was raped?"

Allison slowly shook her head. "I think that's something the doctors are discussing. Personally, I think they'd better tell her. After all, it's her body she has a right to know!"

"Yes, I agree with you on that. If I'm invited to the discussion, I'll give them my opinion on that subject. She should know everything it's her choice to get an abortion."

Tina exclaimed, "Surely she would! Why would she keep something forced on her by some maniac?"

"Um, some people don't believe in it, no matter what," a CNA said.

After report, when the team leaders and all the other staff left, leaving only Allison and Marg in the office, Marg sat studying something on the computer and said, "Really, I don't see how they can keep her here on the ward, Allison. She's in a private room and she's a charity case. Her blood work came back clean this last time. Once she's awake what's to keep her? Somebody on the hospital board'll complain about that."

In disbelief, Allison sucked in a breath and exclaimed, "Marg! Surely you don't mean that! Truly! She needs that room because she's in so much danger!"

"Yeah, I think I'm pretty realistic, actually," she said, nodding. "I mean, come on think about it, they found nothing in her blood work, it was clean. She woke up, so the concussion isn't keeping her comatose any longer. She has a headache, she's sore, but there's pain medication for that. She only has that broken arm, it's been set and it'll heal right. The two lacerations were stitched and are healing well. The scratches are healing and none of them became infected. Probably they'll be healed in a few days. The swelling is finally going down. The bruises… well, they'll fade in time."

Still looking at Marg like she had three heads, Allison exclaimed, "But the woman's in total pain! Since she woke up, we've given her something for pain every time she's allowed. Besides, she still has her IV and catheter."

Marg shrugged and progressed to another page on her computer. As she continued to read, she said, "Actually, it's only a matter of time, Allison. When she starts eating, they'll pull the IV. If she's awake, they'll take out the catheter. The stitches on the two lacerations won't come out until next week, but that won't be something to keep her here. The meds and rehab they can do in a nursing home just as well, if she still doesn't know who she is."

Her eyes wide, Allison looked at Marg. Shaking her head and barely whispering, Allison said, "You're heartless!"

Marg shook her head. "Just realistic. I think you'll find she's on the discharge list real soon, maybe even tomorrow."

"Oh, no! I hope you're wrong!"

Marg shrugged. "Yeah, I hope I'm wrong, too, but it happens."

Allison whispered, "Yes, I suppose it does. I sure hope it's not on my watch!"

Marg didn't say anything, but continued to read the notes on her computer screen. Considering that Allison was the day charge nurse and most orders were written by doctors during the day, Jane Doe would probably be released on Allison's watch. Unfortunately, it was a fact of life in a busy hospital. A hospital board member was bound to complain.

Marg wondered what would become of the poor woman. Now that there was no deputy watching her room, the woman was vulnerable. She couldn't ever remember seeing a case of abuse that was so severe and so extensive. It really was surprising the woman hadn't died of exposure. Probably only because that man had seen the car leave was why she was alive! As far as anybody knew, the abuser was still on the loose! Maybe this was the first time she could remember being glad for working twelve hour shifts. It was light at both ends.

A few minutes later Allison closed her computer and reached into the drawer where she kept her purse. She sighed, "Guess I'm out of here! Those two admissions were a bit rough. Keep the peace for tonight. I'll see you, Marg."

"Will do, see you in the morning."

Melody brought in Jane's supper tray Tuesday evening, but as she started to lift the lid from the dinner plate, Jane whispered, "Melody, what happens to me?"

"What do you mean, Jane?" Although, she was pretty sure she knew what Jane was asking, still it didn't hurt for her to say.

"I... can't remember anything! I don't know who I am, or where I'm from. I... hurt so bad, am I safe? Will someone come after me? I know I look bad, but somebody did this and dumped me off!"

# Four

Melody felt that scratchiness behind her eyes again. She cleared her throat and whispered, "I don't know, Jane. Dr. Simon hasn't told us anything, he's just saying he's glad you're getting better and that your pain is not as bad. You know you've gone from that first pain shot into your IV to only taking pills these last two times. I'm sure you hurt really badly, but I know you don't want to get addicted."

"But I know I can't stay here forever! Where will I go?"

Melody cleared the frog from her throat. She hated even the thought of sending her anywhere, but it probably would happen, maybe even sooner than any of the staff wanted it to happen. "Marg said something about sending you to a nursing home for a while. You could get pain medicine and rehab there."

As if she was totally defeated, Jane sank into her pillow, closed her eyes and whispered, "Oh, oh, I… I wish I knew…."

Melody patted her arm again and waited for Jane to look at her again. "I'm sure you do, Jane, but it'll come. Surely your memory will come back soon. It'll only be a matter of time until your memory comes back."

"I wish…."

Thursday, Eric's group came back to base. When he walked in the office for his next assignment, Sandy sat at the desk with little Jon sitting on her lap. As the door opened, she looked up and said, "Eric, I'm sure you want to know, but the young woman you found in the woods finally woke up late Monday. Stan's been keeping us in the loop, but he said, unless she can remember anything, she's being discharged to a nursing home tomorrow." Sandy scowled. "Can they do that if she's in pain like that?"

The news upset him he wasn't sure why it upset him as much as it did. The woman meant nothing to him he'd never seen her before he'd found her in the woods. He set his backpack against the door and walked to the chair close by the desk. He fell into it, planning to stay a few minutes, but the news that she was being discharged upset him a lot. He scowled and asked, "She can't remember anything? Really? How horrid! How can that be? Did Stan say why she couldn't remember?"

"No, that's what Nancy told me. She said she's got amnesia."

Eric scowled. "But if she woke up isn't she in pain? I mean, there wasn't one place on her that wasn't black and blue! Her arm... man I... I saw the bone! Her head... it looked like the guy had bashed it in!"

"Yes, lots of pain, but they can give her pain medicine in a nursing home. At least that's what Dr. Stan told her." Sandy shook her head. "It seems so heartless to just ship her out! Will she be safe in a nursing home?"

"Oh, my! We may lose track of her in a nursing home!" Eric exclaimed.

He sat thinking for a minute, before he said, "I know there are some nursing homes that don't do much care at all! Did he tell Nancy which nursing home it was?"

"I know about some of those places, but Nancy didn't tell me, I don't think she knew. I'd take her in, but I couldn't give her proper care or give her medicine. Nancy or Marcy could care for her, but they both work. This all makes me sick! It happened here in Vansville! This place is a sleepy little town! How did some criminal find this place?"

After thinking about it for a minute, Eric said, "Sandy, I really don't have any answers. Pray with me?"

"Yes, of course!"

They joined hands and Eric said, "Father in heaven, Jane Doe woke up, but she can't remember anything. They're going to send her to a nursing home if they don't find something out soon. Lord, we pray You'll have Your way in this situation. How can she be safe until she can tell who did this to her? Would they keep her safe in a nursing home? Surely she isn't safe until whoever did this to her is caught!" Eric took a deep breath. "Father, God, You are in control! May Your Name be glorified, in Christ's Name, amen."

"Lord God, bring the man to justice who did this awful thing! He not only abused her terribly, but he left her to die! Lord Jesus, bring this person, whoever he is, to his knees! I pray in Your Name, amen," Sandy added.

They opened their eyes and Jon pointed to Eric and said, "Ick."

Sandy looked at Jon, he wasn't even fourteen months old, but he was looking at Eric, as well as pointing to him. "Little One, I think you almost said Eric's name! That's ER-ic."

Jon's little head went up and down. "Ick."

Eric smiled and Sandy hugged the little boy. "I love you Jon," she breathed.

Jon turned back to Sandy, his smile stretching his face. "Wuv, Mama." The tiny boy laid his head on Sandy's shoulder, put his other arm around her neck and nuzzled her neck.

Eric's heart turned over. He was thirty years old. He'd never met a woman he wanted to spend his life with, but he wished for a family of his own. His brother had been married, but threw his wife away. Thank goodness they hadn't had any children! Children always suffered from a divorce. He'd never married, hadn't met anyone he felt like he couldn't live without. He'd been working on a criminal justice degree, but joined the military and let them pay for the last two years of college. He'd had a good life, but not fulfilling by any means. He'd been deployed to a war zone, but he wouldn't even begrudge that, he was defending his country.

He glanced away from mother and child, feeling the scratchiness behind his eyes. He cleared his throat then had to swallow, as he looked at the little boy. "I guess I'll be going, Sandy, since you've given me my next hike. See you."

"Have a good day off, Eric. See you on Saturday."

"Thanks Sandy, I have some errands to run tomorrow."

A few minutes later, Eric left DeLord's house with his next assignment in hand. Since the weather had been nice, he'd walked the few blocks from his cabin to DeLord's for this hike. However, now he was questioning his intelligence, one more step with a huge backpack on his back was foolish when he had a car he could have brought to ride back in. After all, he'd been either hiking over rough terrain or sleeping on cold, unforgiving ground for almost a week. He turned the corner onto Isabel's parking lot when both Isabel and Ruth came out of her house. Ruth had her keys in her hand and Isabel had her large purse over her shoulder. Those two things made it obvious that the two women were going somewhere.

They headed for Ruth's car, but Isabel saw him turn from the sidewalk onto the gravel. "You walked home after your hike?" she asked, incredulous, when Eric was close enough she didn't have to yell. "What is wrong with your car?"

Eric sighed and walked a few more steps, then lowered his backpack to the walk up to his cabin. Leaning it against his leg, he shook his head and said, "Yes, it seems like one of my more stupid moves right now. Carrying that backpack any further than necessary seems rather stupid! Nothing's wrong with my car, I think it's my head that has something wrong with it! Where are you two off to?"

"We're going to see Jane Doe in the hospital. Dr. Stan told Nancy she'll be discharged tomorrow and we wanted to see her before then," Isabel said, her hand on the passenger door handle. "We want to be neighborly, you know."

Eric glanced at his watch. It was hours before visiting hours ended. "Yes, Sandy told me just now that they were sending her to a nursing home sometime tomorrow. Could you wait a few minutes until I clean up and I'll go with you? I'd really like to see her again. She's being discharged, where will she go that's safe? Is there a good nursing home in Blairsville? Can she get good care at this nursing home?"

"Why, of course, young man! We'll wait for you." Isabel exclaimed. "We were just going now so we could get home before supper. After all, you were the one who found the young woman. I don't blame you for wanting to see her."

Smiling at the two women, Eric said, "Tell you what. If you'll wait, I'll spring for supper. You know we'll be in the big, booming metropolis of Blairsville, we can eat out! You know that's my best way of feeding friends."

Ruth chuckled. "Eric, we'll wait, no supper needed."

Eric picked up his backpack and took a step toward his cabin. "I know, but I'd like to. After all, you ladies keep my place spotless and keep the place comfortable, it's the least I can do once in a while."

Isabel laughed. "Okay, fella, you twisted my arm, but hurry. I turn into a pumpkin soon after dark, you know."

Eric switched the heavy backpack to his other hand and took a step up the walk. Chuckling and knowing how late Isabel was known to stay up, he said, "Ah, is that why the lights go out in your house so early now that the days are getting longer!"

"Of course!" Isabel called to his back. "Hurry all you can, fella, I sure do love to eat somebody else's cooking, now that you mention it."

"I'm on it, Isabel!" He stepped up on his porch, the cabin key in his hand. Before he shut his door he heard two car doors close on the parking lot.

It had been a strenuous hike, the young people kept him, along with their leaders on their toes for the whole hike, but now that he was going with the ladies to see the woman he'd rescued. His steps seemed just a little lighter. He grinned, there was another reason; he could eat something besides one of Alex's frozen dinners. He had to chuckle, now that there was only himself who was single, the supply didn't turn over quite so fast at the store as it had when Natt kept his freezer stocked with TV dinners. Eric looked around the spotless cabin and sighed. He really wouldn't mind to stay home, but he felt he needed to see Jane Doe.

He hurried straight to the bathroom, still dragging his backpack. After a refreshing shower, he shaved quickly, then started his washer and dumped his dirty clothes in as the tub filled. He hurried into his bedroom, dressed comfortably and pulled a comb through his hair; he'd need a cut soon. He hurried out to meet the ladies who were in Ruth's car waiting. They had waited long enough that Ruth had the air conditioning running.

He opened the back door and slid in. Isabel pulled her seat up immediately, since Eric's long legs hit the back of her seat. As soon as the door was shut, Isabel turned with a grin and said, "One hundred percent improvement, Sonny. You clean up pretty good. I like that clean shaven look the best." She shook her head. "I know it's all the rage with men your age to keep that five o'clock shadow all the time, but I like to see a man's face."

Eric chuckled. He was a bit beyond the macho man image, but it was nice to hear he still passed muster with an old lady. "Thanks, Isabel."

"Of course! You'll even make a good impression at any restaurant in town."

"Wow! That's exciting!"

Isabel grinned and nodded. "You wait and see!"

Jane had been frustrated most of the day. Her bruises were slowly changing colors and fading some and the swelling was slowly going down. Much of it was gone from her face, but she still had no memory. That was the most frustrating. It felt like there was a steel door bolted across her brain. Nothing could get out and surely nothing much was going in. The nurses had told her she was in Blairsville Hospital in Blairsville, Georgia, wherever that was.

Did she live close by? Well, if she did, why didn't anyone know her? And this town of Vansville, they kept talking about what a tiny town it was, nobody could believe somebody had beaten her up so badly and left her in a town so small. She pulled out the mirror on the moveable table and made a face at the reflection. Whoever had done this had really done a number on her! Would she ever remember who that somebody was? Maybe her brain didn't want her to remember him, but surely it wouldn't keep all the important stuff boxed away!

Last evening, after visiting hours, when the ward was quiet, Dr. Simon had sat down beside her bed. When she had asked him, he told her what amnesia was and why she was probably suffering from it. It was a mental state where her mind was blocking out some happenings that her mind didn't want to process. By the look of herself in the mirror, it was pretty obvious what her mind was blocking out.

He told her that usually the state cleared up, sometimes right away, sometimes it took a while, but something else he said, sometimes the person never remembered what happened during the incident. No one ever knew, not even the person who suffered from the mental state what the outcome would be. It didn't mean Jane was crazy Dr. Simon was quick to tell her that information. Given how she felt she wondered. An empty brain for a woman as old as she had to be was sort of crazy.

"Maybe not crazy, but I sure feel like a baby who has to learn everything again. Well, no, I don't have to learn how to eat, read, talk…" she grumbled and closed her eyes. Maybe she'd take a nap and by some miracle when she woke up she'd know everything! She tried to think, but it felt like the door was sealed shut. She couldn't remember her name, her birthday, where she lived, what she did. She had to be far from home, surely she had friends who'd be searching for her, wouldn't she? But she'd been here for nearly a week and nobody had come. She wasn't much good, really.

With her eyes closed she remembered something else Dr. Simon had been really hesitant to tell her. Tears formed behind her lids and leaked out. He'd told her she'd been raped. Now she understood why she hurt so much in that place, even inside. He'd told her that was why she'd hurt so badly, it was something she'd never experienced before.

Only a few minutes after she closed her eyes there was a knock on her door. For some reason, she didn't understand just why, when someone knocked on her door her heart rate hit the top of the charts. It didn't matter who knocked, until she saw them, her heart thundered in her chest. It felt like her blood was roaring in her ears. Swallowing down the panic, she said in a tiny voice, "Who is it?"

"Some folks to visit," came the reply from a female through the door.

Jane swallowed, because she didn't recognize the voice, she answered reluctantly, "Come in." Surely it hadn't been a woman who'd beaten her. No, of course it wasn't, Dr. Simon had told her she'd been raped, it surely hadn't been a woman. Did she know a man who would do this to her? She shrugged, with an air-filled brain, who knew what men could do?

An old lady pushed the door open, a younger woman, who had to be her daughter, since they looked so much alike, followed her and a man her age followed them. He closed the door behind them then leaned on the door. Jane's eyes looked at all three people. She tried to make her mind process the people, but nothing came to her mind. Had she known these people before? Did they know her? It seemed even worse when a man she didn't know came in the room. Tentatively, she asked, "Do I know you?"

Isabel walked right up to the bed, laid her hand on her shoulder and gave her a lovely smile. "Of course not, Deary. You've never seen us before. The reason we've come to see you is that this young man, who lives in one of my cabins, was the fella who found you in the woods. Since he found you so close to where we live and we heard you're being discharged tomorrow. We thought it was only neighborly to come see you before that. By the way, that's Eric, this is my daughter Ruth and I'm Isabel. We know they're calling you Jane Doe, but that's only because you can't remember what your real name is."

Jane turned fearful eyes on Eric. "You… you found me in some woods?" She shook her head. "I wish I could remember."

He took one step closer to her, but didn't come any closer, much to Jane's relief. The look on his face was only compassion. She knew she had nothing to dread from him. His smile was friendly, as he said, "Yes, this car backed into the trees behind my place, stopped for a few minutes, then peeled out. It was nearly dark, but he never turned on his lights. When I went to investigate, I found you unconscious. They tell me you don't remember even your name?"

"I... I know."

"I'm so sorry! I know you're wanting to remember, but everyone else wants you to. I guess it's something that just takes time."

As Isabel looked at Jane and watched her, she had some thoughts. When there was a pause for a few seconds, she asked, "You don't know if you were coming to Vansville or if you were kidnapped and brought there?"

Shaking her head, Jane said, "I have no idea. My memory starts after I woke up here. It's like learning everything all over again. I feel sort of like a baby."

Eric had a thought about that. This lady was no baby, maybe someone thought of her as a 'babe', but no infant. Now that the bruises were fading, he was convinced she was the most beautiful woman he'd ever seen. Now his question was even more appropriate, one so beautiful would be a temptation to any man who looked only at a woman's face and body. Yes, she was beautiful, but he also wanted to know more about the woman, was she a believer, did she love his Lord? Who knew, at this point?

Bringing his thoughts back to the here and now, Ruth asked, "Are you afraid?" She walked around the bed to stand by her arm that was in the cast. Looking at Jane's hands, which were twisting themselves together, as if she was worried about something, she said, "It sure looks like you're afraid of something."

"Maybe," Jane said, tentatively. "These nurses said I was beat up very badly and I guess I was. I've seen the bruises all over my body, and my arm... My heart speeds up every time someone knocks on that door until I see who is at the door."

"Well, of course!" Isabel exclaimed. "It's understandable! If you can't remember who did something to you, of course you're scared! Why, it only stands to reason!"

"I...I guess that's right," she murmured.

Eric stood back from the bed and watched the three women interact. He could tell Jane was trying to be friendly, but underlying everything, he knew she was scared. Of course, he'd seen her bruises, how it looked like she'd been tossed away! Maybe she didn't remember, but her body was in 'fight or flight' mode, but she couldn't do either. The car hadn't stayed in the woods long. How could someone pull an unconscious adult across the car in that length of time? Only pulling her from the trunk made sense. He wished he had been closer.

Now that the swelling was nearly gone and the bruises were fading, anyone could tell what a beautiful young woman she was. Her hair, one side was shaved, but the rest was a true blond, with natural waves and resting on her shoulder. Her eyes were a sparkling blue, maybe even had a little green, maybe the color was brine, like ocean water. Unconsciously, he licked his lips, he really admired her. Of course, she had survived a hideous act of violence. What if he hadn't been on his porch? A shudder went up his back. As cool as it had been that evening, if he hadn't seen that suspicious car and went to investigate, she most certainly would have died!

Some time later, after they'd talked for another few minutes, but seemed to have exhausted all topics, Eric stepped up to her bed and said, "You look like you're getting tired, Miss. Could I pray for you before we go?"

Jane scowled, but she nodded, "I... I guess it's alright."

Eric took her right hand, then covered it with his other hand, bowed his head and closed his eyes. "Father, God, the nurses say Jane's to be discharged to a nursing home in the morning. We pray You will keep her safe, put Your loving arms around her, bring back her memory in Your time. Bless her, we pray, we know You love her. Amen."

"They told you I was being discharged?" she asked.

"Yes, do you know where?"

"No, all they've told me is to a nursing home. I wish I knew something, knew somebody, but they say it's because I have this amnesia that I can't remember anything."

"Well, you rest, Deary. We'll pray real hard for you to get better and to remember. I guess that's very, very important."

"Thank you."

Isabel, Ruth and Eric left the room and Eric pulled the door closed, but Jane let out a long sigh. Having those people here had totally zapped every ounce of her strength. She found the control and lowered the bed, closed her eyes and decided she'd nap. She knew she'd get pain medicine and a snack before they left her alone for the night. When at first she'd woken up she couldn't get enough to drink, but now she was ravenous all the time. In answer to her thoughts her stomach growled loudly, even though she'd eaten everything on her tray. She was glad it hadn't done that when her visitors were here. That would have totally embarrassed her, especially in front of that man. He'd been the one who found her. He seemed nice enough…

Eric pulled the door closed, but he was very concerned for the young woman. Right now, she was close to the nurse's desk, only a door beyond the small utility room, but when they transferred her to some nursing home, would that be true? It was a good possibility it wouldn't. She was a young woman, a very beautiful young woman, even with the bruises that were fading and the swelling that was going from her face slowly. The nursing home staff might think she could take care of herself. For a while she'd need pain medicine and possibly some rehab, but not for ever. What would happen to her when she didn't need that? A nasty thought entered his mind. *What would happen to her if she was sent to a custodial nursing home! Suppose the perp found out where she went?* Eric didn't want to think about that, he'd had a great aunt whom the family had shuffled into one of those awful places.

The three started up the hallway toward the nurse's desk that was beside the door into the floor waiting room, Eric was a few steps back, since he'd also closed Jane's door. However, Isabel didn't wait for Ruth and Eric. Like someone on a mission, she walked right up to the nurse's desk and asked, "As I understand it, you folks are discharging that girl in room four-twelve tomorrow. To what nursing home will you send her?"

Tina shook her head. "That's something we're not supposed to tell anyone unless they're family and Jane doesn't have family that any of us know about."

Isabel scowled at the woman and adjusted her purse strap on her shoulder. However, she brought her other hand down on the counter as a fist. Looking the nurse in the eye, she said, "If you know, and we know, she doesn't have family, but there are people who're interested why can't you tell us? Perhaps we'll want to visit again."

"Umm, it's hospital policy," Tina said, reluctantly, not looking at the old lady.

"Listen, young lady," Isabel crossed her arms across her chest and rested them on the high counter. Looking fiercely at the nurse, she said, "I want to know! Who can I ask who will tell me that information? That 'hospital policy' stuff is an easy crutch to fall back on!"

"Ah, I'm not sure. Perhaps her doctor." All Tina knew was that there was an order in Jane's chart not to tell where she was going from the hospital. Jane hadn't had many visitors, in fact, the young man who was with these two women had been her only other visitor.

Isabel leaned on the counter more heavily, stretched as far as she could toward the nurse, as if she was settling in for the long haul. "You get him here. Surely the man's still in the hospital! This is something I want to know before we leave!"

Tina looked at her charge nurse who shrugged, but didn't speak. Marg picked up the phone and punched in some numbers. Without speaking, she hung up and said, "The house doctor has been treating Jane, I've put in a page for him. He should answer soon. That's the best I can do, Ma'am."

"Fine! I'll wait right here." Isabel didn't move.

Marg cleared her throat. "That's fine, Ma'am."

Ruth leaned over to whisper into Isabel's ear, "Mom, come on, don't make a scene. So she's being discharged tomorrow…"

Isabel only turned her head, but didn't move from leaning on the counter. Giving Ruth one of her most powerful 'Isabel' scowls, she said to her daughter, "Listen, Ruth, if you don't like it, go on to the lounge, I'll be out when I have my answer. Eric, if you want to wait with her that's all right, you go ahead."

Eric shook his head. "Isabel, I think it's important too, I'll wait with you. That girl needs to be kept safe! I'd hate for that perp to find out where she was!"

The phone on the desk rang as Ruth pushed the door into the lounge open then walked into the big room, leaving the other two behind. Marg picked up the phone and said, "There are some people here who want to know where Jane Doe will be sent. Can you come up and talk with them?" When she hung up, she said to Isabel, "He said he'll be right up."

"Thank you, Miss. I appreciate that very much." However, Isabel didn't move, so Eric stood behind her.

A few minutes later a middle-aged man wearing a lab coat walked onto the ward from the back elevator. "What is the problem?" he asked. "I'm Dr. Simon, I'm Jane Doe's doctor, what can I do for you?"

"Young man," Isabel said before either of the nurses could open her mouth. She turned and looked at him. "I have asked these people where Jane Doe will be sent when she's discharged. It's important that I know."

"You're not family."

Giving the younger man her sternest 'Isabel' look, she pulled in a deep breath and said, "No, but I am an interested party. You can also be sure I was not the person who did this atrocity to that young woman. This young man found her in the woods behind my cabins the other day. I want to know where you are sending her. Will she be safe? Will she be watched so the mad man who did this awful thing to her can't hurt her again? Besides, what kind of facility is this? Don't you think it should be a safe place for her? Besides, if she was hurt so badly that the bruises haven't even gone away, why is she being sent out?"

Dr. Simon cleared his throat and pulled his hand over his face. He wasn't high man on the hospital medical staff. It wasn't his decision. "Well… um… we have considered all that, Ma'am. The Sheriff's Department is quite concerned about her safety. We don't usually, but we did consult with the Sheriff about her placement. Since the person who did this hasn't been apprehended, we will be sending her to the rehab center right next door for a few days. It is quite safe there all the entrances are either locked or guarded. There are precautions the staff will take. When she doesn't need pain medicine or rehab, if she's still suffering from amnesia, she'll be discharged to another facility later. Of course, if she remembers or if someone were to recognize her, we would be glad to discharge her somewhere else."

"I see, thank you, doctor." She looked at the two nurses still behind the counter and said, "See, that wasn't hard. You could have told me that, now couldn't you?"

"Umm, yes, Ma'am, yes, I guess we could have," Marg answered. *The ethics committee might have come after us, though and pulled a license or two.*

Isabel gave all three of the staff her bright smile and said, "Thank you very much, Doctor. I may see you again."

"Um, yes, Ma'am," Tina whispered. "Thanks for coming to see Jane. Needless to say, she doesn't get many visitors."

Isabel nodded. "Yes, I'm sure that's true." Now that she had her answer, she turned quickly and said to Eric, "Come on, Eric, you didn't hear it, but my stomach's been growling for that dinner you promised us."

Eric chuckled. "Is that so, Isabel?" and ushered her from the ward.

The doctor watched them leave and as the door closed behind them he sighed, "That lady was something else! I sure hope she won't leak that information to the wrong people! Jane could be in some serious trouble."

"I know," Marg agreed. "She wouldn't take no for an answer, though."

The doctor nodded. "I know, some older people are like that."

After they chose the restaurant and waited for service, Ruth took a swallow of her water and said, "Mom, what's so very important that you learn where they're sending Jane Doe? We don't know her we have no idea who she is! Eric's the only one who ever saw her before. We knew she was being sent to a nursing home, why was it so important to know which one?"

Isabel nodded. "Perhaps you don't know and I don't think Eric saw a connection, but that young woman looks like Derek Casbah. At any rate, I intend to contact him."

"Derek Casbah! You mean Ramon DeLord's step-dad?" Ruth exclaimed.

"Exactly."

Eric scowled. "Ramon's step-dad? He has a step-dad? I thought he only had his mom who lives here in town."

Isabel knew what she wanted for her supper, so she laid her menu down and looked at Eric. "That's right. They don't get along much, so he doesn't talk about him much. The man was married before he married old Millie. I don't know anything about his other family, but that girl looks too much like him to not be a relation."

"Haaa," Ruth said, thoughtfully. "So he had another family?"

Isabel shook her head. "That's not what I said I don't know about that. I do know he was married before he made the mistake of marrying Millie. I'll see what he says when I call, but I do intend to call him tonight!"

Ruth shook her head, but didn't say anything. Sometimes she wondered where her mother got her spunk. She surely hadn't passed it on to her daughter. Ruth picked up her menu again to look at the choices. Of course, her mom had lived in Vansville all her married life and since she became a widow. Knowing everyone in a little town was a bit different from living in a city like Detroit where she always kept her doors locked even on warm summer days.

After the three visitors left her room, Jane was too wide awake for a nap, so she turned on her call light. Tina saw it come on, so she ran down the hall. No one ever let Jane wait long to answer, she still was scared and her pain was still quite severe even though she insisted on taking only pain pills. There was the possibility that someone could have let the word drop. She was close to the nurse's desk, but the back exit stairs weren't that far away.

As she pushed open the door, Tina asked, "What is it, Jane?"

"Those people were very nice, but the man prayed for me. At least that's what he called it. What was that about?"

"You mean he bowed his head, closed his eyes and mumbled some words?"

Jane scowled at Tina she didn't like her dismissal of what the man had done. "Yes, well, he bowed his head and closed his eyes, only I could understand what he said."

Tina waved her hand and said, "Oh, don't take what he said for anything. I don't believe that stuff. He talked about God?"

Contemplating what Tina said, Jane thought back to the people who'd visited. She looked at Tina, but she scowled and said, "Yes, he did, well… no, he talked *to* God. Who is this God? He asked some things this Person should do for me that nobody could do!"

Waving her hand dismissively, Tina said, "See, that's just the thing… You can't take stuff like that for anything important. My way of thinking, people who think like that just use religion like a crutch. Most all the time we're better off taking things into our own hands. That's my philosophy in life… take care of number one."

"I… I liked the guy, though. He seemed nice enough and…" she hesitated a moment, "He was the person who found me."

Tina patted Jane's hand. "Don't think much about it, you probably won't see the guy again. Remember you're getting sprung from here tomorrow."

Looking seriously at the nurse, Jane remembered Eric's prayer for her safety. Hesitantly, Jane said, "Tina, will I be safe?" Looking at her puffy, bruised arm, then at the huge cast on her other arm, she asked, "Really, will they keep me safe in this place? I look pretty banged up." Tears sprang to her eyes. "I'm scared, I'm still weak, I couldn't defend myself. Really, I'd be a sitting duck!" she whispered.

Tina swallowed and said, "I… I know, Jane. We've hoped you'd remember something about what happened, who did this, where you're from, something, before you left. It'd really help, not only to keep him away, but the sheriff needs to know, so they can hunt him down. If you knew where you're from we could contact somebody and they could come for you."

Jane let out a long breath. "Doesn't seem like that's gonna happen. That's another thing, he asked his God to keep me safe."

Tina shrugged. "Maybe that's good. Can't hurt, I guess. We all want you to be safe."

"Yeah, I know," she murmured, closed her eyes and settled back on her pillow.

Tina, of course, hurried from the room. She used to go to church as a child, she'd loved Sunday school and had learned all the stories in the Bible, but when she went to nursing school, she'd turned her back on all of it. Too many bad things happened to good people. Life was hard, where was God when it hurt? Where was God when Jane was hurt?

Isabel hadn't turned into a pumpkin when Ruth drove onto the parking lot at their home, even though the evening was long. Eric was tired, he said goodnight and headed for his cabin, but Ruth and Isabel took longer to head into Isabel's house. Ruth put her purse in her room, but came to Isabel in the kitchen just as the older lady lifted the handset from the wall phone.

"Mom, you're going to call that snooty man?"

"Ruth!" Isabel exclaimed, looking so directly at Ruth that the younger woman became uncomfortable. "I never took you for being like this! Of course I'm calling Derek! If she is some relation, he needs to know! Besides, he's well able to care for her."

Ruth grumbled, "I think you should leave well enough alone! I mean… they are discharging her to a good place, aren't they?"

"Well, I'm not! If it'll keep that girl safe, then I'll do whatever I can! And right now, that's calling Derek Casbah!"

"Umm, yeah," Ruth whispered and hurried into the living room. Her mother was not one to be crossed when she was in such a mood.

Derek had come home late from the bank, as he usually did and eaten a solitary meal, also as he usually did. Mrs. Beecham had kept his supper warm for him and he was always grateful for her consideration. He and Millie hadn't spoken a civil word to each other in months. He'd given up talking to the woman, she'd snap at him no matter what he said or how he acted. That's why he stayed late and ate alone.

He'd cleaned up after himself, so that Mrs. Beecham didn't have to come back from her apartment to clean up after him. Finally, his obligations were over, so he went downstairs to sit for a while in his great room and relax. The TV remote was in his hand, he was surfing the channels, but finding nothing of interest. He clicked off the TV, leaned back in his recliner and turned his head so his eyes could rest on the beautiful scene Sandy DeLord had painted. That young woman inspired him, how could she not? She was so vivacious and everything she did was extraordinary and yet she sat in that wheelchair hour after hour, day after day. Since he'd known her he'd wondered if he'd been in the same circumstance how would he be reacting.

Millie was in her suite of rooms working on her computer, trying to find yet another avenue to spend Derek's money. Not that she could spend much, her credit cards were maxed out every month and Derek refused to advance her any more. He also didn't pay them all off each month, so she never knew exactly how much she had. That was definitely a frustration for her. She sighed the man hadn't always been so cantankerous! But it had been a long time.

A note flashed on the screen, 'This card is overdrawn.' Millie pounded her desk and sighed, then punched in another set of numbers. She was determined to get exactly what she wanted. It was time, it was her due! She'd make sure she had everything she wanted tonight! before she went to bed. If that was late, well so be it! Life… and Derek Casbah owed her!

Derek had a cordless phone on the table next to his chair, so when it rang, he picked it up. "Derek Casbah, could I help you?"

He heard someone pull in a deep breath and say, "Mr. Casbah, this is Isabel Isaacson…"

Very graciously, Derek asked, "Yes, Mrs. Isaacson, what can I do for you? I'm not sure I've ever talked to you on the phone. Have you had a pleasant day?"

Isabel took another deep breath. For the unfortunate young woman at the hospital she must do this. There was absolutely no one else who had noticed what she had. Since neither Ruth nor Eric really knew Derek she must be the one to tell him. He needed to know! "Mr. Casbah, I need to ask you some questions that may be uncomfortable, they already are effecting me, but I feel obligated to do this. I sincerely hope I don't offend you."

"Mrs. Isaacson, ask your question, I'll try to be gracious."

Derek heard Isabel take a deep breath before she said, "Thank you, sir. I know you were married before you married Millie. Did you have a family then?"

Derek hesitated for a second. That was not a question he expected to be asked by someone from Vansville, especially by an old, Christian lady who had lived here all her life. He didn't know her well, but people in town spoke highly of her. He pulled his free hand down over his face, cleared his throat and swallowed. Should he answer her question? What was the purpose? Why was she asking?

Finally he answered, "Yes, Ms. Isaacson, I was happily married. After fifteen years of marriage, my wife was killed in an accident, but we did have children together. I hired a nanny to help me raise my two children, but they are grown now, of course. Why do you ask?"

"Do you keep in contact with your children now?"

"Unfortunately, when I married Millie, my children weren't receptive, they didn't like her." He sighed, "Sometimes I wish I'd listened to my children at the time, but I didn't. Why do you wish to know?"

Isabel agreed with him about Millie, but instead of voicing that thought, she said, "Did you hear about the young woman who was left unconscious in the woods behind my house last week? I think it was Friday."

Concern showing in his voice immediately, he said, "Ah, no, I can't say I did. You say a woman was left unconscious in those woods? That's terrible! There in Vansville? Why, it's such a little town! My goodness! What's become of her?"

Isabel took another deep breath. "Well, of course, she was taken immediately to the hospital, but that's the thing. She was terribly abused, with bruises and scratches and broken bones and all. The ambulance transported her immediately to Blairsville Hospital, of course, but she was hurt so badly, she didn't wake up for several days.

"However, when she did wake up, she couldn't remember anything, not even her name. I think they're calling it amnesia, but she still can't remember anything before she woke up the other day, even now. The person who did this was long gone and until she can help us with possibly a name or where she's from, several of us think she's still in danger."

"Well, yes!" Derek exclaimed, still not sure why he needed this information.

"At any rate, she's being discharged from the hospital tomorrow to the rehab place right next to the hospital. Anyway, my daughter and I went to see her late this afternoon. Of course, she doesn't have white hair as you do, but she looks very, very much like you."

Over the years Derek had had several young women approach him, especially at the bank in Blairsville claiming to be his daughter or granddaughter, he had seen right through that each time, but this was a first. No one had ever approached him on someone else's behalf. He had great respect for Isabel Isaacson he didn't think she'd be out to con him. However, he needed to be careful in this situation, as usual. He gripped the phone and was silent for several minutes.

Finally, he took a deep breath. "Isabel, I have a deep respect for you, so I'm taking what you've told me seriously, but you realize that in the position I'm in that I must be careful. I haven't had any contact with my children in probably ten, maybe twelve years. I was not invited to any wedding either of them might have had, so especially with my daughter, I don't even know a married name. Any children they might have had is something out of my knowledge. What does this woman look like?"

Isabel swallowed a sigh, wishing she had a glass of water beside her, unfortunately she didn't. Of course, Ruth had left her completely alone, since she didn't approve of Isabel's call and she'd let her know in no uncertain words. Actually, Isabel wasn't comfortable talking to Derek, especially since she'd never had to do something like this ever before. She was sure he did have to be careful, after all, he was a wealthy man, and that was from before he moved to Vansville a dozen years ago. He was also a bank president.

She took a deep breath and said, "Well, she is quite pretty, even with all the fading bruises she still has on her fac. She has lovely blond, wavy hair. They had to cut some of it away because of a terrible gash on her head that they had to clean and stitch. She has blue eyes and that's what drew me. They are the same shade as yours. She hardly smiled, but her face could have been a younger version of yours."

"You say she'll be discharged from the hospital tomorrow? Since she can't give any information, what will they do with her?"

"Her doctor told me they will send her to the rehab center connected to the hospital tomorrow. If she doesn't remember after several days, when she's well enough to be off pain medication and is finished with rehab, they'll send her somewhere else. In light of what happened to her, I was quite concerned as to where that 'somewhere else' might be."

With her description, Derek's heart rate accelerated. "Yes, that is quite a concern. From what you say she was very badly abused. Perhaps I could see her at the rehab place. I could get away for a bit tomorrow. If she doesn't know her own name, what are they calling her?"

Isabel chuckled, but very seriously said, "Actually, it's very innovative. She's being called Jane Doe."

Derek chuckled slightly. "Ah, yes. Very. All right. I'll go tomorrow and ask for her."

"Thank you, Mr. Casbah. Perhaps she was trying to find you, you know."

"Yes, I guess that is a possibility." *But if her brother had anything to do with it, she wasn't even in the neighborhood.*

"Thank you for your time, Mr. Casbah. I hope this didn't trouble you too much, but as I spoke with her I was struck with how much she looked like you. You have a good night."

He laughed. "Now you tell me that! This is quite something to think about. I'm glad I wasn't on my way to bed when you called; I think possibly this'll keep me awake for a while. I'll have a look myself and see what will happen." He chuckled again. "Perhaps I should take a good look in the mirror before I go, do you think?"

Isabel also chuckled. "Yes, perhaps you should."

# Five

"By the way, Mrs. Isaacson, I'm Derek, if I might call you Isabel?"

Isabel let out a silent sigh. "Yes, that's quite all right, Derek."

"Thank you for your call, Isabel."

Derek leaned back in his chair. He looked back at the beautiful picture over the fireplace. It was how he did most of his best thinking at home. Millie had commissioned it, but Derek was the one who enjoyed it. Millie rarely came down to the great room in fact he'd often wondered why she'd commissioned a painting for this room. Perhaps just to spend more of his money! In fact, except for taking meals in the dining room and leaving by way of the garage, she rarely went anywhere in the house.

A young woman with blond, wavy hair, with eyes the same shade as his… Goose bumps sprinted up and down his spine. He and Isabel didn't know each other well, but she said this young woman looked enough like him that she believed she was some relation of his. Was this something for <u>Ripley's Believe It or Not</u>? Yes, he'd go to see this young woman tomorrow, Isabel Isaacson had tweaked his curiosity.

After he walked in his cabin, Eric needed something to relieve his agitation and settle him so he could sleep. He poured some of his tea into a mug, set it in the microwave and heated it. It wasn't cold outside, but he hoped the warm liquid would help him sleep. He really was quite agitated and worried about the young woman at the hospital. It hardly seemed like the hospital staff was too concerned about her safety.

She'd been admitted to the hospital Friday night. She hadn't woken up until late Monday. She still had lots of bruises and some swelling. He was sure she still had pain. Now it was Thursday and they were discharging her tomorrow! With everything she'd suffered, how could she be well enough to leave the hospital? A terrible thought came to mind. Had someone complained that a woman who had to be a charity case, since she knew nothing, was in a private room? Wow! That would be a heartless act if he'd ever heard of one!

It had been Friday evening when he'd called the sheriff about finding her, but that didn't mean that someone wasn't laying low just waiting for her to be in a more unguarded place where she would be more vulnerable. He understood the sheriff's department couldn't supply 'round the clock guards, but he was very concerned. They had done well by keeping watch for the entire weekend. He wished he could guard her himself. After all, he was an ex-marine!

"What was it about that young woman that made Isabel decide she needed to call Derek Casbah?" He'd seen the man at church several times, but Jane Doe hadn't brought his face to mind. Isabel must be much more observant than he was. He sighed women seemed to almost have a sixth sense about some things.

He remembered looking at what he could see of her while they visited. The swelling in her face had decreased more than half and much of the bruising had faded, but there were still several places where the bruises were still very evident. He sighed, there wasn't much anyone, not even in a hospital, could do to make bruises fade, they pretty much had to do it on their own. Still, he was very concerned for her safety. Sometimes in a nursing home people were forgotten. He'd known of a bedridden woman who had starved to death in a nursing home! Someone who was up and around could be left to fend for themselves. If the wrong person came on the ward and wasn't detected... oh, my! She could be in such danger!

Now that he was in his cabin, with the quietness around him, he thought of all kinds of things that could happen to her. If he erased the bruises from her face and also the residual puffiness that still filled her cheeks, she was a beautiful young woman. It was easy to see why some criminal had taken advantage of her, then raped her and beaten her unconscious so she couldn't identify him until he was away from her.

However, just the way the nameless man had left her in the woods made Eric decide the criminal meant for her to die from exposure.

He remembered how cold he was when he got back to his cabin and she had only rags on her body. If the man ever found out she hadn't died he could come after her! Had they known each other? Had they had a lover's spat? A spat? Hardly something so benign as a spat would produce the kind of damage Jane Doe had received! On the other hand, she could have been traveling and he'd somehow stopped her.... His mind could conger up many scenarios.

He took his hot tea to his bedroom, got ready for bed, but opened his Bible to read until he relaxed enough to sleep. After reading several Psalms and finishing his tea, he crawled under his light covers to pray, then hopefully fall asleep. "Father, God, keep Jane Doe safe, I pray...."

Not long after breakfast, Jane made her way slowly to her bathroom using hand-holds all the way from the bed to the bathroom door. Her knees felt like Jell-o, but she was determined to make the trip on her own. Even with an empty brain, she knew she was no baby. The staff had helped her stand beside the bed yesterday afternoon. It had taken her several minutes to get everything to work together, but she'd finally made it to the bathroom, with Melody walking right beside her with her arm around her back. She'd been up once more before bed last evening. She felt a bit shaky, but if she held on to something, she walked fairly well. However, she was determined! especially today, since she was being discharged.

Once inside the bathroom, with the door closed, she sat on the toilet for several minutes before she felt strong enough to stand at the sink to wash up. She was getting stronger each day, but she was still very weak and extremely sore. Her legs felt like they were made of putty. Yesterday they had removed her IV and the catheter. At least she wasn't hooked up to anything now. She'd even fed herself her supper! It had taken a while she'd had to rest after only a few mouthfuls. But she was so hungry, she ate everything. Even though she'd eaten everything on her supper tray and had a bedtime snack, she'd been ravenous for breakfast and had also eaten everything on her tray only moments ago.

Looking in the mirror, she made a face at herself, most of the swelling had left her face, but there were still many places that were discolored from the bruises. Her right arm still felt like someone had taken a sledgehammer to her shoulder. She took the comb Melody had given her and tried, not very successfully, to comb some of her hair over the area where they'd had to shave away some hair to clean and suture her scalp. The place was healing nicely, it didn't need a dressing over it any longer, but hair didn't grow that fast. Of course, the gash was on the left side of her head and it was her left arm that was in the huge cast, so trying to comb hair on the left side of her head with her right hand that was still a bit weak and with such a sore shoulder it was a trick. She surely hadn't laughed about it!

After she'd done the best she could, she set the comb down and looked at her right arm, it still had bruises, but her left arm was inside a huge cast. Dr. Simon said it would be several more weeks before she'd be free of a cast. They'd had to set the bones in surgery, then stitched up the open wound and left a window in the cast. The window was big enough to see all the stitches, but they'd have to cut off the cast to remove them; then apply another cast.

"Whoever did this sure did a number on me!" she muttered.

The nursing staff didn't know about the tape that had covered her mouth and bound her wrists, the ambulance personnel had kept that information to themselves. Not that they intended to keep the hospital staff in the dark, they just hadn't mentioned it. That meant that Jane didn't know about it either. They did know about her being raped, the ER doctor had examined her and recorded it in her chart. When the nurses read her chart, several didn't want to tell her, but Dr. Simon felt Jane needed to know. After all, he didn't think that was any kind of secret to keep from an adult woman. It should be her choice what she would do about the information.

The shift had changed, so Melody came to her door and said, "Jane, it's Melody, are you presentable, can I come in?"

Glad to hear the voice of her favorite nurse, Jane exclaimed, "Sure! I'm in the bathroom, but it's okay. Come on in."

Melody pushed open the door into the room, then closed it and stepped into the doorway to the small bathroom. "Jane! It's good to see you up! How are you this morning?"

Jane made a face at herself in the mirror, but Melody could see it. "Still very sore, but I'm getting by with only pain pills. Dr. Simon said I'm going next door to the rehab part of the hospital. What do I wear to this new place? Surely not this hospital monstrosity! I mean, three arm holes in a sack?" Jane picked up the top edge and let it fall in disgust.

Melody laughed. "That's a good description! I'll have to remember that, I may need to remind someone that at least it covers you all over. I found you some underwear and sweats. Those X-ray footies should be okay for your feet. It's not like you're going far, there's even a covered connection between the hospital and the rehab building. It's not raining or cold today, so that's a plus. Besides, we'll take you in a wheelchair."

Jane made a face. "Oh, I just love riding around in a wheelchair! Makes me feel so in charge of my life, you know! This place where I'm going, can I be dressed?"

Melody thought about that for a minute. "Yes, actually, the part where you're going sort of expects its residents to be dressed."

"Good, I've felt like an invalid long enough."

Melody patted her arm. "Remember, girl, you were unconscious for nearly four days. You're entitled to be an invalid, at least for a little while."

Jane waved that off. "Mmm, but that's all past now."

Now that Jane was on her feet, Melody realized how beautiful she was. She'd even fixed her hair so the bald spot wasn't near as noticeable. Since the wound wasn't bleeding, they'd removed the dressing from her head. They'd have to remove the stitches some other day, perhaps next week. If she didn't have the cast on her arm or all the discolored bruises on her face, neck and arms, she would be Miss America!

Melody was a slight woman, but this young woman was regal. She probably was close to five foot eight or nine, but there wasn't an ounce of fat anywhere. Melody shook her head. It was no wonder some man had taken advantage of her! If only something had been found with her, some clue who she was. It really was terrible she'd have to be shuffled around until she could remember. No one who had been in had any clue who she was. They'd hoped, at least she'd hoped, that Jane would remember her name and her home town before she was released. However, it'd have to happen within an hour!

"Well, girl, I guess as soon as you're dressed in these non-descript things we'll be ready to take you next door. Are you ready for that?"

Jane shrugged. "Maybe."

Giving Jane a bright smile, Melody said, "They're waiting anxiously for you over there. There's a place just for you."

"Mmm, I'm sure! Didn't your mama ever tell you it's not good to tell lies? Besides, if you lie, you always have to remember what you said."

Melody chuckled. "I think I've heard something like that before."

Derek didn't tell Millie about his conversation with Isabel. She had already been in her room with the door closed when Isabel called. They really hadn't been communicating much in the past year, so he had no qualms about keeping her in the dark. Millie spent much of her time in her bedroom suite, with the door closed and Derek had no desire to knock. Repercussions of that could send the top off one of the nearby mountains and he had no desire to try to put a mountain top back on. Sometimes, actually, quite often, he wondered what he'd ever seen in the woman he'd asked to be his wife years ago.

Actually, he wasn't sure what he would do if somehow the woman at the hospital turned out to be someone in his family. Besides, he hadn't been in contact with his son or daughter for so long he had no way of knowing how to reach them now. Isabel never said how old this woman was. Was she old enough to be his daughter or a granddaughter? Well, she had said she was a young woman. Remembering his children's ages, if his son were married, his child wouldn't be any older than perhaps preschool. So, a granddaughter wouldn't be a young woman. She couldn't be a niece, he was an only child.

By elimination, this would have to be his daughter, if they were related. How could that be? The last he knew, his daughter was several states away! The last time he'd seen her was the night of her high school graduation. That had been in Louisiana! This was Georgia! How could his daughter be here? Had a criminal transported her across that many states? His heart skittered in his chest. At one time he and his daughter had loved each other to distraction, but then everything had fallen apart. Of his own doing he'd been left with... Millie. Yes, God had forgiven him, he'd gotten back into church and his life straightened out, but he had to live with the consequences. He knew he had been and they weren't pretty!

The next morning, he straightened his tie, grabbed up his suit jacket and left the house. He rarely ate breakfast at home, even though Mrs. Beecham made delicious pastries fresh every morning. Millie was usually in a fowl mood in the mornings, if she got up in time before he left for the day and he could never be sure on any given day. He had no desire to start his day off with the woman and her ravings. He raised the garage door and backed his BMW convertible out, then left for Blairsville and the closest drive-thru for a coffee and Danish. It was a habit he'd perfected for almost four years.

As he drove away from the house he had to smile, he had taken an extra long look in the mirror when he combed his hair after his shower. Isabel had told him the young woman at the rehab center looked a lot like him. Yes, before he'd met and married Millie his hair had been wheat blond. It had been the bane of his existence for many years. For some reason, young women seemed to love his hair! Now his hair was pure white. Could he lay the change at Millie's feet? Perhaps.

Millie was awake and heard the garage door go up. She had taken a long shower this morning, using all her oils and lotions then intentionally stayed at her dressing table until Derek had left. She was glad she'd insisted several years ago that they needed to have separate rooms. She had no desire to put up with him in the mornings. Besides, he was always irritated with her about her make-up. Of all the nerve! She needed her makeup! Her makeup and her clothes made the woman she was. And of course her hairdo that her hairdresser did each week! She had no desire to see him or speak to him this morning especially. She would not miss his constant, irritating chorus telling her to hurry every chance she had! How could she hurry? When she showered, she needed her special formula soap, her organic shampoo, her special foundation. All those things were so important to her looking her absolute best. Of course her clothes! Sometimes she had to change her outfit several times before she felt right about being seen by anyone! Today especially she had to look her absolute best!

She finished with her morning routine then clunked down the stairs in her platform heels to the kitchen for her usual cup of black coffee and the homemade Danish Mrs. Beecham made for her. Without a word, she took them back to her room. Not that they weren't good, but she was the housekeeper after all! That's what Derek paid her to do, wasn't it? After a few swallows and several bites to keep her stomach from growling again, she pulled out her luggage from her walk-in closet and started packing. Fortunately, she had a large set, her closet was full and she intended to leave nothing behind. Not to mention her cosmetics and lotions. By the time the man came home tonight from his precious bank she planned that her room would be totally empty and she would be miles away, enjoying herself immensely. That was why she'd stayed at her computer so late last night. She planned to forget about this miserable little town and move on to bigger and better things!

There had been a time when she wanted to leave her husband and move in with her son, but no more! She had no use for his wife. If she could have, she'd have prevented the marriage in the first place! Yes, she'd painted a beautiful painting, one she loved, but it was too big to take with her. Besides, she hadn't decided where she'd live after this. Her grandson… well… She'd have to forfeit that. Leaving him almost brought tears to her eyes, but of course, she couldn't let her eye make-up be ruined. She loved that boy, even though she had to see his mother every time she saw him. Besides, having a grandson made her feel *old*. Her new image that she was creating today was *not old*!

Besides, who wanted to be married to some *old* man? For goodness sake! The man's hair was white! No white-haired man could be considered young enough for her! Besides, she had no use for the man. He actually went to *church*! Nobody who was anything went to church any more! God, church, any of that stuff was not for her!

About ten o'clock she finished her breakfast and stuffing her luggage. Everything she valued was in her luggage, even her laptop was in its case ready to go. Now it was time to load her Jaguar. Of course, she had to do this quietly and watch where the housekeeper was. Mrs. Beecham was not to have a clue! Well, she'd use the front door and the other woman stayed pretty much in the kitchen. The old woman knew it wasn't unusual for her to go to the garage several times before she was ready to leave on any given day.

She loaded as much as she could on her biggest rolling suitcase and headed for the front door. She had to make three trips before she had the last things in her car. She was beginning to worry that Mrs. Beecham would discover what she was doing, since she took so long. Of course, her heels went perfectly with her outfit, but they were a bit hard to navigate stairs, while pulling luggage down behind her.

Just before she was ready to leave for good, she went in Derek's office, dropped the keys to his precious house on his desk and decided to write him a note.

"*Derek: I have left, I won't be back, don't try to find me. I'm through with you!*"

Moments later, Millie backed her car out of the garage, but then powered down her window. With the garage door opener in her hand, she pushed the button for the door to go down, but as it started down, she threw the little box inside onto the floor where her car had been parked. She would do anything to keep anyone from suspecting that she was gone for good. She powered the window up again, let out a sigh and continued to back around on the asphalt. Only a moment later she pulled the stick down into drive and nearly left black marks. It was a long driveway, but she was onto the country road in only seconds.

"I'm finally shed of him! He didn't appreciate me anyway!" As she drove the country road into Vansville, a thought entered her mind. *Would Ramon go with me? Would he bring the baby? No, of course not! He's stuck on that* **cripple**! Never looking at Ramon's house or any of the other buildings in the little town, Millie pushed her foot down on the gas and left her life in Vansville behind. She would not miss it, not at all! Soon, she was on the open road, it felt great! She was on to new places, new things and a new life! She was *not old!* From now on, she had no reason to tell anyone her true age.

At noon, Derek left the bank downtown, drove through a fast food drive thru then went the few blocks to the medical complex. He hadn't had reason to visit the place except that one time when Millie had bashed her car into the tree at Isabel's. When he'd picked her up she insisted she had whiplash and must be treated immediately, so Derek had taken her to the emergency room at the hospital in Blairsville, but the emergency doctor looked at her, raised his eyebrows at Derek, then sent her for an X-ray and sent her home, telling her to 'take two aspirin and call her family doctor in the morning.'

He had to smile, she'd been furious. Actually, her car was in much worse shape than she'd been. He'd had to spend several thousand dollars to get it fixed, then nearly turned himself inside out making her understand he wasn't buying her a new car. The body shop was the best in the county and had made her car look like new, but she'd nearly refused to drive it.

He followed the signs, first for the parking garage and left his car, then for the rehab center that was connected to the hospital. He straightened his tie and pulled out his comb to press down the hairs that the wind had whipped up in the open garage. He walked in and went directly to the desk he could see from the front door. The woman looked up, but her mouth dropped open, she snapped it closed, swallowed, but still not a word or a sound came out. Usually, when a visitor came in, she stood up, but this time her knees felt like water.

Derek didn't seem to notice her actions he walked confidently to the desk and said, "I guess, Ma'am, I need to ask for your help."

Finally, the woman cleared her throat and was able to croak out. "Umm, yes…"

Derek turned and leaned on the desk in front of the uncomfortable woman and continued, "I understand you admitted a woman today who's been a patient in the hospital. I believe they've called her Jane Doe."

"Uh, yes. Sir, she's in the room down the hallway, but I need to call someone to accompany you to that room."

"May I go see her?"

"Well, perhaps you should wait until someone can go with you this first time? Actually, that's our policy here at the rehab center." She'd spoken so softly the first time Derek hadn't understood what she said.

"Really? That's necessary?"

Acting very uncomfortable, the woman said, "Well… let me call someone immediately. Have a seat right over there."

Derek shrugged, then turned and found a chair close by. "Sure, not a problem, but I do need to hurry. You realize I'm on my lunch hour."

However, the woman immediately picked up the phone and with trembling fingers was able to punch in some numbers. When a voice answered, she whispered, "Angie, come quick! There's a man just came in who looks like our new Jane Doe. It's uncanny, really! He's asked to see her, too."

Angie scowled as she replaced the receiver. A man who looked like Jane Doe? How could that be? The hospital said no family had come or called. No one knew her, no one had ever seen her before, but someone was here who looked like her! How could that be? Actually, she was reading Jane's chart at the moment, so she had instant knowledge of everything anyone said about her, including the visitors she'd had last evening. That old lady had spunk!

Actually, the old woman who'd come last night as a visitor had been a bit demanding to know where Jane was going. Knowing Dr. Simon as she did, Angie was quite surprised that he'd told her. Dr. Simon was a stickler for policy and following orders. He'd been the one to write the 'no tell' order!

She was the charge nurse on duty, so she left her desk in her office immediately, taking the chart with her and stopped at the desk of the woman who called her. From behind the desk she observed Derek sitting several feet away. She swallowed a gasp and whispered, "Ruth, you're right! But I know him he's the president of the bank downtown. I never thought about him when we admitted her until right now!"

"I tell you! I thought I was seeing things!"

Angie walked out from behind the desk and said, "Mr. Casbah, what's brought you here today? I've never seen you except at the bank."

Derek smiled and stood up. He came toward the nurse with his hand out and said, "Hello, Angie, good to see you. Actually a friend told me about a young lady she thought looked like me who was being admitted to this facility today and urged me to come see her."

Angie nodded and started walking. She turned from looking at Derek and swallowed before she said, "Mr. Casbah, come with me. If this young woman isn't some relation of yours there must be two of you in the world and the other guy's her dad."

Derek gave Angie a long look, but all he said was, "Hmmm."

Angie led the way down the long hall, but Derek was right on her heels. She turned left into the last room on the hall, but stepped aside immediately so Derek could step into the room. He took a step over the threshold and stopped abruptly. Sitting on a chair, looking out the window so that only her profile showed to Derek, was a woman who twelve years ago was his eighteen year old daughter. Feeling his legs turn to butter, he quickly leaned against the doorpost and tried to pull in a breath.

When she became aware of the people in her room, the young woman turned her head and Derek whispered, "Carolyn!"

The young woman stared and as usual, her heart rate went off the charts. Looking at her, but leaning on the doorpost was a man who looked like the reflection she'd stared at in the mirror this morning. His eyes were the same shade as hers, they were shaped the same. The only difference she could see, her hair was blond his was white. It was uncanny! It seemed like her heart not only was going miles a minute, but it felt as if it turned over. Who was this man? How could he look so much like her?

"Carolyn," he murmured again.

Angie had been looking at her patient, but she turned and looked at Derek. "Did you call her Carolyn? You know her?"

Still looking at the young woman, Derek swallowed hard, but continued to look at the young woman. In little more than a whisper, he said to Angie, "As you say, if she isn't my daughter, then there are two of us and he's her dad. Believe me I do not have a twin. The only way she couldn't be my daughter would be for someone unrelated to me who looked like me."

"Wow!" Angie looked back and forth between them. The young woman stared at Derek, but there didn't seem to be any recognition in her features. On the other hand, Derek's face was stark white in fact, she could almost bet there were tears in his eyes. "Jane?" she asked the young woman, "What do you say?"

"I... I," she swallowed, but a scowl worked its way across her face. "I... he, um looks like what I saw in the mirror this morning."

"But you can't say you know him." Jane shook her head. "Mr. Casbah, you're sure this is your daughter?"

After taking some time to feast his eyes on the lovely young woman, Derek pulled in a breath and said, "Angie, I have been estranged from my children for too many years. The last time I saw my daughter she was eighteen at her high school graduation. I know people change as they mature, but this young lady very well could be my daughter Carolyn, yes."

Looking at the young lady, Angie asked, "How does Carolyn sit with you?"

"Better than Jane," she answered immediately.

"Okay, Carolyn it is." Looking again from one to the other, Angie said, "But if she doesn't remember, maybe we'd better not do the Casbah. What do you think, Mr. Casbah?"

Derek shrugged. "I guess Carolyn Doe will pass."

"Would you like to stay and talk for a few minutes?"

Derek sighed and looked at his watch. "I'm on my lunch break, so I should leave soon, however, I have some questions I need to ask you."

"Fine, let's go to my office."

Derek turned to 'Carolyn' and said, "I'll be back later to talk with you, Carolyn. It is so good to see you, believe me!"

The young lady nodded and looked back out the window. Her heart was still beating faster than double time! If this man was her dad, shouldn't she know him? Why was there so much dead air space in her head? Yeah, she knew she had amnesia, but still… He called her Carolyn, why didn't it sound familiar? He did look just like the reflection she'd looked at in the mirror this morning… but still… When would she start to remember? Why couldn't she remember even the simple thing like her name?

Tears came to her eyes and dripped slowly down her face. He hadn't seen his children in twelve years? Children, did that mean she had siblings somewhere in the world? Why hadn't he seen them? He didn't know if she was married, but neither did she! Actually, there were lots of other things she didn't know – her birthday…

The hospital garden outside her window cheered her. Her heart rate was off the charts! Now what would happen to her? This man claimed to be her father, was he really? She shook her head it was obvious she didn't know him. Would she be safe with him? Who knew! At that moment she remembered the young man who had prayed for her last night. Was his God answering his prayer? A feeling of awe settled over her. Perhaps his God was watching out for her! He'd only said those words to keep her safe last night. Maybe this was the answer. Her tears continued to slide down her cheeks. Who would have known to get this man to come see her today? Was it one of those women last night?

Derek followed Angie down the hall. "Thanks for taking me to her room."

"Mr. Casbah, that was unreal! She has to be your daughter!"

"It does seem too uncanny for any other possibility."

"Absolutely!"

They arrived at the receptionist's desk. Angie pulled the newly made chart from the rack and took it with her into her office. She motioned him to a seat then she closed the door and took a chair close by. "What questions did you want to ask?"

Derek took the seat, he still felt a bit weak in the knees. He clasped his hands and looked at the young woman who he'd gotten to know at the bank. He realized his knees were not only weak, but his heart rate was galloping. He pulled in a breath and asked, "How long must she stay here? Will she be safe? Could she be released to me?"

"About her safety, all our doors are locked. Staff must use their name cards to get on the ward there is a special viewer at the back by the timeclock. Visitors are allowed only to this front desk until they can be escorted to whom they want to visit. Jane… I mean Carolyn was brought here for two reasons she still needs some pain medicine, at least some to keep her comfortable. The other reason, since she's still suffering from amnesia, she has no idea where she's from so we had nowhere to send her, other than a nursing home. Here the two hospital house doctors could continue to treat her. As far as being released to you, that could happen at any time, especially because you claim to be her father and I most definitely agree that the family resemblance is very evident. As I recall, she's not on strong narcotics and she is moving quite well considering. You have the option of taking her?"

Derek looked at the young woman and smiled. "Angie, I have a huge house in the country. I have a housekeeper who is there except at night when I'm there, but she also has a suite of rooms. I have a security system that would put Fort Knox to shame. Surely we could provide any help she needs any time, day or night. The young lady seems capable enough to be responsible for her own medicine, don't you think? My only problem would be to contact my housekeeper and clear it with her."

Angie shrugged and looked down at the chart in front of her. It was only a stalling tactic. "Well, then, I see no problem. You say you're on lunch break. Would you make this contact and then come back today or what?"

"You would have to get a discharge from the doctor? I could contact my housekeeper yet today, so we could be ready for her later, yes."

"All right, I'll contact the doctor on call, but we'll wait for you to contact us."

Derek stood, smiled at Angie and held out his hand. "Sounds like a plan, Angie. Thank you for your help. I'll be in touch."

Angie shook his hand and nodded. "Glad this has worked out, Mr. Casbah. It was stressed in her information from the hospital that she needed to be kept safe. Even the nurse who brought her over here spoke strongly about it. We would do our best, but there are so many long term residents here who also have visitors and only so many staff to work with them and also keep them safe. Surely a private home with a security system would be the most secure."

Derek smiled and took one step toward the door. "Yes, that was my feeling, too. We can keep the place like a fortress, if we need to."

Angie reached for the door and asked, "By the way, how did you find out about our 'Jane Doe'? We've been instructed very strongly to keep her placement as quiet as we can."

"A friend of mine who lives in the little town I live in came to see her last evening and insisted she had to know where Carolyn was being sent. She called me to tell me."

"That was very good of her!"

"Absolutely!" *You can't know how much!*

Derek left immediately for the bank, but he drove rather slowly for the few blocks. Once he was back at the bank, his time usually wasn't his own. Some employee had a problem or there was a customer who wouldn't see anyone but him. It never seemed to fail, especially on a Friday. It didn't really matter if he had life-changing happenings in his own life.

He was convinced that young woman he'd just seen was his long estranged daughter. When he was married to her mother they had lived as a happy family in Louisiana. When his wife died, his son was ten and his daughter seven and a half. He'd hired a nanny to help him raise them until his daughter was eighteen, planning on college. Even then, it had been another few years before he'd married Millie. As that relationship became more serious, his son had demanded he either get out or give her up. Being the dumb ox that he was, he'd moved out.

He had purchased the house in Vansville before he'd married Millie, but for some reason he'd never figure out, she didn't want her name put on the deed at that time. Now he was glad. On several occasions she'd threatened to leave him. Still, she hadn't wanted his house, only happy enough to live in it and make demands about it. He shook his head, Millie couldn't be too bright! If her name were on the deed, if there was a divorce, he would have to sell and split the income with her, it would be a large sum she would receive and that would keep her very comfortable for many years. As it was, if she left, she'd have nothing.

He pulled into the bank parking lot, but kept the car running while he dialed his home landline on his cell phone. It was a very warm May day, so the air conditioning helped keep the car cool. Once spring had come, it came with a vengeance! He knew Mrs. Beecham didn't like to answer the phone, but she would if he let it ring. Millie, of course, could be home or not. Finally, after five rings Mrs. Beecham picked up.

"Hello, Mrs. Beecham," Derek said.

"Oh, hello, Mr. Casbah!"

Scowling, Derek said, "You sound as if you're out of breath, or upset, Mrs. Beecham. Has something come up to disturb you?" After all, the woman was going on eighty. He didn't want to be responsible for a stroke or a heart attack! She was an excellent housekeeper and the meals she made were exceptional!

The older woman swallowed loud enough that Derek could hear her, before she said, "Well, I am a bit upset, actually. You see, Mr. Casbah, I needed to go to the garage to the big freezer for something to fix for your dinner this evening. Of course, I heard your wife leave this morning, I thought nothing of it, but when I went by her empty spot I found her garage door opener on the floor…"

Knowing the ramifications of that statement instantly, Derek exclaimed, "Yes, that would be very unusual, Mrs. Beecham!"

"Uh, actually, I did something I probably shouldn't have done after that. I went in Mrs. Casbah's room and Mr. Casbah… oh, my! She's left! There is nothing in her room! Her closet if completely empty! Her dressing table…"

He took a minute for his brain to process this new information. "Well, under the circumstances, I'm glad you did! I tell you what… I have a few things here at the bank I must do, but I should be home soon. Did she leave a note or anything?"

"I... I didn't find one, but of course, I never go into some of your rooms except to clean, so it's possible she has left one and I didn't find it."

"Yes, that's true. Actually, the reason I called was to tell you something and also ask you a question. First of all, I believe I've found my daughter! She's been in the hospital here in Blairsville, then been discharged today to a nursing home. I've talked with the staff at the nursing home and she could be discharged to me if I can provide adequate care. That's my question for you. Would you be willing, for a raise in your salary, of course, to at least watch out for this young woman during the day, while I work?"

"Why... why... Mr. Casbah! I would have no problem with that, not even a raise is needed! You pay me very, very well now," she sputtered. "Goodness, you take really good care of me and the lovely apartment you have for me!"

"Well, as soon as I take care of some things here I'll be home and we'll discuss this. Is that all right with you?"

"Certainly, certainly!"

"Great! I'll see you very soon, Mrs. Beecham."

Derek closed his cell phone then went in the back entrance to the bank. He contemplated what the implications were to the news Mrs. Beecham had told him. Actually, with all her clothes gone and her room emptied, there was only one implication, she had left him! If Millie had left, taken everything, her clothes, her make-up, she probably took her credit cards and was planning on using them as long as she could. He had all the numbers and the necessary information on both his office computer as well as his laptop. Maybe she thought she'd swindle him out of thousands, but she was now on her own!

He went in his office. Fortunately there was plenty of glass in the room, but it was on the two outside walls, not facing into the bank, no one could see him if he closed the door. He had closed it when he left, so he left it closed. Immediately he sat down at his desk and checked his extension, there was no light flashing saying he had a call he must return. What an unusual happening! On a Friday that was unheard of!

Quickly, he activated Millie's credit card accounts. He had all three set up so he could view them all at the same time on his computer. There had been several entries last evening, one of them being to a cruise line! However, looking at the transaction time more closely, he realized that that transaction had taken place so late in the evening it hadn't been posted until after midnight. Since that was true, she might think she'd be cruising somewhere, but it wouldn't be on his dime!

He clicked his bank account number on all the accounts and with one stroke of his mouse, paid off everything that had been entered until today, then cancelled the cards as of midnight this morning. When the words on each account came up 'Paid in full' he grinned and breathed out a sigh of relief. As far as he was concerned, she was the last of the big spenders and he'd cut her ability to spend his money to shreds.

As soon as that was done, he contacted his lawyer to draw up divorce papers. She had left him, he was more than happy to be shed of her! In fact, it was an easy transaction, since there was no house, no children and because she had left him there would be no settlement. After his chat with the lawyer, he breathed a sigh of relief. She'd spoken several times of leaving him, but it had never happened, she relied too heavily on those credit cards. Obviously, she was too interested in doing things on her own to worry about leaving him.

She probably didn't even think about him finding out about her leaving until much later, perhaps not even today. Thank goodness Mrs. Beecham was so observant! He must remember to thank her soon. Perhaps Millie thought she'd be on that cruise ship today enjoying all those amenities before he found out.

"Well," he muttered, "she may be on a cruise ship, but they'll catch up with her when they find out she hasn't paid. She's relied so much on her credit cards; she probably doesn't even have any cash with her at all!" He smiled a bit. "She's taken her Jag; it's a high performance car and guzzles the gas. That woman isn't known for being conservative behind the wheel. Wonder what she plans to use to pay for the gas?" Well, that wasn't his problem now.

Back at the rehab center, Angie called Dr. Ramoz on his beeper. She put the call in immediately she couldn't believe what had happened! When he answered, Angie said excitedly, "Doctor, you will never believe this!"

"Okay, I'm all ears."

"Our Jane Doe had a visitor this noon."

He processed that silently for a minute, before he said, "I guess that's not too unusual. It was noted in her chart at the hospital that she had several visitors last evening. One of them especially was very adamant that she talk to Dr. Simon. She insisted she had to know where we were discharging her to. Against his own advice he told her. So if her having visitors isn't so unusual, what's on your mind?"

"Doctor, her visitor this noon was the bank president from the big bank downtown! If Mr. Casbah had blond hair instead of white, he could be Jane's brother! Actually, he recognized her as his long lost daughter, Carolyn."

"Wow!"

"Yes, wow! Actually, he says he can easily put her up and care for her, so he wants her released to him today!"

"My, oh, my!" Dr. Ramoz cleared his throat and was quiet for a few seconds. "Tell you what, I'll contact Dr. Simon and consult him on this, but I'm pretty sure it could happen. Since you know the man and can vouch for him, I really don't see a problem still I'll talk with Dr. Simon, since he was the one to admit her and also wrote the order for her release to the rehab place. And, I might add, wrote the no talk order. We'll surely need to send some prescriptions home with her. By the way, how did he find out about her and how well can he keep her safe? Well, I guess that really isn't any of our concern, he's taking her to a private residence? He knows about her abductor?"

"Yes, Doctor, one of his concerns was about keeping her safe. He says he can keep his house safe as Fort Knox. It was a friend from Vansville who told him about her. Doctor, she was one of her visitors last evening and she saw how much they look alike! He is quite well off and says he can keep his house locked up like a fortress. His major concern was to keep her safe. I need to wait to hear from Mr. Casbah, but that's all. Yes, she's still taking those pain pills quite regularly, so I'm sure she'll need something to take with her."

"Fine, not a problem! I guess that answers all my questions. We don't have to be concerned that he might have any connection with her abductor?"

"Oh, absolutely not!"

"Fine I'll give Dr. Simon a call."

Angie put down the phone, then rushed out of her office and opened up the intercom for the ward and said, "All staff please come to the desk as soon as possible." One of the staff was in the hallway and had her arms full of dirty laundry. She made a face, stopped in the utility room, then changed directions and came toward the desk.

# Six

Soon, four other staff stepped behind the desk and joined Angie and the receptionist. Scowling, the male nurse sighed dramatically and leaned on the desk. He asked, "What's this about, Angie? I mean, I was stressed out with exercises on my new patient! You know it's important the first time to get things right, our patients need that reinforcement."

Giving the young man a withering look, Angie said, "Our new patient, actually, the new patient you're talking about, who doesn't really need any exercises, in room eleven may be discharged today, oh, by the way, we've changed her name, it's now Carolyn Doe."

"*Carolyn* Doe?"

"Yes, she had a visitor over lunch hour. He's nearly convinced that the lady we've been calling Jane Doe is his long lost daughter. She didn't recognize him, so we're keeping the 'Doe' but we'll call her Carolyn until he comes for her."

"Humph! Amazing!"

Looking at the receptionist, Angie said, "Yes, if his hair had been blond like hers, he could have been a twin brother."

The receptionist nodded. "That is absolutely the truth!" she exclaimed. "If he'd touched me with a feather when he came through the door I would have fallen over!"

"Really, Henry," the man said, knowing she hated being called that, "A feather? I mean, I know you've been on a diet...."

The receptionist gave the man a look and muttered, "Humph!"

Angie continued, "Actually, he hasn't seen her in years, so he doesn't know what her life's been like, so he didn't know if she was married or not. Still, he's willing to take her to his home. He'll be calling about that soon."

"Wow!" the other nurse exclaimed, "All this time they've tried to find out something there at the hospital, but she comes here and somebody knows her."

"I know, but you should have seen the two of them! Amazing!"

"How many years? Why?"

"Hey, I don't ask personal questions!"

"Yeah, I guess that would be sort of personal."

"Actually..." the male nurse said, "I was kinda hoping she'd stick around a while, I could do with a beauty on my arm like that." He let out another dramatic sigh, "Here I won't even be able to do any of those exercises on... I mean, with her."

Angie scowled at the man. He was not your typical medical person, with tattoos covering the parts of his body anyone could see. He had earrings in both ears and his hair was long and done in dreadlocks. She was surprised he didn't wear black scrubs. "You would, huh? Well, put your hopes back in the box, 'cause it ain't gonna happen, not with Carolyn."

"D..." he swallowed, as Angie looked daggers at him.

"My ears are tender, Keagan. You know and have been corrected several times that that language is not appropriate here on the ward."

"Yup, I've been told..."

Derek sat at his desk for several minutes after hanging up with his lawyer. He pulled in a deep breath, leaned back so his chair back nearly touched the wall and put his hands behind his head, then looked out the window but saw nothing. Millie didn't know it yet, she as of now, was on her own and probably penniless, since she hadn't darkened the door of this establishment, at least not today. He couldn't say he was unhappy that she had gone. He wouldn't have divorced her if she hadn't made the first move, but since she had, well, he was shed of her.

He was glad Mrs. Beecham had noticed the garage door opener and checked to find her room empty and also that he had called her. Otherwise, on any usual day, he wouldn't have known about her leaving until he came home late for dinner and she could have been far away and on some cruise at his expense by that time.

He sighed, and sat forward again. Probably he needed to inform her son, she likely hadn't. Derek shook his head. The woman was so selfish, what had he ever seen in her? It hadn't taken many months after they had tied the knot for her to show her true colors, but even though he was far from God back then he knew divorce wasn't right, so he put up with her. He'd given her three credit cards and at first had paid them off each month. He'd bought that huge house soon after they started going together, then much more recently he'd moved out of the master suite and taken the smaller suite next to it, just to keep her from complaining so much.

Derek was one of the few people who had Ramon's private number, so he dialed and wondered how he and Sandy would take the news. He shrugged it was something he needed to know. He knew Ramon hadn't had very many dealings with his mom in recent months, but that wasn't the issue. He knew of no one else who could tell them.

After two rings a deep voice said, "Hello, DeLord's, this is Ramon."

Ramon had such a deep voice and he was very laid back, so much different from his mother. "Ramon, Derek. This seems a bit awkward for me to be telling you, but I think you need to know what I just found out that your mother left this morning. I haven't been home as yet, but Mrs. Beecham found her garage door opener on the floor of the garage and her bedroom suite totally cleared out. I assume she's left me a note somewhere, but I've not been home yet to find it. Did she notify you?"

There was a short silence before Ramon said, "I am a bit surprised, not that she left, really, but that she didn't contact us at all! I thought she really loved Jon, but, well, I guess…" There was another pause he had to gather his thoughts for a minute. "Still, she's been an unhappy person most of her life, really. That being said, I'm not surprised for both things, that she finally left and that she didn't let us know."

There was another pause, this one longer than the first one, before Derek said, "Umm, I'm not real sure how to say this, but if you're willing, I'd like to take on the role of granddad, if that would work for you and Sandy." He was astonished he couldn't believe how fast his heart was going! He anxiously waited to hear what the young man would say.

Ramon chuckled, but he didn't hesitate. "You know, since Sandy came to town, you've sort of grown on me. I know without even asking, that she would like to adopt you as a dad-in-law, so that sort of puts you in that granddad spot, doesn't it?"

Ramon could easily hear the emotion in Derek's voice, as he said, "I'd be honored, truly! I didn't feel right before with Millie in the picture, saying anything about it, but I've watched that little tyke. He is so precious! You two are doing such a great job raising him! Seriously, I'd be honored to be considered his granddad!" He cleared his throat, then swallowed and continued, "Actually, I have something else I need to run by you."

Derek didn't continue immediately, so Ramon said, "Yes? What is it? Is it serious?"

Derek was still so over-charged he had to swallow again. "You remember the young woman Eric found out in those woods behind the clinic last week, wasn't it?"

"Yes, Nancy Roads has been keeping us up to date on her. Sandy has been really upset that she was being discharged to a nursing home. We all know people in a nursing home don't get treated as well as they do in the hospital. Well, I mean…"

"Yes, I know that's true. I was astonished last evening when Ms Isabel contacted me. She told me she went to visit her in the hospital. When she saw her she was convinced that the young woman looked like me, so I went to see her this noon." He cleared his throat again. "Actually, I'm convinced she's my long estranged daughter! Why she was close to Vansville, I don't know, but I'm convinced. She has amnesia, so she knows nothing. However, I'm going to bring her to my place this afternoon."

"Wow!"

"Yes, that was my feeling when I saw her this noon! When my daughter was growing up, she did look very much like me, now, well, the likeness is uncanny! I'm going to my place now to see about getting things ready so I can bring her home perhaps this evening. I agree with you totally about a stay in any nursing home. She'll be much safer at my place."

"Keep us posted!"

"Yes, I'll do that, Ramon. I felt you needed to know about Millie. I'm not really surprised she didn't tell you herself."

"Thanks. Um, yes, I guess I did need to know. After all, she is my mom, but as you know, we were becoming more and more estranged."

Derek chuckled a bit, as he said, "Yes, except she'd rant and rave after she'd slam down the phone about how you've been treating her and had no respect for your mom."

Ramon sighed, "Really!"

"Oh, absolutely!"

Ramon chuckled and said, "I remember once she called and I hung up on her. She kept calling, but I wouldn't answer, so she'd leave message after message on my machine. I finally unplugged it, but the next day I had all those messages to delete. I had to listen to each one in case someone wanting a hike had gotten a call in between. Believe me, I was really frustrated!"

"I can believe that! Was that when you were going with Sandy?"

"No, not really, but I had spent an evening with her at her cabin. You know how Mom hated that I spent time with her!"

"Oh, do I ever. Well, no more."

"Yes. I'm only sad she's never come to the Lord."

"I'm with you on that, Son." Just that word stunned Ramon so much he was speechless. Derek obviously didn't realize the significance and hung up.

Once Derek hung up, he'd been on the phone for over half an hour, but there hadn't been any beeps on his office phone while he talked and his cell phone was also quiet. Since no one seemed to notice that Derek's door was still closed and even Marlene hadn't tried to contact him, perhaps he was dispensable this afternoon. He had no qualms to make that a reality! Quickly, he grabbed his suit jacket from the hook by the door and with his briefcase and laptop in hand he retraced his steps and quickly left the bank by the back door. He breathed in the warm fresh air. Life on the outside could be great!

It was still sunny! *Imagine that!* Actually, a lovely day - something he rarely knew when he worked a normal day and never when Millie necessitated long hours. He sank into his car, no one had haled him or run after him, amazing! This day was turning into one amazing day! There hadn't been too many of those in his life recently.

He quickly left the parking lot and considered turning off his cell phone, but he didn't. Instead he left Blairsville without a qualm and headed for his home outside of Vansville. Now that his appearance didn't matter, he powered down the windows and let in the fresh air as he drove. Mrs. Beecham would be wondering what to do. That dear lady had weathered many days of Millie's less than stellar behavior. Now that was over.

Soon, he touched the garage door opener on his visor and let himself in the garage. As of this day, he was an unmarried man. His housekeeper was an elderly widow and he hoped to bring his daughter to his home. What a motley crew! As he turned off the car he wondered where and what his son was doing now. Did he and Carolyn have ties? Did he know she was gone? Had he been agreeable? Did he know anything about this trip she'd made? Had she found him – her dad - on the internet and was on her way here or had some abductor found her and by accident dumped her here? What a crazy world this was!

He sat for several minutes in the garage, then hit the door opener again, grabbed his things from the passenger seat and exited the car. If he was bringing Carolyn home today and that was his desire, there was lots to do and letting Mrs. Beecham into the loop was one of those things. He hoped he wasn't putting too much work on her after all, she was no spring chicken!

Mrs. Beecham met him just inside the garage door into the kitchen, waving a small piece of paper. She also held a duster in her other hand. As she waved the paper, a set of keys fell from her hand. As soon as he reached her, she handed the note to him, her face wreathed in concern. "Mr. Casbah! Mrs. Casbah did leave a note! After I spoke with you, I took my cleaning supplies into your office and there on your desk was this note." She looked down at her feet and saw the keys. "Oh, and her house keys! Mr. Casbah, I'm so sorry! Really how terrible!" The look she gave him showed her true feeling about the split. Mrs. Beecham was a widow from a long marriage, after all.

Derek reached down for the keys before the old lady could, then took the short note from her hand and read it, not surprised at all. Obviously, Mrs. Beecham didn't know the real relationship between him and his wife for her to tell him she was sorry! Well, he wasn't. They had gone to several things together, but that was mostly for show, now that would stop. There hadn't been much love lost between them in most of the years they'd been married. In that time all he'd done was pay off credit cards. He was glad that would stop. He'd had no qualms about canceling her credit cards, especially the one on which she'd paid for a cruise! He wouldn't mind taking a cruise! He'd been hold up in that bank for years.

He looked up at the lady and smiled. He stepped through the doorway and said, "It's all right, Mrs. Beecham, actually, Mrs. Casbah hasn't been happy with me for a long time. Let's have a seat here in the kitchen and let's talk about bringing Carolyn home. Would you think Millie's suite would be a good one to rearrange for my daughter?"

Derek took his regular chair at the big table, but Mrs. Beecham wasn't used to sitting with her employer, so very reluctantly, she pulled out another chair and slowly sat down. Giving her employer a baffled look, she said, "Mr. Casbah, you won't try to reconcile? I… I know you've been married for several years."

Derek made himself comfortable in the chair, smiled at the older lady and wanted to put her at ease, so he said, "Mrs. Beecham, Millie and I have been married in name only for several years. I'm really surprised it's taken her this long to leave me. No, I'll not try to reconcile. Besides, she left me no clue where she might have gone, so no, there isn't a reason to. It's obvious by this note that she wants nothing to do with me or her grandson, either. So, can her suite be fixed up quickly enough that I could bring my daughter here yet today?"

It was obvious by the expression on her face the lady was having a hard time reconciling what Derek had said about his wife. Finally, she realized he'd asked her a question, so she answered, "Oh… oh, yes, of course. I can get to it immediately. I've already put a roast in the oven for your dinner. Of course, at the time I didn't realize Mrs. Casbah wouldn't be eating as well. So to clean and change the bed linens will be no problem."

"I understand Carolyn has been eating soft food, but the way you fix a roast, it will melt in her mouth, so I have no problem with that."

The older lady blushed. "Why thank you, Mr. Casbah. Believe me, I enjoy cooking for you, you always compliment my meals and my housework."

Derek stood when the housekeeper stood. He wondered what his wife's suite would look like starkly empty. He couldn't remember what it had been like before they'd moved into the house. At that time the suite had been their bedroom, but even then he'd had to use the closet in his present room for his clothes. She always had so many clothes and many bottles of different things for purposes he had no idea what she used them for, that the place almost looked cluttered, but he'd never enquired about any of it. His feeling was if he kept his nose out of such things he was better off. Besides, he had enough to do to keep up with her constant spending. He nearly let a huge sigh pass his lips he wouldn't have to deal with that any longer!

Instead, he focused on Carolyn. What was Carolyn like now? When she was eighteen, she was into sports she'd been an excellent swimmer and had won a full swimming scholarship to the University of Alabama. Not that he couldn't have paid for her to go to any university she'd wanted to go to, but it was the prestige of it and besides, her brother, Lance had poisoned her mind against him so that she had accepted the scholarship and insisted, along with Lance, that he hit the door. He shook his head as he followed Mrs. Beecham. Like a fool he'd done that, he'd left his children, but only after his daughter's graduation from high school and married a woman he should have left well enough alone.

He had only seen Carolyn briefly at the rehab center today, but she'd been a beautiful woman. He hadn't really looked hard, he'd been too overwhelmed, but he could almost bet she didn't have any makeup on, but her skin, where the bruising had faded, was flawless. At eighteen, she was still very much a tomboy, she'd rather be at a pool perfecting her dive or her stroke rather than sit at a mirror to primp.

He remembered even in high school she'd won several competitions in the pool he'd been instrumental in getting installed and that had drawn the scouts. Was she still like that? If she was it would be a very welcome relief! She would be the exact opposite of Millie. It had been a lot of years since he'd been thirty-five, he'd have to be very sensitive. He shook his head. This was Carolyn he was thinking about. He and Carolyn never had any trouble connecting, it was her brother, Lance who'd never let him into his life.

Hearing Mrs. Beecham step on the bottom step brought him out of his musings. He followed her onto the second floor. When she reached Millie's suite of rooms she bustled in to start working, but Derek slouched against the doorframe, looking at the spacious room his wife had left. Actually, it was more spacious than he'd remembered now that all of Millie's things were gone. All he could decide was that she was a very unhappy woman. She'd had everything, everything this world could give her, yet she was never happy. Several years ago he'd come back to his Christian heritage, something he and his first wife had instilled in their children, but Millie would have nothing to do with religion or church. He'd given up trying to convince her. Even Sandy, who had tried for a long time had finally given up.

Drawing him from his musings, Mrs. Beecham asked, "Mr. Casbah, what should I change? Would you prefer the room be rearranged or just cleaned and the linen's changed?"

Derek sighed, "Mrs. Beecham, I'm not into that kind of stuff. Just your basic bed, nightstand, dresser and closet, along with a bath are quite adequate for me. Just give the place a good cleaning and change the linens. Surely Carolyn will want some say in things. We'll wait for her and see what she has to say."

"Fine, fine! I'll get that done in a jiffy. When will you bring her here?"

He smiled at the old lady. "I think the rehab center is waiting to hear from me, so how long will you need to do this, do you think?"

"Oh, no time at all, Mr. Casbah! Probably if you were to contact them and then go after her will be plenty of time." The lady immediately went to the bed and started stripping off the bedding. She wadded it up in her arms to take to the utility room. She'd picked up her duster along the way.

"Now, about the increase in your salary, Mrs. Beecham…"

The lady wouldn't even let him finish, before she waved her hand and scowled at her employer. Immediately, she said, "Mr. Casbah, please, you pay me very well, I really will take it as a great privilege to care for this young lady."

"All right, I'll go call the rehab center now."

"That will be fine! I'll get this room cleaned and clean bedding on the bed in no time!" she said and started for the hallway. "Oh, by the way, there is that lovely quilt that you loved so much but Mrs. Casbah wouldn't tolerate. I believe it's packed in a trunk in the guest room. Could I use that as the bedspread for this bed? I think it would look truly beautiful."

Derek's face lit up. "Oh that would be great, Mrs. Beecham! I would be happy for you to use it. I'll get my end taken care of right away. I'm sure we can have Carolyn here by dinner time today. I'm anxious to bring her home."

The old lady smiled at her employer. "I'm happy to do this, Mr. Casbah. I hope your daughter will be happy here."

"I'm sure she will be, once she's feeling better. I thank you kindly."

"Yes, of course, Mr. Casbah."

Angie came into Carolyn's room after telling the staff her new name and the developments over the noon hour. She knew the young woman would have plenty of questions, so she sat down on the bed only a few feet from her patient and placed a gentle hand on her arm. She knew the young lady was still fragile. "Carolyn, what are your thoughts?"

Carolyn turned slowly and looked at the nurse. Angie could almost feel her fear. Shaking her head, she finally said, "Angie, I really have none, only lots of questions. I don't know this man, other than we look eerily alike. I think I saw that face in the mirror this morning! Did I live close by? He said he hadn't seen me in many years. Why? Shouldn't a man have contact with his daughter sooner than that? Was he the cause of my beating? Will I be safe with him? On the other hand, what do I wear? For all I know, these clothes that someone gave me this morning are the only clothes I have to my name! I have so many questions and absolutely no answers! With an empty brain, I have no idea what I think or what feelings I could have!" Her voice dropped to a whisper, "Other than that I'm scared spitless!"

Realizing that Carolyn really had no frame of reference to go on, except the people she'd dealt with since she woke up, Angie said, "I really have no real answers to your questions, either, but I can tell you a little bit about the man who came to see you this noon."

"Yes, please!"

"Mr. Casbah is the president of the largest bank in this city. He is a good man, I've had professional dealings with him several times and he has worked with my husband and me very conscientiously and has helped us every time. We specifically ask for him each time we need help. He's a talented man, he goes to the symphony often, of course that's in Atlanta, but if I'm not mistaken, he liberally supports them. He supports several youth activities here in the city. He's a church going man and supports the tiny church he goes to."

Angie sat and thought for just a minute. "The only negative thing that I know, he is not in a happy marriage, that's the only thing I see as a problem. The way I see it, you could do far worse and no, I'm sure you have nothing to fear from him. Nothing. From what I've read in the information sent to us by the hospital, the Sheriff's Department has no idea who did this to you. Still, I can understand your fear, I'd be afraid, too!"

Carolyn was quiet for several minutes processing what Angie had told her about the man who claimed to be her dad. Finally she smiled at Angie. "Okay, I'll take your word for it. Still, this sweatsuit I have on that the nurse in the hospital gave me along with the underwear it's hiding and these footies they put on me because I was cold, are every stitch of clothing I have. Umm, perhaps that's not enough?"

Angie laughed. "You got that right! Lets see…"

A voice came through the speaker in Carolyn's room. "Angie, you're wanted on the phone. Shall I direct the call there?"

"Sure, that's fine."

The phone rang and Angie picked it up, but before she could speak the voice said, "Angie, Derek Casbah. I've been informed by my housekeeper that the room will be ready for Carolyn by the time I get her here. Can she be ready in say, forty minutes?"

Angie chuckled. "Mr. Casbah, since Carolyn has nothing but the clothes on her back, she is more than ready. We were just discussing what she wears away from here."

"Oh, my! What is it she has?"

"A sweatsuit and some X-ray footies."

"Hmmm, a slight problem."

Angie laughed. "I should say."

"We'll see about taking care of that when I arrive."

"Great, thanks."

"That's the man coming for me?" Carolyn asked, a touch of fear in her voice, as soon as Angie hung up.

"Sure enough! He said he'll take care of your clothing needs when he comes."

Letting out a long sigh, Carolyn, whispered, "Okay."

Angie patted her hand. "You'll do just fine, I guarantee it! Until he comes why don't you lie down and rest, it certainly won't hurt you."

"Angie, I sincerely hope you're right!" The young man's prayer last night floated into her mind. It seemed God was taking care of keeping her safe… today!

Derek disconnected and sat staring out his home office window for several minutes, then dialed another number. This time when the deep voice answered, Derek said, "Son, could I speak with your wife, please?"

Ramon wasn't used to his step-dad calling him son, but it felt … well… rather good. As he thought about it for a minute, he hadn't been called 'Son' in a very long time, his mom didn't. After a second hesitation, when a smile spread on his face, he said, "Sure, here she is…. Dad."

Sandy came on the line and said, "Derek, what can I do for you?"

Being a bit hesitant, after all, a bank president wasn't used to asking favors, he said, "Sandy, I wager you've never had someone ask this of you before, but would you do me the honor of accompanying me to the rehab center to pick up my daughter? I just now found out she has nothing but the clothes on her back. I'm sure she would feel much more comfortable if a young lady went with her to purchase clothes than a man she doesn't know."

Sandy laughed. "You're right, probably on both counts. No, I've never been asked to do something like that, but I'll be glad to if you let me drive my van and you go along."

"Sandy, for me that is not a hardship. Thank you. Perhaps to save time, I should come to your place and ride with you."

"Of course, that's fine." After a moment's silence, Sandy added, "Should I bring your grandson along?"

After a swallow, Derek whispered, "I'd love that, but perhaps this time we should focus on Carolyn, okay?"

"Sure, that's fine. See you in a few."

Derek hung up and wondered if he'd lost his mind.

It was closer to an hour later when Derek walked into the rehab center. He had changed from his business suit and now looked much more like an ordinary dad. Angie met him at the front desk with several sheets of paper and a small bag. Sitting in a wheelchair close by was Carolyn. The only addition to what Angie had told Derek on the phone, Carolyn had a pair of tennis shoes on over the lime green footies. With a bright pink sweatsuit on, she was quite a sight, but she smiled bravely at Derek.

Derek smiled at Carolyn, but he could see in her eyes the fear she was feeling, so he said compassionately, "Hello, Carolyn." Carolyn didn't speak, she only nodded at Derek. It seemed like the cotton in her mouth had glued her tongue down.

"Mr. Casbah, Carolyn is all ready." Angie smiled at the white-haired man. Her eyes strayed to the uncomfortable young woman sitting not far away. "We can't say she's raring to go, but she's ready. We were even able to rustle up a pair of tennis shoes left behind in a locker in the catacombs, they aren't the best, but at least she can walk without hurting her feet. Oh, here are things for you to sign to get her sprung from this place, some instructions for her care, the appointments the doctors felt she needed to keep and also for the meds she's been taking, and still needs, I might add. Here are also the prescriptions Dr. Ramoz ordered and we requested from our pharmacy."

"Angie, thank you so much." He signed all the papers and Angie gave him copies, then he smiled at Carolyn. "Our chauffeur awaits. The van is parked right out front in the circle drive. I assume that was appropriate."

"I...I'm ready," Carolyn said, tentatively. The results of the beating she'd received at the hands of some unknown man kept her from being excited about leaving with this man.

"Your car's out front, Mr. Casbah?" A CNA came up behind the chair.

"Actually, my daughter-in-law drove her van to pick us up then we'll go and she can help Carolyn with getting some clothes."

"Your daughter-in-law?" Carolyn asked. Neither he nor Angie had said anything about a son, married or otherwise.

Sheepishly Derek smiled. "Actually, my second wife had a son and it's his wife, but my wife ran away today, so I've officially adopted him and his family." He chuckled. "We took care of that transaction after I was here to see you before. Since we did that, she was more than happy to come along as our chauffer."

Wondering why his step-daughter-in-law would be the one to drive to pick her up, Carolyn asked, "So she is about my age?"

"A bit younger, but I know you'll like her. I haven't met one person who doesn't like Sandy, so I know you won't be the first."

"Sandy?" Angie asked. "Do you mean Sandy DeLord?"

"Yes, she's the one!"

"Oh, Carolyn, Sandy is the most wonderful lady you'll ever meet!"

"I… I'm… well, okay," she said, tentatively.

As the CNA began to push the chair, Carolyn looked up at him. "I really have no idea what will happen, you know."

Compassionately Derek said, "I know, Carolyn, but I'm also very sure you'll be in good hands. Believe me, my every intention is to keep you comfortable, happy, loved and safe. That, my dear, begins right now, so lets be off, shall we?"

Neither Carolyn nor the CNA who took her out was prepared for the scene that greeted them. Sandy was seated in the driver's spot, so they couldn't see her at first, as they started down the walk toward the waiting van. However, she had the big passenger door open and the lift on the ground. That was what they saw when they left the building, both women scowled as they approached the van, following Derek. Derek didn't hesitate he stepped on the lift, then turned and held out his hand to Carolyn.

"Sandy's in here, I'll make introductions as soon as we're inside."

The CNA set the brake on the wheelchair so that Carolyn could stand. Carefully, Carolyn braced herself on the armrests and stood. She felt like her insides were shaking like a leaf in a stiff wind. Derek moved to take her hand and help her onto the lift. He was very gentle with her and smiled, understanding her hesitant moves.

Carolyn became even more puzzled and apprehensive when the lift began to move. "What's going on?" she exclaimed.

When the door was closed and the CNA had returned inside, Derek gently put his arm around Carolyn, hoping the contact wouldn't upset her and took her the few steps to the front of the van. A young lady was smiling up at her and before Derek could say anything, she said, "Hi, you must be Carolyn! I'm Sandy and I'm so thrilled to meet you. Once you get settled in at Derek's place, you will have so much company! You'll probably toss us out so you can get a moment's peace. I know for a fact that our friends will absolutely love you to pieces! Vansville's a great place to live."

Looking at Sandy, then at her wheelchair, then at the controls of the van, then back to Sandy, Carolyn's scowl deepened. Each of those stops took several minutes. Carolyn finally cleared her throat and said, "Ahhhh. Yes, I'm Carolyn at least Mr. Casbah seems to think that's my name. I really can't be sure. I'm pleased to meet you."

With another grin, Sandy said, "Have a seat and let's go shopping! We'll give Derek a run for his money, how's that?"

Derek chuckled. "You won't mind if I come along, will you?"

Sandy laughed and said, "Oh, no, Derek, I suspect you'll be needed to hand over your plastic a few times."

Derek laughed. "Sandy, you're not only a whiz on the piano and with a paint brush, but you have a quick wit, too. Let's be off!" He looked at Carolyn and said, "Care to sit up here with Sandy or in the back with me?"

Sandy shook her head immediately. "Oh, she must sit up here with me! Derek, we need to get started on our girl talk. I need to know her a *little* bit before this shopping spree!"

Derek helped Carolyn into the front bucket seat then slouched onto the back bench. "Lead on, fearless one, lead on!"

"Yes, sir! We're off!" Sandy chuckled again and pulled the stick into drive. Carolyn watched as Sandy pulled another lever and the van surged ahead. This van was unlike any van she'd ever seen before.

By the time the girls had exhausted several clothing stores and Carolyn was wiped out, Derek had called Ramon and insisted he drive Derek's car to his place and of course bring Jon. They would all eat Mrs. Beecham's roast and Derek could spoil his new grandson while everyone was there. Derek was convinced that his house hadn't seen such a lively time since he'd hosted Roger's wedding rehearsal dinner at his place many months before. He knew Millie's presence had always put a damper on anything he wanted to do, but no more! He couldn't remember feeling such relief and freedom! Both Jon and Carolyn were yawning and falling asleep by the time Derek sent Ramon and his family home.

When they had arrived at the big house after the shopping spree, Derek and Ramon had taken the boxes and bags to the suite Carolyn would have, but she would have to put her things away, any woman, no matter how fussy they were, wanted to know where all her things were. However, until Ramon's family left, Carolyn hadn't been to her room yet. Seeing how tired she was, Derek immediately turned off the porch light and led Carolyn upstairs to the room Mrs. Beecham had cleaned and made ready.

They climbed the stairs and Derek said, "Carolyn, here's your room. Ramon and I've put all the boxes and things in here that you and Sandy purchased today. Don't feel you must put things away tonight, tomorrow is soon enough. I can tell how exhausted you are, do what you need to do and fall into bed. Morning can take care of the rest. Your bath is through there and I know Mrs. Beecham has put clean towels and such in there for you. I do hope you are very comfortable in this room. It's a privilege for me to have you come and live here with me."

The young woman sighed, "Thank you, Mr. Casbah, I'm more than happy to see a bed. Thank you for all you've done for me."

Derek, lightly patted Carolyn's shoulder and exclaimed, "Nonsense! I'm extremely happy to do it. Please, will you call me Derek? Since we don't really know for absolute sure that you're my daughter, let's do that until we do, okay?"

"Yes, that's fine, thank you."

"Good, sleep well." He left, closing the door behind him.

Carolyn watched the door close and heard the latch click. She looked down at the outfit she had on and wondered if she even had the strength to take it off and find the nightie. She looked at the bags on the chairs in the sitting area and sighed. Finally she walked over to them, found the bag she thought it was in and was relieved to find it immediately. She only went to the bathroom momentarily, didn't even brush her teeth, then came back and fell into bed. Sleep came quickly and was deep and dreamless. Her body obviously knew it was safe.

Friday evening, after he ate his unappetizing meal, Eric gathered up his things for his hike that left Saturday morning. He wondered what had happened with Jane Doe since he'd seen her at the hospital. Of course, he'd heard Isabel tell Ruth that she was sure the young woman was some relation of Derek Casbah, but he didn't know anything else that might have happened to her, because he'd been doing some errands in Blairsville all day today. He didn't know the banker well he'd met him casually at church and spoken to him there on Sundays when he was able to go. Was there a connection? Did Jane Doe know the man? What had he done? Was he visiting her as if she was his daughter? Perhaps Sandy could tell him tomorrow.

This year, since there were three full time guides beside Ramon, he took only two or three day hikes and those only when they began and ended during the week, but Sandy had insisted she feed the guides breakfast before they left for each hike. Today, when Eric walked in DeLord's house, Sandy exclaimed, "Eric, guess what!"

"Sandy, it's hard to guess. What has you over the moon?"

"First of all, Derek discovered that Jane Doe is his long lost daughter, thanks to Isabel. She insisted he needed to see her, so he went to the rehab center. They do look nearly identical. So now instead of being Jane Doe, she's Carolyn Doe. Yesterday afternoon, he invited me to take her shopping for clothes. Then he invited his new adopted family to share dinner at his home with him and his daughter."

"Uh, who's his new adopted family?"

"Why, Ramon, Jon and me, of course."

"I thought Ramon was Millie's son and they didn't get along."

"That's true, but at about the same time Derek was finding out about his daughter, he found out Millie had run off and left no forwarding address."

Eric was piling the eggs and bacon on his plate, but he stopped and stared. Finally, he said, "Wow, Mr. Casbah had one busy day yesterday!"

"That is true, but I've never seen him so happy."

After they prayed over the food, Eric said, "So he was convinced, just by seeing her that he was her dad?"

Sandy nodded and said, "Eric, if you'd seen them together there is no question that they are related. As the nurse said, 'If he's not her dad, then there's another man just like him in the world and she was his daughter.' Actually, it was uncanny, their voices sounded alike, accept to be male and female." Sandy shook her head. "Their eyes are the same shade of blue and the way they both smile, they have to be father and daughter."

Ramon also nodded. "I agree, it's uncanny!"

"I guess God answered our prayers really fast! We both prayed that she be safe and that the Lord would take care of the situation. He sure did that!"

"Yes, so much better than we could ever imagine."

After a mouthful of delicious omelet, he said, "I believe that wholeheartedly!"

Eric shoveled the last of his breakfast in his mouth as the Westminster chime started its full chime in the living room. He and Ramon stood up with their coffee cups and headed toward the office for Eric's paperwork for this hike. Ramon's next hike was scheduled for Monday, but Eric had seven hikers to take out for a week long hike today. Soon they heard car doors slam and voices out on the parking lot, so the two men slapped each other on the back and Eric headed out, glad to be headed back into God's beautiful creation. The weather forecast for the week was encouraging it should be a good hike. Eric would count on it. It was later in the summer that hurricanes came ashore and gave them a drenching.

Unlike Millie, Carolyn had enquired last evening when she should be up for breakfast. Derek had urged her to sleep in, since she was still officially convalescing, but she had insisted she wanted to eat with him. He was not opposed, so Saturday morning, Mrs. Beecham had her special Danish rolls and coffee ready for the other two people in the house. She was happy to accommodate two agreeable people.

After Derek said a blessing, Carolyn appreciatively took a bite of the wonderful smelling pastry and said, "Oh, my, Mrs. Beecham, this is wonderful! This Danish is like your roast, it melts in your mouth!"

"Why, thank you, my dear!" she exclaimed. Self-consciously, she continued, "Actually, it's been my hobby for all my life, to cook and bake. My mother had me working in her kitchen when I was eight years old, it's something I love." She chuckled. "My late husband was rather insistent on a clean house, too."

As soon as Mrs. Beecham left, Carolyn asked, "Derek, you say Sandy is your step-son's wife? Why is she paralyzed? I was totally shocked when

I met her. Actually, I was probably rude it startled me so much to see her behind the wheel of a vehicle and in a wheelchair. Really, she is an amazing woman!"

"Yes, Sandy is a wonderful young lady!" Carolyn nodded enthusiastically. "Except to see her in that chair, you wouldn't even think about the fact that she is paralyzed. Ramon has told me, only because I asked him, that she was dropped in the hospital nursery, hit her back on the changing table and therefore has never walked a day in her life."

Carolyn's eyes turned to saucers. She gasped, "Oh, my! She is the most upbeat person I've ever met! She's amazing! She isn't bitter at all! How can she not be?"

Without knowing her life for so many years, Derek said, tentatively, "Carolyn, I'm not sure what your beliefs are and perhaps you don't know your own beliefs now either, but Sandy has a strong faith in God and loves the Lord Jesus as her Savior. Because of that, she's given everything about her life to Him and He's fulfilled her more than abundantly. Believe me, she has helped many of us here in town and has also led several people to the Lord."

"Wow! Yesterday you said something about her piano playing? Really? How can she play the piano if her legs don't work?"

"Carolyn, that young lady not only plays the piano better than most pros I've known, she teaches piano to fifty students! She played for us once at the symphony in Atlanta and received a standing ovation. She's also given several smaller recitals here in Vansville and Blairsville. She has a little black pouch that she and her brother rigged up many years ago that she hangs on the back of her chair. She uses her shoulder to press it, but it's hooked to the sustaining mechanism on a piano. That painting over the fireplace in the great room, she painted that as well. From a photograph, no less."

"Yes, she is totally amazing! She puts me to shame! I'll suffer only a short time."

Thinking of all that Carolyn was bound to go through, Derek said, "Well, maybe not so short a time, Carolyn."

"True, but not a lifetime."

"Yes, I'll give you that."

Derek looked at the clock and sighed. "It seems I must visit my place of employment for a few hours this morning, but I'll be home quite early. Relax, Carolyn, you're still recuperating. Be sure if you go outside that you can get back in, but as you know, we have no idea who did this awful deed to you, so be very careful!"

"I will. I don't think I'll venture out, really, but thank you."

# Seven

Sunday morning, Carolyn woke up before dawn sick as a dog. She hung her head over the toilet in her suite and retched until there was nothing more to lose. She still wasn't very strong from her beating, so because she felt even weaker, she fell back against the tub, stretching out her legs in front of her. Tears were sliding down her cheeks, partly from the vile taste in her mouth, but she knew what this meant. She was pregnant with someone's baby. Pregnant by violence and by someone she had no idea who.

The tears came more freely. What would Derek do now? He'd been so kind to her since he'd brought her here to his home, but now that she knew she was pregnant, what would he do? Would he urge her to have an abortion, to keep the baby, give it up for adoption? Would he even want her to stay? After all, he was a bank president. Not having any answers, she went back to bed, morning was soon enough to deal with such hard questions.

Derek's bathroom was back to back with Carolyn's, it woke him up to hear her. He lay on his back and heard her retching. The sound brought tears to his eyes. Now they were pretty sure she was pregnant. The poor girl, she'd been through enough! Now on top of it all, she had to know that what she carried in her body was the result of terrible violence and probably hatred. Perhaps that hatred wasn't against her in particular, but against women in general, but she was suffering for a man's hatred and ability to master and hurt a woman. He wished he could get his hands on the man he'd like to treat him as he'd treated this beautiful young woman. Finally, there was silence on the other side of the wall.

What would she do? Would she want to get rid of the baby? If she did, it was undoubtedly his grandchild, but did he have the right to make her keep the baby for that reason? After all, he hadn't been part of her life for so many years! As a Christian man, he wanted to preserve life this was a baby, made in God's image. On the other hand, it was not the result of love between a man who loved his wife and the baby the result of their love. Would she want to keep a child that would forever remind her of this terrible experience? Would she not want to have an abortion, but rather go through the pregnancy and give the child up for adoption? These were all questions he had no answers for. All was quiet in the next room, he turned over, he had no answers, morning was soon enough to deal with such hard questions.

Carolyn lay in bed after the sun came up wondering what would become of her. Her brain seemed like there was a chain-link fence, so high and impenetrable, nothing could get out or in, either. What did Derek do on a Sunday? What would she do? Did he go to church? Would he expect her to go with him if he did? Sandy had gotten her a lovely dress-up outfit, but she was still bruised now she knew she was pregnant. If she went to church what would people think of her? Add all these questions to the ones she'd thought about at four o'clock, it would take all morning to figure it out! Maybe she didn't want to figure it out. Still, she supposed this was not something that should be swept under the rug. Derek seemed like a level-headed man surely they'd discuss things in a civil manner.

She heard some faint noises coming through the wall and realized it was Derek. Since she didn't know who she was and therefore didn't know if she was truly his daughter, he had asked her to call him Derek until they knew for sure. The man was every bit as kind and noble as Angie at the rehab center said he was. So far, she hadn't gotten up her nerve to ask why he hadn't seen his children in so long, but maybe today would be the day to find that out. He seemed like such a nice man, why hadn't they kept in touch? Besides, Angie said he was in a bad marriage, but so far she hadn't seen a woman who could be his wife and neither Mrs. Beecham nor Derek had spoken about her. Well, he had mentioned she'd run away. With this man? This kind, big hearted man and she'd run away?

Finally, she let out a long sigh, threw the covers back and sat up. Last evening Derek had given her a huge plastic bag to put over her left arm and cast so she could take a shower. Swishing off at a sink was acceptable in the hospital where there wasn't a shower and yesterday she was still feeling the effects of the big day on Friday, but today, she wanted to take a shower, besides, she needed to wash off the evidence of the nasty business that happened at four o'clock. She didn't remember getting anything on herself, but she could still smell it. It was not something to keep around! Besides, there was that lovely shower in the bathroom only a few feet away begging her to come in and let the water run over her.

Surprising herself, she had no trouble figuring out how to get her left arm covered and keeping any moisture from coming in contact with the cast. It wasn't long before she stepped into some nice warm spray. She sighed with the wonderful feeling of warm water on her body. She had a little trouble washing her hair one handed, since her right shoulder still hurt, but that was a minor inconvenience, the cleanliness felt terrific! Besides, Dr. Ramoz said the cast would come off this week so the stitches could be removed, then a much lighter cast would be applied. Besides it didn't really fit anymore, her arm had been so swollen that now her arm rattled around in the cast and she must keep a sling on it to keep everything in its proper place.

Not knowing what would happen today, she put on underclothes and her long bathrobe and headed out of her room to find what there was for breakfast. Derek had told her last night that Mrs. Beecham had Sundays off. Someone usually picked her up to take her to church and she was gone the rest of the day.

As she reached the table in the kitchen, Derek sat at the table with a huge mug of coffee and between him and another chair sat a huge platter of the delicious pastries Mrs. Beecham had made, probably the day before. Derek looked up at her and smiled. Her heart turned over, this man was every kindness she could imagine. Carolyn smiled back at him, something she hadn't felt like doing in quite a few days.

"Carolyn, there's coffee in the carafe, if you want it, there're three kinds of juice in the fridge and here's all these pastries I hope you'll help me eat."

Carolyn opened the cupboard door and pulled out a mug and a glass, then poured some coffee and orange juice. As she sat down, then bit into a delicious confection, she swallowed and asked, "I know you don't go to the bank today. What is it you do on Sunday?"

"I go to the little church in Vansville. Just recently, we got Sunday school going and I'm one of the teachers. After that, of course, is the church service and the minister is a young man who is terrific. There is also an evening service which I usually go to, but not always. If you like you are welcome to go with me or you can stay home, whichever you feel most comfortable doing, it's entirely up to you."

Carolyn took another bite of the delicious confection then took a swallow of orange juice to wash it down. Putting the pastry down on her plate, she slowly wiped her hands and said, "Derek, I... I spent some time at four o'clock in the bathroom throwing up all my cookies. You know what that means, right?"

Compassionately, Derek reached over and put his hand over hers, then curled his fingers around her hand and squeezed it. Looking at her directly, he said, "Yes, I heard you, Carolyn. I assume that means that you're pregnant, unfortunately. I know we were all hoping that wasn't the case, but things happen we can't control." It was easy to see the anger come into his eyes. He shook his head and said, "Like I said to myself at the time, I wish I could get my hands on whoever did this to you and maybe wring his neck!"

Carolyn smiled briefly at Derek's vehemence, but then she scowled and said, "This doesn't bother you?"

He squeezed her hand again then his anger showed just a little as he exhaled a huff. Fiercely, he said, "What bothers me is that the man took out his hatred of women on you! Yes, it's unfortunate that you're pregnant, but it's no more unfortunate than what he did to you and tossed you away!"

"So I... I, um could go to church with you? Since I really don't remember what my life was like before, I'm a little unnerved, but I think I'd like to, is that alright?"

"Carolyn, of course! Absolutely I have no problem with you going with me! In fact, I'd love to have you go with me. You would be in the class Ramon teaches. He's not a very old Christian, but that's good, he studies hard and does a good job. If someone asks a question he can't answer, he'll stop and let someone else help him out or he'll write it down and study up on it himself. Yes, you are more than welcome!"

"I... thank you," she said simply.

By now, both Derek and Carolyn had finished their breakfast and Carolyn looked at the clock. "What time would we leave?"

Chuckling, remembering how long it used to take Millie to get ready to go anywhere and how long it had taken Carolyn to dress yesterday, he said, with a grin, "I suspect we should leave in an hour, since Sunday school starts at nine and it's about a fifteen minute drive. Would that be time enough for you?"

She looked at the clock again and exclaimed, "Of course! I have no problem with that, Derek. Goodness, that's plenty of time! My major problems will be to comb my hair to cover that bald spot and to pull the top over this cast! It's so huge, but I managed it Friday at the store, so it shouldn't be any harder today." She chuckled a bit and said, "Sandy helped me pick out a lovely outfit. I'm anxious to wear it."

His eyes twinkling, Derek said, "I'll meet you by the door to the garage in fifty-five minutes. Agreed?"

"Great!" She started to get up, then looked at him and asked, "Why did you chuckle about my question?"

Grinning, as she sank back into her chair, he said, "Carolyn, the day Sandy and I brought you home, my wife left. She'd left a note, but didn't elaborate, so I have no idea where she has disappeared to. Believe me, she was a very unhappy woman and had been for a long time. She and I hadn't lost any love over each other in several years, so I am not devastated that she left. In fact, the note she left me was very terse and to the point." He took a deep breath and said, very dramatically, "However, when she commenced... to begin... to get started... to get ready... to begin... to make herself ready... to go anywhere..., regardless of where it might be, be it the symphony, the salon to get her nails done, her son's place, wherever, one could plan on waiting at least two hours, possibly three, before there was any visible sign of the woman." He had dramatically dragged out each word.

By now, Carolyn was laughing. "I see, so if I'm all ready in say forty-five minutes you won't think I've abused your time."

"Absolutely not!"

Still chuckling, Carolyn stood up, cleared her dishes to the sink and smiled at the man who probably was her dad. She left the kitchen and headed toward the stairs to finish dressing. "Derek, I promise I won't take two hours," she said, over her shoulder.

Derek chuckled. "That's great! In fact, it may take me that long to run the razor over my whiskers and pull on some clothes for Sunday."

Roger stood at the door welcoming all those coming for the opening song for Sunday school. As Derek and Carolyn walked up, he first shook Derek's hand, then looked at Carolyn, held out his hand and said, "I do believe we haven't met, but that doesn't mean I don't know who you are. Welcome to our services, Carolyn! I'm so happy you came with Derek today. I do believe you could pass for twins; that's if Derek had your beautiful blond hair. Oh, by the way, I'm Roger Clemens and as I tell everyone, I'm Roger to all my friends and I haven't met anyone who's not a friend here in Vansville."

Carolyn took the man's hand and smiled. Perhaps he was the pastor, but he looked like any clean-cut thirty-something young man. "Thank you. I'm happy to be here. I can't tell you if I've ever been to church before, but Derek has been so kind I feel right at home."

The grin he gave her set his eyes twinkling, as he said, "Great! I hope you feel right at home with the whole crew of us."

"Roger, Carolyn goes in Ramon's class, isn't that right?"

"Right. You can walk her there, since it's on the way to your class."

"I'll just do that in a few minutes."

Everyone coming in the auditorium found a seat, the praise team was warming up for the first song and Roger turned to turn on the over head projector which showed the words. As soon as the words were showing on the wall, the praise team with their instruments played a chord. Everyone stood up and the noise began. Carolyn surprised herself, she knew the song so she sang along, reading the words on the wall.

As Marcy had predicted, now that Sunday school had started in the Vansville church, attendance for the services was growing each week. Of course, Ramon and Sandy started going there the first Sunday classes started. Both of them were teachers, Ramon taught the young adults; Sandy had a full class of children who were mostly her piano students. Marcy and Natt had a nursery class and that made Marcy happy, since she could have time with her little nephew. Derek and Ramon split the adults. Derek's class stayed in the auditorium, while Ramon's class met in one of the portable classrooms. Fortunately, both the auditorium and the classrooms were good sized to hold the large classes.

As the adults gathered briefly in the auditorium, Roger looked around. He could count on one hand the empty seats and more people would be coming for the worship service! Marcy had been so right when she'd come to church that first time after moving here from Philadelphia. Soon they'd have to punch out some walls to accommodate all those who were coming! It was a good problem to have. The worship team led the singing for Sunday school, since Sandy had the children's class and they met from the beginning.

Roger sat in the back of the auditorium. He was not a music person, so it was not his responsibility to pick or lead the song for Sunday school. As the song started, he looked around then bowed his head. With tears in his eyes, he murmured, "Father, God, I am so humbled that You have decided to use me here in Vansville church. Yes, there were a few faithful adults who came while I was in my desert, but how You have blessed this place since I came back to You!"

Derek and Carolyn sat with Ramon and Sandy during church. Nancy and Raylyn kept the babies and toddlers for the second hour, so both Lenny and Jon stayed in their class for church. However, Derek leaned over to Ramon after they'd found their seats and said, "Say, since Mrs. Beecham has Sunday off, how about coming out to the house for dinner? I cook a mean steak on the grill and Carolyn says she wants to make a salad."

Ramon had his mouth open to answer Derek, but Sandy hadn't moved to the piano as yet, so she looked hard at Derek and said, "Okay, Dad, but we bring dessert! There will be no argument on that!"

Derek swallowed, it had been so very long since someone had called him Dad in a way that even sounded loving. He had to swallow again, before he could say, "I won't argue with that, Sandy. I know how awesome your desserts are."

"Okay, just so we're clear of that!"

Derek chuckled. "Yes, Ma'am!"

Ramon chuckled. "Guess we'll see you then, Dad."

Sandy stayed at the piano after the last hymn and played softly as people walked out. Roger stood at the back door, but soon Raylyn and Lenny joined him to greet everyone who was leaving. Most everyone stopped to give attention to the loveable toddler. Heidi, of course, was outside with her friends running on the church yard. At one time she was the only child who attended, but now there were so many Roger was contemplating the need for junior church to be held in one of the classrooms.

Corky and his wife came toward the end of those leaving the church, but Corky said, "Roger, my man, you got more chairs ordered?"

"Why no, Corky, why?"

"As I see it, young fella, we're about to run out of places for people to sit down. You gonna let 'em sit on the platform with ya?"

Roger chuckled, remembering the prayer he'd prayed when Sunday school started today. "Hadn't really thought of that, Corky! I guess it's a possibility."

"Well, I ain't got no more empty classrooms up my sleeve, but you's about to pack this place out! Got some ideas?"

Tears glistened in Roger's eyes, as he said, "Corky, what's happened here is beyond my imagination! I'm so in awe of God's work, I can only thank Him."

Derek stood behind him and said, "Corky, Roger, you come up with some ideas and you know there's funding readily available."

"Thanks, Derek," Roger said around the lump in his throat.

Corky turned to Derek and looked at Carolyn. He nodded to Derek, but said to Carolyn, "Young lady, I haven't met you, but I'd say you's some relation to Derek. We's downright glad you come today!"

Carolyn smiled. "Thank you, sir, I'm Carolyn."

Corky nodded. "A real pretty name for a real pretty lady."

Carolyn blushed. "Thanks." *Even with the bruises?*

"Of course! See ya all later!" The older man gallantly put his hand around his wife's elbow and escorted her down the ramp.

Not too long into the afternoon, Derek, Carolyn, Sandy and Ramon sat at the table on Derek's deck eating dinner. The good smell from the grill still lingered in the air and all the adults enjoyed the meal. Jon sat in his high chair, but soon, his tummy was full and he wanted down! Like a boy with a mission, he toddled around the table to Derek.

He stood at Derek's knee patting his leg. "Up, up!" When he didn't think Derek responded fast enough, he slapped his leg harder and demanded, "UP! UP!"

Ramon couldn't remember ever seeing a smile on Derek's face any wider as he scooted back and held out his hands toward the little boy. "Okay, I got it!" he exclaimed. "I'd say the boy wants up!" As he lifted the little boy from the deck and stood him on his leg, but keeping the little boy snug in his arms, he gave him a loving kiss and said, "So, now that we're on this grandson and grandpa thing, what'll we call ourselves?"

Very seriously, Jon looked at Derek. Jon put one little hand on Derek's cheek and Derek had a hard time pulling in a breath. In fact, for a minute his smile slipped a little. However, Jon didn't seem to notice, with the other hand pointed to himself and said, "Ja," then pointed to Derek and said, "Pa, Japa." Without any hesitation, Jon leaned against Derek and put his arms around his neck, then whispered in his ear, "Ja-pa."

Tears started streaming down Derek's cheeks. The others at the table had to clear their throats. Derek was so choked up he couldn't speak. Jon leaned back, looked at Derek and shook his head. "Ja-pa, no cry." Before Derek could stop the tears, Jon wiped his cheek.

Because he couldn't make his speech any louder, he whispered, "You are so precious! Ja-pa is just fine!"

Still from Derek's arms, the little boy turned and pointed around the table. "Mama, Dada, Ja-pa," but then he scowled at Carolyn and pointed to her, but didn't say anything.

"That's Aunt Carolyn," Sandy said.

Jon shook his head. "An-tee."

Soon, Jon wanted down, so Derek placed the child on the floor of the deck. Immediately, he toddled over to Sandy, climbed up on her footrest then held up his arms. Sandy pulled the child onto her lap. Only minutes later, Jon made himself comfortable, pushed his thumb into his mouth, closed his eyes and was soon fast asleep.

"Such a precious child!" Derek murmured, as he watched him sleep. He pulled in a deep breath and looked out at the lush green lawn out beyond the manicured gardens. Silently, he said, *What Millie will miss!*

"So, Dad, you've spent long days at the bank for years now…."

Before he could continue, Derek waved his hand in front of him to erase the words, then shook his head vehemently and said, "Millie made me do it! Believe me, that won't happen any more! Millie was more than happy that I stayed away and because of her personality and attitude I was happy to be gone, but since she's not here, I will be much more."

"That's great!"

Sandy's hand was unconsciously stroking her little one. "So, Carolyn how about you?"

Carolyn shook her head and looked at the lovely young lady. "Sandy, I have no idea! I know I'm an adult woman, but that is all I know, really. I think my mind has decided to go on an extended vacation."

"I have an idea! Ramon has a group going out tomorrow at eight. Come by any time and we can see some sights!"

Carolyn looked at Derek, then at Sandy. "Um, how do I do that? I, ah, don't have a car and I don't know where you live."

Sandy laughed then covered her mouth, wanting to let Jon sleep. "Silly! I'll come after you! I'll bring my camera along and we'll see some places. There are so many awesome places to view God's glorious handiwork; it'll take us all day. I'll pack a picnic lunch and we can make a day of it. How's that work for you?"

Carolyn grinned. "Super!"

"Excellent!"

Monday morning, Carolyn woke to good smelling coffee and baking. She quickly showered and dressed, then nearly ran to the kitchen. Derek sat at the table nursing his coffee and when she saw Carolyn, Mrs. Beecham bustled around, poured a cup of coffee and brought it to her. Derek took a sip of his coffee then pushed the platter of pastries over to Carolyn.

"Eat up! These are fresh, just out of the oven."

"Oh, I will! Mrs. Beecham, you fix the best pastries!"

"Thank you, Ms Carolyn!"

"Of course, Mrs. Beecham! Except they aren't wrapped in cellophane they could pass for the Danish you buy in any store. They are delicious."

"I'll agree, Mrs. Beecham," Derek added.

"Thank you so much, both of you!"

Soon, Derek looked at the clock, sighed, drained his mug, then cleared his place and stood up. "Well, ladies, I guess duty calls. I will see you this afternoon." After a short pause, "It will be long before the sun sets!" he exclaimed. "Believe me!"

"That is very good, Mr. Casbah, you have worked long hours for many years," Mrs. Beecham said. "I'll be glad for you to come home earlier."

Derek chuckled. "It'll be a new experience you won't have to keep stuff warm."

Mrs. Beecham chuckled. "That was no problem, Mr. Casbah."

Later, as he sat at his massive office desk, Derek thought about Sandy's question, wondering what Carolyn would do with her time. He knew it was a spur-of-the-moment thought to go on a picnic and sightsee, but he wondered what Carolyn would do with her time day after day. Until she got her memory back she couldn't drive, she couldn't get a driver's license. She didn't know what she did for a living; of course, he didn't know what she'd done for a living since she graduated from college. Besides, there wasn't much here in this neck of the woods for her to do anyway. Sandy ran the business for DeLord's Hiking Service. She couldn't always be taking off to drive Carolyn around and entertain her.

He took care of some bank business, but the thought of what Carolyn would do wouldn't leave him alone. When a thought came to him he pulled a phone book from his desk and opened it to the yellow pages. Thumbing through, he finally found the name of a man who had gotten a loan from the bank for a business he'd wanted to start. At present, the business was going well Derek decided to support him, so he dialed his number.

When the man answered, Derek said, "Sam, Derek Casbah. Tell me, man, how many pools are you behind?"

The man laughed. "I'm sitting here working out some plans for a guy who enquired about a project only on Friday my helper is putting the finishing touches on a place we finished up on Friday. We're waiting on a guy to get financing before we start on another. Actually, we aren't very far behind at all. Why, what can I do for you, Derek?"

Derek was doodling on his notepad and said, "I have some ideas, but I need some advice, when could we get together?"

Obviously, Sam pulled his calendar in front of him before he answered, "Could free up some time this afternoon."

"Great! Meet me at my place about five?"

"Sounds like a plan, if you'll tell me where your place is."

Derek chuckled. "Yeah, that would help, wouldn't it?"

After he gave the directions, Sam said, "Got it down, Derek. I'll bring my books and pamphlets and we'll have a session. See you then."

A young man drove his car into the two car attached garage, then pulled his briefcase from the passenger seat and giving an appreciative sniff, made his way from the garage into his house. He was home early today. His wife and little daughter met him in the kitchen. After a kiss, she asked, "How was your day, Honey?"

"Not bad for a Monday. How was yours?"

She grinned, "Brenda and I went shopping!"

The young man groaned. "Oh, terrific! How much am I broke for on that credit card?"

The lady chuckled at her husband's expression. "We bought a new car seat, since Brenda's outgrown her old one and a panda bear."

He shrugged. "Not too bad, not too bad. A fake panda bear, I hope?"

His wife chuckled. "Oh, no worries there Honey."

Holding her arms wide, Brenda said, "Daddy, we bought this panda bear, the hugest panda bear in the store! You home for supper? Read me a story?"

He bent over and picked up his little daughter and gave her a raspberry on her cheek, then walked her around the table to her booster seat. While she giggled, he said, "Yes, pumpkin, I'm home for supper and I'll read you a story, but I know you must eat your supper first and that story can't be until after your bath."

"I know, Daddy. I glad you're home!"

Linda smiled at her husband. "Come sit down, dinner's ready!"

After they sat down for dinner, the young man asked, "By the way, have we heard from Carolyn lately? She was due to call, wasn't she?"

"Yes, she should have called last week, but she didn't. I've been waiting to call her, but maybe you'd better."

Lance looked at the calendar hanging on the wall by the sink and said, "Well, let's wait till Friday maybe the month's just slipped by her. Of course, she moved this month, she's probably been covered up."

"Okay, maybe we ought to do it Thursday, we're due in Birmingham on Friday, you know, you're taking us to the big city for the weekend, remember."

He chuckled. "Ah, yes, that's it in a nutshell."

"Daddy," the little girl said, enthusiastically, "we go with you to the big city!"

"Yes, you and Mommy can spend the day in the pool!"

"Oh, yippee! Is Aunt Carolyn going too?"

"I don't think so, Pumpkin, Aunt Carolyn moved, remember? She has a new job and doesn't live close any more. She can only call sometimes."

"Oh, yeah," Brenda sighed. "Can we go see her, Daddy?"

"Probably not for a while, Pumpkin, we'll have to take time off now, she lives too far away, but we'll go, I promise."

"That's great!"

Lance noticed Brenda wasn't doing much of a job on her supper, so he said, "I know somebody who's gonna miss out on a story if she doesn't finish her peas."

Brenda sighed, "Daddy, you're no fun!"

"Maybe not, but I ate my peas right down."

"I know, I do it now."

"Okay, it'll be bath time pretty soon then story time."

"I finish real quick, Daddy."

When Sandy brought Carolyn home that afternoon, there was a big truck in the driveway. Immediately, Sandy could tell that Carolyn became agitated. "What is it, Carolyn? I guess Derek has somebody here? Hmm, it looks like the logo on the truck says it's Graham's Pool Service. Would he be installing a swimming pool?"

Still focusing on Sandy's first question, Carolyn said, "Umm, I guess it's nothing, but Sandy, I get scared every time I see somebody new."

"Why, of course, Carolyn! That's understandable. You were beat up and left, you don't know who it was, sure you have a right to be scared, at least until you know it's not somebody after you. Shall I come in with you? Would that help?"

"Would you? I'd feel better."

"Of course! Let's both go down on the lift, it's better in numbers."

Breathing a sigh of relief, Carolyn said, "Thanks so much, Sandy. You don't know how that helps me."

"Of course! Don't think a thing about it, Carolyn. I can't imagine how you feel! Do you feel like you have a sieve for a brain?"

Chuckling, as Sandy hoped she would, Carolyn said, "I believe that says it all! The bad part is, my heart works just fine, but when someone new is around, it takes off, big time."

Sandy laughed. "At least it doesn't leave you high and dry!"

Carolyn grinned. "No, thank goodness!"

Sandy took Jon from his car seat and placed him on her lap. Carolyn had watched Sandy enough times working the inside mechanism for the lift that she went to the buttons and pushed the right one to open the door, then lower the lift for them to get on. Jon crowed, he loved going up and down on the lift, especially when he sat on his mama's lap. Since Carolyn stepped on with them, she smiled at the little boy.

Mrs. Beecham was the only one inside when Sandy, Jon and Carolyn came in. She was putting her last minute touches on dinner. Before Sandy or Carolyn could ask, the older lady said, "Mr. Casbah asked some man to come out. They're in the back yard doing some sort of measurements. I guess Mr. Casbah has thought of some project he wants to start, so he had that man come out."

Carolyn could easily see Derek and a man she'd never seen before from the kitchen window. She looked from Mrs. Beecham to Sandy and said, "I think I'll stay in here. It doesn't look like they need my help."

Mrs. Beecham shook her head. "No, Mr. Casbah said he and that man could do everything that needed to get done this afternoon."

Sandy had Jon on her lap, but she said, "Since they're busy, I think I'll go home. Probably the phone has rung off the hook, since it's Monday, but I'll see you again, Carolyn. We did have fun today, didn't we?"

Carolyn smiled. "More fun than I've had since I've been remembering. I don't think I've seen anything like those views you showed me. Believe me, your dessert yesterday was super, but lunch today was great, too.

Thanks, Sandy and Jon, you're such a good boy!" She let out a long sigh. "I'm a bit tired though, I think I'll go upstairs."

Jon bounced on Sandy's lap and gave Carolyn a radiant smile. "An-tee-Car! Bye, bye, An-tee-Car!"

Both Carolyn and Sandy chuckled at Jon's name for Carolyn. As Sandy started her chair toward the door, Carolyn followed her. Enthusiastically, Sandy said, "Oh, it was great we'll do it again one day soon. Maybe we can talk Raylyn into bringing Heidi and Lenny along. Bye, Mrs. Beecham, you have a good evening!"

"Thank you, Ms Sandy, I'll do my best."

Carolyn watched Sandy enter the van, close the big door and then a few minutes later leave. She sighed, they did have a good time, but Sandy was responsible for that. Carolyn didn't go back to the kitchen she went upstairs to her room and closed the door. For now, she didn't want to be where the new man was.

When Derek and Sam came inside, Sandy was gone and Carolyn was safely in her room with the door tightly closed. She had no reason to suspect that the man with Derek was the man who had hurt her, but men in general and men she didn't know in particular were not her favorite people to encounter right now. Maybe she'd get past that feeling some day, but for now she was more than happy to let someone else deal with the men. She lay down on the bed and stared at the ceiling. Would her brain always be empty? Only a few minutes later Carolyn's eyes went closed. She still didn't have much stamina – a nap was a welcome thing.

Derek and Sam were talking as they came inside and Derek took him immediately to his office. They pulled up chairs to the big oak desk to look over Sam's books and pamphlets for pool designs, costs and when it could be installed. Sam waited quietly while Derek looked over several different designs. He'd been living hand to mouth for so long and only recently could splurge a little. He wondered how the rich and famous lived. He didn't envy Derek his money, but he was glad he'd get to have some of it.

When Derek finally made his choice, Sam said, "Derek, I think that's an excellent choice. You have the ideal place for such a pool to be installed. Since there's no waiting for financing, I think we could start tomorrow.

With curing the cement and all, we should be done and gone before the end of the month."

"Excellent! I'll be glad to tell Carolyn."

Sam shook Derek's hand and said, "Thanks for the business, Derek. It means a lot to me, not only that you supported my first thoughts, but now with some business. I'm sure you know an upstart like me needs all that."

"I'm glad to do it, Sam. I'll see you soon. I'm really glad things have been working for you these several years."

"Believe me, so am I! Those first couple of years we were glad for my wife's job, but now it's a bit easier, we're not living hand to mouth."

Derek smiled. "I'm glad."

Derek had heard Sandy's van when she brought Carolyn home, how could he not hear that sweet child! As soon as Sam left, he went looking for Carolyn, wondering why she hadn't come looking for him. He searched through the empty living room, great room, the kitchen. Mrs. Beecham was in the kitchen putting last minute touches on her dinner. He knew she wasn't in his office; he and Sam had done their thinking and planning there and only left it moments before. Finally he went upstairs to the bedroom suites. Being quiet, he heard her soft sobs. They quickened his steps.

He stopped at her door, waiting a few minutes to make sure what he heard then he knocked gently and said in a quiet voice, "Carolyn? What's wrong, my dear? Am I really hearing you cry? What is it?"

Through a hiccup, she gasped, "Da… Derek, I'm so afraid! I'm terrified to meet a… a man I… I don't know!"

Derek's heart sped up he'd heard her almost call him Dad. It had been so long since he'd been called Dad by a loving child. Carefully, he turned the knob, when it turned, he asked, "May I come in, Sweetheart?"

"Y… yes, come in."

He stepped in the room and pushed the door nearly closed, then turned to Carolyn and held out his arms, as he walked toward her. Eagerly, she reached for him going into his arms as he came to her. Into his chest, she whispered, "I'm so afraid!"

In that instant, Derek knew without a doubt that this was his daughter. She might still have amnesia, she might never know him, but he knew beyond any doubt that this was Carolyn his darling daughter. When she was growing up, they had had a special place in their hearts for each other. He felt it now as he held her. Even after his wife's death, it hadn't changed how they'd felt for each other. He had grieved, but he'd taken much comfort in the love of his little daughter. He knew she'd missed her mommy, but they had comforted each other.

Lance, on the other hand, had become bitter. So very bitter! He and his mother had been close. As a ten year old boy it had devastated him. He had suffered, but he'd done it alone, he refused to take comfort from his dad. Even though, heaven knew he'd tried his best to give it. He'd loved his son; he'd wanted so desperately to give him comfort too. His son was his first born, his pride. The boy had been an over-achiever like himself, but he would not accept his dad's love or comfort. That had grieved him.

Bringing his mind back to the present and knowing that Carolyn needed his undivided attention, he stroked his hand from the back of her head down through her hair onto her back. He held her for several minutes without saying anything. He was content to hold her and she seemed content in his arms. Finally, he murmured, "It's okay, Carolyn, it's okay. You've had a terrible ordeal, but you're safe here. We always have the doors locked only the people we want get to come in. Sam is gone, now. By the way, he and his helper will be putting in a swimming pool in the backyard starting tomorrow. What do you think of that?"

Still with tear tracks on her cheeks, Carolyn pulled away from him enough she could look into his face. Her face wreathed in a smile, she asked, eagerly, "Really? You're serious? A swimming pool?"

He had wanted to see and hear her reaction he'd gotten what he'd hoped for. This was the most excited she'd been since she'd come to his home. He smiled, so glad he'd thought about putting in the pool right away. "Yes, he'll be here tomorrow morning. Does that excite you to have a swimming pool?"

"Oh, it sounds terrific!" She scowled. "Why?" Wondering at her own excitement then noticing his grin, she asked again, "Why?"

Still holding her loosely in his arms, he swallowed, then cleared his throat and said, "Carolyn, come, let's sit a minute. When you graduated from high school was the last time I saw you. Your brother told me to get out of your lives. You had graduated with high honors and had a swimming scholarship from Louisiana University."

"Oh... oh, my!" she whispered. "I did?"

"Yes, you most certainly did."

She laid her head back on his chest. He started stroking her back again. Finally, she asked, "Why did you leave your family?"

This was the question he'd been waiting for her to ask. He wasn't anxious to have to answer, but he knew he must. She truly had amnesia if she didn't remember the circumstances. To him, that time in their lives was something he'd never forget. He didn't share it, it wasn't something most people needed to know, but Carolyn was family, if she didn't remember something so important, he had to tell her. He was glad he'd taken her to the loveseat near the window, pulled her close and took a deep breath before he said, "It's a long story, my dear."

"I'd like to hear it, please," her blue eyes were clear and innocent as she asked. She pulled back from his chest and added, "Do you mind?"

Derek took a deep breath this was not something he'd ever shared with anyone, not in a very, very long time. He never thought he'd ever have to share it with one of his children. "No, it's something you really should know and since you don't remember I need to tell you. Your mom and I were married fifteen years and they were happy years. The first four we pursued our careers, I was in banking, your mom loved to teach. She was the girls' athletic teacher in our local high school. When she became pregnant with your brother, she continued to teach, only took a maternity leave for a few months before summer vacation that year."

He stopped, took a deep breath, before he could continue. It was hard talking about that time in their lives. He hadn't realized it would be so hard. Finally, he continued, "She continued to teach, it was her passion, she loved the girls, she loved athletics. Two and a half years later you were born. We were happy, a boy and a girl, we felt our quiver was complete. At first, you were a bit sickly, so your mom extended her maternity leave then decided not to go back at all. She became a stay-at-home mom. That was entirely possible because I was doing very well in my own field. Finally, though, you straightened out and became more healthy than your brother. You too, loved sports, but swimming was your passion."

Swallowing again, trying to get enough moisture into his dry mouth, he finally said, "One night, more than seven years later, in the dead of winter, during a terrible ice storm, her mom called to say her dad had wandered off. Her children had noticed some signs of Alzheimer's beginning to show in their dad. However, the lady was frantic. I was away at a banker's convention. Your mom called me, but told me she'd be fine and not to come home, since I was a hundred miles away. She left you two with her sister-in-law and went with her brother to hunt for their dad. They found him, brought him back to his home, then they left to get you two at his house." He had to swallow again and Carolyn saw tears glistening in his eyes.

Finally he spoke again, but only in a whisper, "They never made it to his place. Glen hit some black ice, hit a cement bridge and went over the side into the small river below. Your mom had been badly hurt from hitting the bridge, so hypothermia claimed her quickly in the icy water. Glen was able to drag himself out, but he nearly died from exposure."

Derek pulled in a deep breath he could feel the tears clogging his throat. He swallowed then had to swallow again. He had really loved his wife. Finally, he went on. "I came home immediately, of course, we had the funeral and you two children grieved. You and I had each other, we were special to each other, but your brother refused anything from me. It was almost like he blamed me for her death. I hired a lady to keep my house and be with you after school, but Lance hated everyone I hired. Actually, I couldn't please him in any way."

# Eight

He sighed before he continued, "When you were in high school I did a very foolish thing, I started seeing a woman. She drew me away from home more and more. I didn't realize it at first, but I wasn't as attentive to either of you. Your brother's resentment grew even stronger. By the time he graduated from high school, he was anxious to be out of our house. He'd stay away if he knew I was at home. When you were a senior, he was going to college not far from our home, but he had opted to stay in a dorm rather than live at home. Millie was taking up a lot of my time, she was very demanding, wanting us to marry. Unfortunately for you two, I listened to her and not to you two. The night after your graduation your brother stormed into the room where Millie and I were and demanded I either give her up or get out of your lives."

Remembering the words he'd said only a few sentences before, Carolyn asked, "But if you and I were special to each other, wouldn't you stay for me?" By now, Carolyn had tears in her eyes as she asked her question.

With tears in his eyes, Derek choked out, "You sided with your brother that night, Honey. Millie left almost immediately for her apartment and I tried to reason with you both, but Lance said some things that hurt me terribly. You didn't say much, but you kept nodding as if you agreed with him. The next morning I did move out. I tried to keep in touch, but all my letters were returned unopened and he must have screened the calls because no one answered the phone, they always went to an answering machine and no one called back. Ever. That was twelve years ago. I married Millie two years later and over the years have deeply regretted it."

Derek took a deep breath he hadn't talked or told anyone about that time in his life for a long time, he was drained. "That, my dear, was a long time ago, but it's the sordid tale of my life. Since Sandy came to town I've come back to the Lord, but Millie would have nothing to do with Him. I wish you could tell me what's happened in your life since then. Believe me, I've thought of you over and over again over the years."

Carolyn nodded. "Yes, I wish I could. Actually, there are a lot of things I wish I could remember." Still content to sit in Derek's arm, Carolyn asked, "So your wife that ran off the other day is Millie?"

"Yes, she'd obviously planned it for some time, but the night before she left she spent several hours on the computer. The only reason she spent time on the computer was to spend money. I think that was her hobby. She had three credit cards which I gave her soon after we were married which she maxed out each month. I found out quickly that I didn't want to pay them all off each month, she would only max them out again in a month. Anyway, the night before she left she'd done it again, putting quite a few items on two of them and a ten day cruise on the other one. Fortunately, that cruise was the last transaction on that account and so late at night that it wasn't posted until after midnight.

"I had been to see you that first time and called Mrs. Beecham about staying with you while you recuperated and she told me Millie had cleared out, so I checked her credit card records. I was able to cancel them and didn't have to pay for that cruise. I haven't heard from her to know if she went on it or not. If she did, it was a free trip for her, because I didn't pay."

Carolyn shook her head. "I can't imagine spending that much money, of course, that's in my life now, who knows what I did in my old life!"

Derek squeezed her shoulder gently and smiled at the lovely young lady. There was no question in his heart of hearts that this was his daughter. He had loved her so much! "Carolyn, I'm sure you haven't changed that much from the way you acted before, while you were in high school. You act like a very conscientious young lady."

"Thank you, Derek." After a sigh, she said, "I know it was hard for you to tell me your story and I appreciate that you did. I am so glad that lady who came to see me that night before I was discharged got in touch with you about me. It's wonderful being here in your home. I can't thank you enough for bringing me here."

The tears he'd been trying not to shed finally broke free and slid down his cheeks. "Oh, Carolyn, it means the world to me! Yes, I'm glad Isabel went to see you and called me. She is also a dear Christian lady, but she is quite a character! She told me I needed to take a good look at myself in the mirror before I went to see you."

Carolyn laughed. "I guess you did."

Derek raised his head and gave a very appreciative sniff. "You know, I think it's dinner time and Mrs. Beecham has done herself proud again. It's a bit faint, but I can smell dinner. Let's go enjoy it."

Carolyn smiled. "Yes, her meals have been great! I even enjoyed that steak you grilled on Sunday. I have no idea, but I wonder if I can cook?"

Derek smiled. "I guess we'll wait on that for another day. Believe me Mrs. Beecham really takes her job seriously. Millie had no interest, but I'm not even sure Mrs. Beecham would show you where there was a spatula!"

Carolyn grinned. "Oh, surely she'd do that! I mean, after all, we may have to flip a hamburger for Jon some Sunday!"

Derek chuckled. "Yes, that's a good possibility."

Mrs. Beecham had fixed a plate for herself that she would take to her tiny apartment then set the rest of the food on the table along with two place settings. Derek ushered Carolyn into the kitchen. Giving a long sniff, then looking at the table, Derek said, "Mrs. Beecham, you have outdone yourself again this evening! We could even smell this delicious meal behind the door in Carolyn's room and that brought us on the run! Thank you for fixing this meal, I'm sure Carolyn and I can do the cleanup after we finish."

"Oh, Mr. Casbah, I can come back to do that!"

Emphatically shaking his head, Derek said, "No, Ma'am! We'll be glad to do the honors. Oh, by the way, that man that was here, he and his helper will be back tomorrow to start putting a swimming pool in the back yard. He said they'll be at it for several days. Would you be able to supply them with water to drink during the day? I'm sure they'll get thirsty, with hot weather nearly upon us."

"Of course! That's no trouble, Mr. Casbah."

"Thanks, Mrs. Beecham."

The older lady picked up her dinner plate and left then Derek placed his hand over Carolyn's and bowed his head. Carolyn also bowed her head, she had much to be thankful for and she silently spoke her thanks to God as Derek spoke their thanks for a good meal. He also mentioned Carolyn's terrible ordeal, but for her, she knew she was safe in this house and with this man. Remembering his arms around her upstairs, she was almost convinced Derek was her dad and she was glad.

She tuned back in as Derek said, "Thank You again for everything, amen."

"Amen," Carolyn whispered.

Reluctantly, Carolyn picked up her napkin, but put it back on the table, instead picked up a bowl to pass. After taking some of the mixed vegetables, she said, "You never mentioned back in my room about going to church back then."

"Oh, your mom and I were faithful to our church even before we were married, Carolyn. In fact, we knew each other not only from school, but also from our youth group at church." He grinned. "Believe it or not, she got a prize on Mother's Day the year you were born for having the youngest baby in the service that year. Yes, we both loved the Lord and after she died I kept up the pretense for you children, but unfortunately, when I started seeing Millie I had let myself put my Savior on the back burner, since Millie had no interest in spiritual things, never did and still doesn't. Lance, however, had long before that pushed anything to do with the Lord from his life. You were still faithful and very much involved in the youth group. In fact, you were planning on being a life guard at a Christian camp the summer after you graduated from high school. That, my dear, was the last I knew about your affairs. I really don't know if you even went to that camp. After your graduation there were still several days before it opened."

Carolyn shook her head. "Who knows what's happened since?"

Derek shook his head. "Until you can remember, I guess it's in a deep, dark hole."

Carolyn sighed, "Yes, I guess that's so."

Derek grinned. "Let's not be morbid, let's eat this delicious meal!"

Loading a spoonful of real mashed potatoes on her plate, she said, "I plan to!"

Eric brought his hikers back to base on Saturday, glad that he could have Sunday off for a change. He hadn't had a Sunday free in several weeks, but tomorrow he could go to church. He fed on God's Word each day, but tomorrow he'd be able to attend Ramon's class and then hear Roger's preaching both in the morning and in the evening participate in the Bible study that he held for everyone who wanted to come. Eric felt privileged that he could study the Bible with other believers. Reading the Bible on the trails was good, but studying with others was best. He agreed with the Bible that told him to mingle often with other believers.

He wondered if Jane Doe had gone to church with Derek last Sunday, but of course, he'd been gone, so he had no idea. He remembered that Derek had said what his daughter's name was, but he couldn't remember what it was, but he had called her Jane several times, so in his mind, she was still Jane Doe. He wondered what she looked like now, surely most, if no all, of her swelling was gone and probably her skin didn't have the dark smudges any longer from all the bruises she'd had. Most of the scratches he'd seen the night he found her were superficial and would be gone by now. In fact, they had been nearly invisible when he'd gone with Isabel and Ruth to see her. He knew she'd be a beautiful young woman. Sadly, he wondered if she was pregnant, nothing had been said about that, perhaps it wasn't common knowledge other than to him, as her rescuer, those that came with the sheriff and the hospital staff, but he knew she'd been raped, it was an obvious realization when he'd found her there in the woods before the sheriff came. He sighed deeply, he felt so badly for her.

He wondered if anything had turned up to identify the man who had done such an atrocity to her. Could the man have worn gloves the whole time he was abusing her? Did men who did that kind of thing think that sophisticatedly that he'd wear gloves to not get caught? Was that car fire related? Had the car been her car or did it belong to the abuser? Either way, why would he have burned it up? Surely if it had been his own car he'd need it to get back home, wouldn't he? Could his questions ever be answered in this lifetime?

After his hikers were gone, he looked at Ramon's house, it was dark and quiet. He decided that the family who lived there was gone. He didn't begrudge them their life, but he did like the job they'd given him. Surely they would be back tomorrow he could get his new assignment sometime then. It wasn't like Vansville was so huge he'd have to drive hours to contact them to find out. He liked the fact that he worked for such good people and best of all, that they were Christians.

When the parking lot was empty, except for the empty cars that belonged to hikers on the two hikes still out and all was quiet, he heard a faint roll of thunder off in the distance. He quickly pulled his keys from the side pocket of his backpack and headed for his own car. The week-long hike had been good, the sun had blessed them with its presence each day, but he had no desire to get wet before he reached his cabin. His clothes were sweaty and dirty, he surely didn't want them caked on his body because they were wet too. Again he was glad he could go straight home and not have to go to the Laundromat. He'd be wet for sure if he had to do that.

Now that he'd heard the thunder, he realized that the black clouds were quickly rolling in from the west. Since it was after four o'clock, the clouds had obscured the sun since he'd brought his group back. As he unlocked the driver's door he noticed a flash of lightning in those clouds, so he quickly dove in the car, slammed the door and started up. He waited for the car on the street to pass before he left DeLord's parking lot, then drove quickly the few blocks to Isabel's parking lot and drove to his parking spot.

There were other cars on the lot probably travelers renting cabins for the night, after all, it was Saturday night. He was always glad to see the parking lot full or nearly so. That meant that Isabel was getting more income, it supplemented her Social Security. Fortunately she wasn't as badly off now that Ruth lived with her, he was glad of that, too.

Another snap of lightning and a roll of thunder greeted him as he yanked his keys from the ignition and opened the door. He grabbed his backpack from the passenger seat and stepped out hurriedly, then slammed the car door behind him. "That storm is coming fast!" he exclaimed. "I'm glad I got those people back when I did, they'll get caught in it before they get home, I'm sure, but they won't get wet." He hurried up his walk and stepped onto the porch just as the first drops splattered on the walk behind him. "Whew! I made it!" he exclaimed. He was happy to open the cabin door, step inside and close the rain out. Hearing it splatter on the roof was calming and refreshing, but he was dry.

He hadn't even gone in his bathroom when the phone rang. "Has to be Isabel," he muttered. "She'd be the only one who'd know I was here already." He picked up his handset and said, "Isabel? I knew it had to be you, you sit in that chair by the window you'd be the only one who'd know I was home already!"

She cackled. "Yes, Sonny, I see you made it before the rain."

"So glad I did! It also makes me glad for my washer and dryer that are here in the cabin. I didn't have to stop at Thomas's Laundromat and get wet washing clothes. What's on your mind, Isabel?"

"So you think I sit in my chair and watch every move people make, huh. Wanna come over for supper in about an hour?"

"Well, if it's still raining, I might melt."

"Listen here, you're a nice guy and all, but it's sweet young *ladies* who melt in rain, not sassy young men. Now, how about it? Oh, by the way, I made cinnamon rolls this morning I don't suppose you'd want some to take home for your breakfast tomorrow?"

"Isabel, I'll be there! I haven't met a soul in this town of Vansville who will turn down the prospect of having one of your cinnamon rolls."

"That's what I thought." The dial tone hummed in his ear.

He chuckled and replaced the handset. "That lady is something else!"

He glanced out the window and realized it was dark as late evening and the rain was pouring down. He wondered briefly about the two groups that were still out on the trails. This wasn't Arizona or the deserts of Afghanistan where you didn't have to worry about a rain storm coming up. Surely they all had rain slickers. He hurried into his bathroom, took a quick shower and filled his washer with a load. His clothes could get clean while he ate with Isabel and Ruth.

About an hour later, Eric ran through the rain, across the parking lot, took the steps to Isabel's porch in two leaps and rapped on the door. He heard, "Come in!" so he did.

Ruth met him in the hallway and said, "I see you didn't get too wet."

On a sigh, Eric said, "No, I had to run, though. I was sure I'd melt if I didn't."

From the kitchen they heard, "You can't fool me! You're not made of sugar, I guarantee that! Maybe salt, but for your size, you'd have a lot farther to run to melt. That's a fact, Sonny!"

Coming to the door into the kitchen, Eric said, woefully, "Isabel, you wound me! Here I've been on the trail…"

Pointing to the chair closest to him with the large spatula in her hand, she commanded, "Sit down in that chair! Don't give me that, you scallywag! You don't melt in rain there's too many minerals in our rainwater and I surely don't wound you, you're too big for that and your hide's too tough."

Eric sighed, "Isabel, I'm crushed!"

"Hardly!" she retorted.

The two ladies brought the dinner bowls to the table and sat down. After saying the blessing, Eric said, "So have you heard anything about Jane Doe?"

"You mean Carolyn?" Eric nodded. "She's adjusting to living with Derek very well. Of course, he's loving her to pieces! The man is blossoming with her there. Did you hear that Millie left town?"

"No, really?"

Isabel nodded. "It was the same day that Derek brought Carolyn home. Believe me, nobody misses her. Would you believe, Derek has unofficially adopted Ramon, Sandy and Jon? As I understand it, he's gone crazy over that baby!"

"So nobody knows where Millie went?"

"Nope. She left no forwarding address and hasn't called, that I know of." Isabel chuckled. "Actually, that surprises me, because she doesn't have the credit cards Derek cancelled out. He told Sandy she'd put a ten day cruise on one of them, but he caught it soon enough and cancelled the card before it was paid for."

Eric smiled. "Good for him! So has Carolyn gotten her memory back?"

"Not the last I knew, but that was Thursday."

Eric shook his head. "That must be a very strange situation! Can they really know if she's his daughter?"

"Well… well… I don't know!"

Ruth scowled and wiped her mouth, since she'd emptied her plate. "I suppose they could if they were really into finding out, they could do that DNA thing. I understand it's not that hard to do any more."

"Yeah, I guess they could," Eric said, thoughtfully.

After an enjoyable evening, Isabel slid several cinnamon buns in a ziploc bag, handed them to Eric and said, "Now, that's too many for one meal, Sonny. You eat all those in one sitting you'll swell up and burst!"

Taking the bag that was bulging with nearly a dozen huge buns, he said, "I'll call it breakfast and lunch, how's that?"

Isabel nodded. "Eaten at two different times, that might work."

Eric sighed, "Spoil sport!"

Grinning at him, Isabel said, "I wouldn't want Ramon to lose his greenie guide."

"Humph! Thanks a lot, Isabel!" Isabel just cackled as Eric headed for the door. It was still pouring, so Eric held the bag close to his chest and sprinted for his cabin. Thank goodness it wasn't October or November, it wasn't freezing rain!

It was still raining Sunday morning. Usually, Eric walked to church, since it was only a few blocks, but sitting in wet clothes in church for two hours was not his favorite pastime, so he drove and found a parking space in Thomas's gaspump lot, since the store and gas station were closed on Sundays. He still had to run across the street in the rain, but it wasn't like walking four blocks in a downpour. It did seem like the heavens opened up once he left his car, however. He ran up the steps to the tiny roof sheltering the front door.

He had just reached the covered entryway of the church when a car drove onto the lot and parked next to his car. The man stepped out with an umbrella then walked around to the passenger side and helped a woman from the seat. It was then he realized it was Derek and Carolyn he was protecting from the weather. Roger shook his hand, but Eric only paid slight attention to him, as he continued to watch as Derek and Carolyn came across the street. He hadn't seen her since she'd been released from the hospital.

"That's right," Roger said, looking where Eric was looking. "You're the one who found her in the woods, weren't you? Last Sunday she'd lost the swelling around her face, but she appears normal now."

"Yes, I've only seen her once since then. I was wondering how she looked now that it's been a while." When they reached the bottom step, Eric whispered, "She's beautiful!"

"That she is," Roger answered in a quiet voice.

As they came up behind him, Derek folded his umbrella and exclaimed, "Eric! You have a day off. Good to have you come today."

"Yes, Derek, that I do and I'm glad to come to God's house instead of being on a trail. Especially with this rain. Fortunately, I got my group back before the heavens opened up yesterday." He looked at Carolyn and held out his hand. "Perhaps you don't remember me, but I'm the guy who found you in the woods. I came with Isabel and Ruth to the hospital the night before you went to the rehab center."

Her smile was devastating as she took his hand and said, "Yes, I remember when you came to see me at the hospital. I remember you prayed for me. You know, it was the very next day that Derek came and took me to his place. You had prayed I'd be safe and God answered your prayer before twenty-four hours had past."

He smiled at her. "I'm humbled, truly!"

"Yes, I was amazed. I wasn't sure what I believed before that, but when I thought about your prayer and how fast it was answered, I decided God was real."

This was the first time Eric had seen Carolyn out of the hospital. Regular clothes, rather than a hospital gown did marvelous things for a woman. She was the most beautiful woman he had ever laid eyes on. To him, she was the most stunning creature he'd ever met. Those three words he'd said to her felt like they had strangled in his throat. He would have liked nothing more than to stand and gaze on her the rest of his life. Of course, that couldn't be, there were too many unanswered questions, questions no one in Vansville could answer. Besides, who was he to think someone so beautiful would even look at him?

He had to look away before he could say to Derek, "I'd be honored to walk Carolyn to Ramon's classroom, would that be all right?"

"Of course, Eric! You're both in that class, that's fine."

"Great!"

Knowing that the adult classes all gathered in the auditorium first and sang a song before they split into their classes, Eric ushered Carolyn to a seat, then sat beside her. She turned to him immediately after they sat down and asked, "What is it you do that I haven't seen you since that evening at the hospital? I know you weren't here at church last Sunday."

"I work for DeLord's Hiking Service. It's rare that I have a Sunday off, usually a group wants to start their hike on a Friday or Saturday and it'll last into the next week sometime. Usually, we only have one day off between hikes. I brought a group back yesterday, so I have today off, but I must be out again tomorrow. We have been so busy this year that the three of us who are full time only get one day off between hikes."

Tentatively, Carolyn asked, "Is that Sandy's hikes? She took me out to see some of the sights around last Monday and told me something about what she does."

After the song, everyone left for their classes and on the way, Eric answered her last question. "Well, she runs the business end, she and Ramon. He works with us part time but there are three of us who are full time guides. We're so busy that the three of us usually only get one day off between hikes. It's quite challenging, believe me. Usually I try to cram all my errands into that one day, but since I knew I'd have today off, the last time I was off, I tried to get all my errands done then."

"Oh, I'm sure it is very challenging! Surely you don't do this in the winter!"

"No, only through October, but we start again in March."

"March, isn't it cold then? I mean, it's here in the mountains!" Instantly goosebumps sprang up on her arms. She rubbed her arms, she hadn't gotten wet under the umbrella, but thinking of hiking in March gave her the chills. "Goodness! You're outside all the time, you sleep on the ground! I can't imagine people wanting to do that in March!"

"Oh, it's cold! Sometimes it's snowing when we take a group out, but they ask for the time, so we do take our turn with these foolish people, they're only two and three days long. Sandy makes sure those die-hards know that."

Softly, to herself, she murmured, "I wonder, in my other life if I'd have gone on a hike. It sounds really challenging!" She looked at the young man walking beside her. She was sure he'd been in some branch of the military not too long ago. He wore his hair very short, he had no facial hair, perhaps when he came back from a week on the trail, he'd have a full beard, but only because he couldn't shave on the trail. She remembered the day he'd come to see her at the hospital, he hadn't had any then either. However the way he walked gave him away... it screamed military, as if someone was yelling 'one! two! one! two!'. Physically... well, it went without saying.... The man was definitely in shape! She didn't dare look into his eyes to see their color, she'd probably melt away!

Eric looked at her and smiled. "Perhaps you did, Carolyn."

As they walked into Ramon's class, Eric continued, "I guess we don't know that answer, but if I were you, I wouldn't want to chance it until the man who did that horrific act to you is caught. From what you said just now, I take it you still haven't remembered?"

Carolyn sighed, as she sat down beside him in Ramon's class. Sadly, she shook her head as Eric opened his Bible. "No, I know the meaning of 'airhead' now. I think that's all that's in my brain, but I feel like a baby. Except to know how to walk, talk, eat and easy things like that, I don't remember who I am, where I came from, what I did for a living or anything before I woke up there in the hospital. It's very frustrating, like I told Derek; I don't know my birthday, nothing! Actually, he was the one who said my name was Carolyn. I liked it better than Jane, so that's what we went with. I guess I'll have to live with nothing until that door opens up, but when that'll be is a deep, dark mystery."

Eric laid his hand over hers, but then lifted it quickly away. It felt as if her skin had scorched his when he touched her. It affected him so he had to clear his throat before he said, "Carolyn, I'm sure it'll come in God's time. Leave it in His hands. He really is in control and He knows what's in our best interest."

Also feeling the spark from Eric's hand, she kept her hand on her leg. "Yes, that's what Derek has told me, too. That's another thing, he's nearly positive I'm his daughter Carolyn. I guess I am, there at the nursing home the receptionist nearly had a heart attack when he walked in. Only about a half hour before he came I'd been admitted and we do look very much alike. Still, until I get my memory back, how can we know for sure?"

Ramon stood up to start his lesson, but Eric whispered, "I like that name much better, too. It's a beautiful name and suits you perfectly."

Carolyn gave him another radiant smile. "Thanks," she whispered back.

It took Eric the rest of the Sunday school hour to get his mind off that smile and back on the lesson Ramon was teaching. He was disgusted with himself, here was a Sunday to spend in church and he was mooning over a woman? While he still mulled over his reaction, Eric tried to think of another time when such a thing had happened to him concerning another woman, but never in his memory could he bring up a face or the name of anyone who affected him like she did. He shook his head, life was complicated enough he didn't need to add the complication of a beautiful woman! Besides, when she got her memory back, surely she'd go back to her life, wherever and whatever that was. Maybe she was even married…

Lance Casbah sat alone in the hotel suite he had reserved for the weekend outing with his wife and daughter in Birmingham. He'd had business to attend to all day on Saturday, a one day seminar he had to lead for his work. While he did that, Linda and Brenda had spent the day either at the hotel or at a mall. He was glad she wasn't a 'mall-a-holic' or a 'spend-a-holic'. Today Linda and Brenda were spending the morning in the indoor pool, since it was raining hard and no one was using the outside pool for fear of lightning and thunder.

While he was alone he took advantage of the quietness in the suite and had tried several times since Friday to call his sister's cell phone. He was perplexed and looked at the phone in his hand. She always kept her phone with her or at least with her things and if she didn't answer, it always went to her voicemail. However, each time he'd tried her number this weekend the canned voice said, 'The number you have dialed is no longer a working number. Check to see if you have dialed it correctly and try again.' He had, several times with the same result.

He pulled the phone away from his ear and quickly clicked it off, those canned voices grated on his nerves. Still staring at his phone, he muttered, "Where could she be? Why isn't her cell number working any more? This is not like her at all! I've never known her to let her time run out or ignore my number before. Besides, she's on a payment plan and I know it hasn't run out! Her payments come out of her account automatically and it's not time for her contract renewal. Besides, we used our phones to communicate between the rental truck and her car when she moved! That was only two weeks ago! What's going on?"

He sat at the desk in the sitting room and looked out at the dismal day and the rain pouring down. Except for the bright spots of his wife and daughter, his life felt rather like the day outside the hotel room. He sat there, staring out the window. He couldn't remember when the last time was when he'd been truly happy. Perhaps it was when he was part of a complete family, before his mom was killed. But he'd been just a boy she'd died when he was ten. Nothing seemed to be right after that, he remembered his dad trying to comfort him. He shook his head, he'd never let him. In fact, as he sat thinking, he wondered why he'd been like that. That witch hadn't come into his dad's life until years later.

There was a feeble knock on the door and a little voice chattered, "D-d-daddy, o-o-open u-u-up th-th-the d-d-door! I'm f-f-freezing!"

Lance, glad for the interruption from his morbid thoughts went immediately to the door and pulled it open. Two drowned individuals scurried passed him into the room from the much cooler hallway. He closed the door and grinned. "I'm not sure I should let drowned rats in here!" Trying to sound annoyed, he said, "Look at this! There're puddles all over this carpet!"

He scrunched down to Brenda's level, took the towel wrapped around her and began to scrub her wet body. She protested, "D-d-daddy! I a-a-aren't n-n-no r-r-rat!"

Still rubbing the little girl briskly, he grinned at her and said, "Well, I don't know, that's sure what you look like!"

Brenda shook her head, her wet ringlets dripping water on his arm. "Daddy, I look like a wet girl, not a rat!"

Lance snapped his fingers. "Hmm, maybe that's it."

Lance wrapped a dry towel around her and Brenda said, "Daddy, that feels good."

"Of course, Sweetheart, right now anything dry feels good to a cold, wet girl."

"Yes, Daddy."

From the bigger bedroom doorway, Linda asked, "Did you reach Carolyn?"

Looking at his wife over his shoulder, he said, "No, I can't figure it out! Some canned voice comes on each time I dial to tell me it's not a working number. I could see if she had it off that it would go to voicemail, but the voice says it's not working."

Linda scowled and pulled the long terrycloth robe around her, glad for the warmth it provided. Once they left the warm pool area, the rest of the hotel had been very cool. "What! That can't be!" she exclaimed, shaking her head, then remembered her own hair was wet and reached for a dry towel. "I know it is! You've got it programmed into your phone she hasn't changed phones in a long time. She wouldn't let it lapse, she wouldn't! That's the only way we get together. Besides, she's on a payment plan, it comes out automatically. She's religious about renewing it every time."

"I know. I've tried five times, but that's what it says each time. Maybe we ought to leave earlier and maybe we could go by her place…"

With a towel wrapped around her hair turban style, Linda came into the sitting room, shook her head and said, "Honey, she's moved! She's in Atlanta now. Surely you remember."

He picked Brenda up and hugged her to his chest, huge towel, wet, dripping curls and all. "Yes, of course…." he whispered. "It was kind of foolish that I didn't remember, you helped her pack up her apartment and I drove the U-haul for her. Surely, it didn't get dropped and damaged and she's had to change phones, but she'd have let us know about that."

"Honey," Linda whispered, "where is it your dad lives?"

Lance shook his head, threw his head back and stared at the ceiling. Realizing that only moments ago he'd thought about his dad. "Don't! Don't even say it! No! Surely she didn't!" After a moment's thought, he added, "but that wouldn't mean her phone wouldn't work!"

Seeing the utter devastation on her husband's face, Linda said, compassionately, "Honey, you need to think about it. She's never gotten over it that you made him leave."

"I… I know-w-w-w!" he wailed.

Brenda patted his cheek. "Daddy! Daddy, don't cry, Daddy!" Brenda started crying.

Hugging his little daughter, he put his face into the towel that now covered her shoulders. After several minutes he had control of himself enough that he managed to croak, "I still don't understand how he could do that to us. He and Mom loved each other so much, how could he take up with that horrid wench and let Mom's memory go? And… and let us go, too?"

Remembering when she'd first met her husband, she said, softly, "Honey, if I remember right, you weren't very nice to him, were you?"

Lance heaved out a huge sigh, "No, perhaps I wasn't. Maybe I drove him away." Remembering clearly Carolyn's graduation night, he said, "I guess I told him to leave. I said some really mean things that night."

"I hate to agree with you, but we were going together then, you were a very bitter young man toward your dad. You hardly wanted to see him."

"I know. I really said some awful things to him." Brenda wanted down, so Lance absently set her on the floor. She scampered into her room to dress and Lance went to his wife. Taking her in his arms, he rested his forehead on her shoulder and said, "I've lost track of him. Would he be close to Atlanta now?"

"Honey, I don't know, but really, it's not hard to find somebody now with the internet. Carolyn's pretty savvy on the internet, perhaps she's looked him up."

"But <u>would</u> she look him up?"

"It's anyone's guess. Maybe she did."

He nodded slowly. "Yes, maybe she did."

Thinking she was walking into some uncharted waters, Linda said, "You know she never got over that you said those things to him and made her agree with you. She loved your dad she'd forgiven him a lot. Was that woman really that bad? Really? You don't know where he is now, do you, Honey?"

Lance shook his head. "No, really, it wasn't his fault so much as it was me. I hated him for what he'd done to Mom's memory. Once the phone calls and the letters stopped I put the man out of my mind. I never let Carolyn see the letters and I always screened the calls. I made her promise never to answer the phone and she didn't. I never once let her know he was still trying to reach us." He sighed, "I really didn't know that woman, just to know he was seeing her. Maybe she wasn't that bad a person, but she was taking Dad away. And with Mom gone… I just couldn't take it."

Linda nodded and put her arms around her husband's neck. "I know that was a really hard time for you, Honey, but maybe now she's trying to find him."

Lance leaned back and looked into his wife's eyes. "Maybe, but why would her phone keep saying it wasn't working any more?"

"I don't know, Honey, but Atlanta is too far away to go there now and get back for work tomorrow morning. You know that. Maybe if you hadn't had that seminar yesterday we could have made a weekend trip over there."

"I know, I really had forgotten for a minute that she'd moved." He scowled. "I really can't think of another way to get hold of her, can you?"

"No, I can't either. We do know where she lives maybe you could call her landlord."

"Good idea, but that number's at home I don't even remember his name. I'm not even sure he lives in the complex where she rented."

"I'll find the number and call him in the morning."

"Yes, that'll be good."

Church was over, again, as usual, Roger had preached a powerful sermon to the full house, but Derek leaned over Carolyn and said to Eric, "You're alone in the world, why don't you join us and the DeLord's at my place for dinner?"

Eric swallowed, very uncomfortable. He had to look passed Carolyn to see Derek and just the sight of her seemed to make him lose all rational thought. "Oh, I wouldn't want to impose on a family get together, Derek!"

Derek put his hand on Carolyn's shoulder and exclaimed, "Nonsense! One more steak on the grill is a small thing, Eric! Besides, you'd be eating alone, wouldn't you? What and eat one of Alex's frozen dinners?" Derek grinned. "You'd be the first man I ever heard of who chose to eat a frozen dinner over a steak."

Eric chuckled. "You got me there, Derek."

"Fine, you've never been to my place, I'm sure Ramon and Sandy must stop by their place momentarily, so hurry and change and follow them out, or even come with them. We'll have a great time, even in the rain." At that very moment they heard a snap of lightning and the lights blinked, as the thunder roared.

Eric nodded. "You twisted my arm, Derek, I'll come."

Derek reached for Eric's hand. "That's my man!"

Eric gave Derek a big smile, one that sent Carolyn's heart into overdrive and not because he scared her. "You are very convincing! Thank you for the invite. Except for TV dinners I don't have anything I could bring."

Derek shook his head and laughed. "None of those needed, man! You can't know how happy I am to be able to invite people on the spur of the moment to my house!" Eric and Carolyn both heard what he didn't say. Obviously, Millie had been a very big obstacle.

Roger stood at the back door shaking hands, but people were leaving in spurts because it was still raining like hurricane weather. Either a husband darted out to bring the family car closer while the rest of the family waited just inside or several others would wait for an imaginary let up of the pouring rain to raise an umbrella and dash outside into the gloom. Since he was alone and had no umbrella, Eric dashed out as one of the first to go to his cabin to change. He had plenty of time to reach DeLord's house before they left.

Ramon was one who dashed out, but the van sat right at the foot of the ramp. Holding a small umbrella over his head, he stuck the key into the outside mechanism to open the door and lower the lift. Roger watched, then opened the huge umbrella Ramon had handed him just outside the church door and held it over Sandy, Jon and the chair, as Sandy pushed the lever into fast forward. They were usually the last to leave and except for Roger's family, they were last.

Besides a huge uncovered deck off his dining room, Derek had a large covered patio that used the deck floor as its roof. It was off the great room that took up most of the floor space below the main floor. In rainy weather this was where the activity was centered for dinner. With the rain and humidity, the cooking steaks and baking potatoes gave off an aroma that drew those who came in the van quickly to the backyard. As they came across the back of the house, from the back door of the garage, Sandy carried Jon on her lap and Ramon hefted a huge picnic basket. Eric walked beside Sandy holding the huge umbrella over her. He'd never seen one so big, but the DeLord's insisted Sandy's chair motor couldn't get wet. Thus the huge umbrella.

On the way to Derek's place Eric had commented on the huge umbrella, because he'd seen it at church. Ramon had told him they'd watched mail order catalogs for some time to find one so big. They couldn't find one big enough in any store where they looked. He also told him about Sandy's experiences when she'd first moved to Vansville. As anyone could observe, the lift on the van had one speed, rain or shine - **slow**.

The moment they rounded the corner, Eric's eyes quickly zeroed in on the lovely blond sitting at the big picnic table close to the grill. In Eric's eyes the lady was a breath of spring. He could sit and gaze at her for hours. But of course, that was something he couldn't or wouldn't do. After all, his life was bound up in the hiking service now. He had one day a week off, most times that wasn't Sunday. Never mind that he felt tongue-tied, his heart thumped and his hands turned clammy in her presence. And her smile...

Since the rain was pouring down, the three coming on the back walk were hurrying as fast as Sandy's chair controls would let it move. At the corner they saw that Derek stood at the grill, holding the huge tongs. He'd just put down the lid, but the smoke and aroma still moved out from the edges. "Oh, man!" Ramon exclaimed. "That smells terrific! I can't wait to savor those steaks!" He took another giant step toward the patio. He held the small umbrella over himself and the basket, but it didn't keep him very dry.

"Japa!" the little person exclaimed from Sandy's lap. "Japa!" he sang again and started clambering down from Sandy's chair. She had to grab him with one hand until she also reached the covered patio.

Derek quickly put the tongs he'd been using down on the table and turned just as a tiny tornado slammed into his legs. Swinging the child up in his arms, Derek exclaimed, "How's Japa's little guy?"

Jon threw his arms around Derek's neck as soon as he was up in his arms. The child grinned at the man but after a slobbery kiss, he laid his head on Derek's shoulder and said, much more quietly, "I good, Japa." After a quick breath, he murmured, "Wuv, Japa."

Derek immediately became blubbery, "Oh, Jonny, I love you, too."

After another slobbery kiss, Jon squirmed to get down, so Derek placed him on the cement. His legs already moving, Jon toddled over to Carolyn and held up his hands. "Up, An-tee-Car." Carolyn, of course, couldn't resist the toddler any better than Derek, so she picked him up. Immediately he put his arms around her neck and gave her a slobbery kiss on her cheek. Carolyn, of course, returned the favor and gave Jon a loving kiss. A minute later Jon turned around and sat down on her lap. From there he looked at the man who had ridden with them from town and said, "Ick."

Derek laughed. "So you've been reduced to Ick?"

"Yep! We had this discussion the day I came back from a hike a bit ago. 'Ick' it was and very adamantly endorsed."

With a grin, Derek said, "Well, I won't say it suits you, but it goes along with the others voiced just now."

Eric chuckled. "Yes, I guess that's so."

Eric chanced a look at the young woman and asked, "So you're anticar?"

Everyone chuckled, but Carolyn said, "Perhaps that's it, but I prefer to make that into 'An-TEE-Car'. I'm not really opposed to cars, it's just that I can't drive one right now, perhaps I did in my other life."

# Nine

Lifting the lid of the huge grill, Derek let out another long whiff of sizzling meat and exclaimed, "Ah, looks like our dinner is about ready! Gather around the table. I see Sandy outdid herself again this week with another delicious dessert! Let's dig in so we can have some soon! Besides, the steaks and potatoes are done to a turn! Since Mrs. Beecham isn't here on Sundays, Carolyn was able to sneak in the kitchen and make us a salad."

Ramon quickly stepped up to the grill. "I'm all for that….Dad."

"Good, you say grace."

After saying the blessing, Derek loaded plates with meat and a potato. Handing them out, everyone finished loading his plate with the other things Carolyn had placed on the bar attached to the side of the house. They all found seats at the large table and dug in. Without the food on the grill, Derek left the lid up so the heat could take off some of the chill.

Ramon still felt strange addressing Derek by 'Dad' and didn't do it often, so he said, "So, Sandy tells me you had Sam here the other day measuring for a pool. I see there's a hole out there, but it looks like God's been filling it sooner, before the cement."

Looking out at the soggy green expanse, Derek sighed, "Yes, that's what Sam and I planned out there. He pulled his backhoe out on Friday, planning to pour cement tomorrow, but he may have to bring it back when it dries out. I haven't been out to look to see if the sides have crumbled in with this rain. I'm also thinking of enclosing the whole backyard, but this rain'll set the guys back a bit. After the rain stops he'll have to decide how soon he can get his work resumed or if he'll have to start over. If it hadn't started raining, he thought he'd be able to get done by month's end." As the rain gave a renewed lashing, Derek sighed, "I guess that date'll be up for debate now."

"So Carolyn's an Olympic swimmer?" Ramon asked.

Carolyn sighed, "I have no idea about the Olympic part, Ramon, but Derek says I went to college on a swimming scholarship. Having a pool so close does sound great!"

Looking out at the heavy rain and hearing it pounding on the roof, Derek said to Eric, "You'll be taking a group of hikers out in this tomorrow?"

Also looking out at the dismal weather, Eric said, "Both Ramon and I have one scheduled. If no one calls we'll both head out."

Carolyn shivered, as the lightning snapped close by and nearly instantly deafening thunder roared. "That doesn't sound like fun at all!"

"No, but it pays the bills. We don't have any more slots for rainchecks either."

Derek looked at Ramon and asked, "You mean you're booked solid until into October? That's amazing! I didn't know hiking was such big time entertainment."

"Yes, we are. You and I weren't close when I started this business, but it hasn't always been this busy or popular."

"Oh, I know. I do remember when Millie would call your number then get frustrated when you weren't there or weren't returning her calls. She'd make a big production about having to talk to that answering machine, but she'd storm around the house like some spoiled child having a temper tantrum!" He rolled his eyes and continued, "And in those ridiculous platform heels… let your answering machine pick up! My, oh, my! That was like you had committed the unpardonable sin. There was no excuse for that." He looked at the lovely lady sitting in her wheelchair and shook his head. "Then when Sandy came along… Once she saw you kissing… Really you don't want to know what all she said or how she acted! My, my, I'm glad you weren't around."

Sandy nodded. "I remember my first encounter. It wasn't nice!"

"You know, thinking back to the ancient history of my childhood, I can remember when she'd act like that each time things didn't go her way."

Derek put his hands together between his knees and shook his head. "Son, you know that's the measure of an unhappy person."

"Believe me, I know that about her! She never was happy with anything I ever did. I remember it even happened when I was in elementary school."

Derek shook his head. "That is truly too bad!"

After eating the few bites Ramon had set on Jon's tray, the little boy climbed out of his highchair, dangled from the armrest for a few seconds, then dropped to the floor. He looked around at the adults sitting around the table then rubbing his eyes, he made a beeline for his mommy, and climbed up on Sandy's footrest. From there he held up his hands and said, sleepily, "Up, Mama, up now."

Sandy's heart swelled, as she looked at her son. She pulled the toddler onto her lap, straight to her chest. From there he hugged her neck a minute then squirmed around to sprawl into a rather uncomfortable looking position. After a sigh and just before his thumb found his mouth, he whispered, "Ni, ni."

Derek wiped his mouth and looked tenderly at the little boy. As he laid his napkin down, he whispered, "He is so precious!" After a few seconds, he shook his head and murmured, "Millie must have wanted out very badly to leave her grandson."

"Yes," Ramon agreed, "we both thought she really loved him, but she didn't even call to tell us she was going away!"

Derek shook his head. "Ramon, it was me she wanted to leave, not him, I'm sure." Looking at Sandy with renewed admiration, he said, "He's such a treasure." Neither he nor Ramon could forget what Sandy had gone through for nine months to carry this child.

Wiping his mouth, but his twinkling eyes shown above his napkin, Ramon said, "But you're a nice guy! Surely…"

"Son, believe me, it's all in the eyes of the beholder."

When everyone had finished eating and very little food was left on the table, Carolyn started cleanup. Sandy whispered, "Carolyn, I'd help you, but this is Jon's favorite nap place."

Carolyn waved her hand at her friend and said, "Don't think a thing about it! I'll have this cleared away in no time at all."

Eric also stood up and started stacking dishes in front of him. "It's the least I can do to help! Goodness, I didn't bring anything or do any of the work. Carolyn, lead the way, I've never been in this great house to know where to go."

Carolyn gave him her brilliant smile and said, "Come on, we'll head inside."

Eric also grinned, his heart hammering like a jack-hammer and picked up his pile of dirty dishes. "After you." The pair disappeared inside the house.

Derek, Ramon and Sandy still sat on the patio. The rain poured down and nearly drowned out Derek as he asked, "Those other two men still have their hikers out?"

"Yup, Duncan and Neal are both due back today, but they'll be soaked! And their poor hikers will be drowned rats!"

After another round of lightning and thunder, Derek asked, "When it's raining like this there's no shortcut back, is there?"

Ramon shook his head and looked out at the pouring rain that was now coming down even harder. A great streak of lightning snapped and thunder roared right behind it. "Unfortunately not, no, they have to follow the route. Sometimes there are trails off the main trail, but unless one could access our program a guide couldn't be sure of the destination. Of course, none of the men take their computers along. The only thing that's electronic that we take on our hikes is the phone for emergencies."

"Yes, I remember some of those emergencies you've had. What happened before cell phones? How did you handle emergencies?"

"I'd leave someone from the group in charge, but leave them there. Since I knew the area so much better, I'd hike out to call Blairsville Hospital to send a chopper. Of course, the chopper would arrive before I got back, because I'd go back home to call. I'm so glad that woman on that hike after Sandy came had her cell phone. Believe me once I realized they'd work out in that wilderness, I had one the next hike out."

"Then you had an accident yourself!"

"Yes, that was such a freak of nature. Who would ever think a tree uprooting would drop a rock on my head?" Ramon looked lovingly at his wife. "But, it brought Sandy close enough, I knew she loved me even though she didn't know herself."

"Really? Why?"

Sandy shook her head. "Derek, I never thought anyone could love me!"

"Sandy! Why not!" he demanded. "As far as I can tell, you are easy to love!"

Sandy shrugged. "I guess Mom's attitude toward this chair had rubbed off on me, even though I didn't realize it. I never thought anyone could look beyond this chair."

"Oh, Sandy, believe me, nobody even notices the chair."

Shyly, Sandy whispered, "Thank you, Derek."

Derek shook his head. "Really, Sandy, there is no thanks needed! I have such admiration for you. I've thought of you for a long time as a great daughter."

"Oh, Derek, thank you!" Sandy exclaimed with tears sparkling in her eyes.

Looking out at the rain pouring down, Derek asked, "Will you call the hikers for tomorrow? Man, that's awful! It'll be a sea of mud and if you have to cross shale it'll be a nightmare for sure! Maybe some of the creeks will be over their banks, too."

"No, but I'm sure when we get back home the light on the machine'll be red. No one likes to start a hike in the rain, even if the weather's supposed to improve later in the week."

After a loud clap of thunder, Derek said, "Any self-respecting group leader should call to cancel, that's for sure."

"We can only hope," Sandy sighed.

Inside, both Carolyn and Eric climbed the stairs to the main floor and put their load of dirty dishes down on the counter. Carolyn absently picked up a plate and turned on the water as she looked out the kitchen window and asked, "Really? You'd lead a group of hikers on a hike that starts in something like this?"

Eric followed her line of vision to the pouring rain. "Unfortunately yes. We never call to cancel. It's up to the hike's leader to make that decision. Remember, my hike is for a week. It'll probably turn nice Tuesday or Wednesday."

"I know, but if it's even a fraction of what this is, it'll be a nightmare! And the mud on the trail! You'd probably sink up to your ankles! Have there ever been accidents because of bad weather, that you know about?"

"Not since I've been working for them, but I guess that year that Sandy came there were two. That was when Ramon found out how important a cell phone was so they could call base to get the helicopter to the injured person in a hurry."

"Oh, my! What happened?"

"The first accident a girl slipped on some wet shale and fell. She had a bad leg fracture. She had to be airlifted to Macon. The second time the group was caught in a tornado and Ramon was knocked out by some flying debris."

"Wow! I'm sure you're glad that doesn't happen often."

"That's for sure, the first time one of the hikers had her cell phone, but Ramon bought his own right away and we've carried them ever since."

"So you'll go even in the rain," Carolyn mused.

"I know and believe me; I really am hoping they've called to cancel. It's just too bad we don't have any more spaces for rainchecks."

Carolyn chuckled, still looking outside at the pouring rain. "Raincheck is a good word for this. Yes, it's hard to believe, like Derek said, that you're all booked up into October. There are three of you who do this?"

"Three who work full time plus Ramon who does it part time."

"It's surprising to be so busy and this is such a small town."

"That's true, but people come from over fifty miles away to hike with us. Well, more than that, we've had several groups from Atlanta."

"Wow!"

A huge streak of lightning snapped followed almost immediately by a loud clap of thunder. Eric swallowed and said, "But still I don't melt. Did Derek take you back Sunday evening for the Bible study last week?"

"No, we didn't go. I was still really tired and weak from being discharged and going shopping on Friday, so I went to bed early and he stayed with me. I've only just in the last day or two felt good enough that I could stay by myself and he's been so kind to have either Mrs. Beecham or him here all the time." She smiled a little, only one side of her mouth turned up. "I think he's paranoid that I'm still not safe. He's got this place locked up like a fortress! Actually, I think that's why he said he's thinking about enclosing the backyard."

"Well, I don't blame him on that one at all, Carolyn!" Eric smiled and said, "Would you like to go tonight?"

"With you?"

"Umm, yeah, that's what I was thinking."

She smiled shyly at him. "I think I'd like that, Eric."

Eric's heart going miles a minute, he smiled back at her. "That's great, Carolyn! It's all really casual for the evening. Roger holds a Bible study. Sometimes it's a large group, but I'll bet it's pretty small tonight."

"That sounds good. I'll be ready."

Eric's smile covered his face and lit up his eyes. "Thanks."

After their company left that afternoon, Carolyn found the book she'd been reading and sat in the great room to read for a while. She opened the book, but didn't start to read, instead she thought about their dinner guests. She knew why she had no problem with Ramon, he was Sandy's husband and Sandy was a wonderful person. She also had no problem with Eric; in fact she'd consented to going with him to a Bible study. Her heart rate didn't go over the moon. Actually, it did speed up a little, she had to admit, but it wasn't because she feared him. She wasn't ready to admit any reason for that action, not yet. Of course, in her heart of hearts she was sure Derek was her dad, he certainly didn't scare her!

Eric came and picked her up, Derek was going, but he made an excuse to need to come later and drove himself. He was glad to see Carolyn get out and of course, Eric was the perfect man to take her. When Eric pulled up there was still a heavy shower, but no lightning or thunder for the moment. Without Millie's car in the garage, they used the second slot for Eric to pull in, so only at the church would they get wet. It was his turn to be gallant and use an umbrella. Of course, since there were so few attending, Eric parked right in front of the church. Roger greeted them at the door, telling them the Bible reference they'd be using.

Eric had been right, even the DeLord's didn't come for the Bible study. The weather was so nasty they decided not to take the van out and Ramon had survived enough rain storms during hikes he decided to stay home with his wife and baby. Roger had also left his family at home, but those that came enjoyed a wonderful time in the book of John, studying Jesus' last hours and the intimate time with the disciples in the upper room. Carolyn truly enjoyed the time and wondered once again if perhaps she'd continued in her faith in her life before her amnesia.

After they left the church, Eric said, "Carolyn, thank you for going with me, I enjoyed your company. I probably won't have another Sunday off for a while, but this was great."

"Thanks so much for inviting me, Eric. You really know your Bible. Perhaps I knew mine at one time and I don't seem to have trouble finding the books and the references. Derek says that as a teenager I was active in the youth group and after I graduated from high school I planned to work at a Christian camp for the summer, but who knows at this point!"

Eric shook his head. "That all has to be so frustrating!"

"Yes, it is, believe me. I wonder sometimes if maybe there's a hole in my brainstem that keeps draining out what's supposed to be there." Carolyn grew very serious and after a long sigh, she said, "Eric?" When he looked at her, she finally said, "I really like your company a lot, but... without my memory, I'm not sure it's a good thing for us to date. I have no idea what was going on in my life before I woke up in the hospital. Maybe I have a boyfriend, although I'd think he'd be looking for me, or if I'm married, but then I'd think my husband would look for me, too. Like I say, it's so frustrating not knowing what went on in my life before!"

Eric took his right hand from the wheel, took Carolyn's hand and squeezed it briefly. It still felt like a live cinder, but he held her hand for several minutes. After swallowing, he said, "I know. I don't want to string you along, Carolyn. My only thought was to invite you to the Bible study. Like I say, I'll probably be out again for several Sundays. Who knows, by then you may have your memory back and you'll be back home, wherever that is. I surely wouldn't want to complicate things for you." *Besides, that husband you're thinking about may have been the man who abused you so badly.*

Slowly, Carolyn pulled her hand from under Eric's. When he'd covered her hand it felt like he'd scorched it! "Yes, perhaps. Thanks for being so understanding, Eric and thanks for tonight. That study was great and such an intimate time in Christ's life, it was good with such a small group. Roger really is good!"

"Yes, it was good and Roger is exceptional. I didn't know him before, but from what he says, I guess he wasn't much of a preacher for five years after he came."

Carolyn scowled. "What do you mean?"

"As I understand it, before Sandy came to Vansville, he only read from a book, but never preached a sermon. That praise team that leads the song at Sunday school did all the music and took up most of the hour."

"Did she go to the church then? I can't imagine she'd tolerate that!"

"No, she didn't, she went with Isabel into Blairsville, but I've heard she hounded that man mercilessly. From what I've heard, he was under conviction for several months. Finally, just before Thanksgiving that year the Lord got hold of him. When that happened things started happening in his life. The way they tell it, it was amazing. Raylyn came from Michigan, they fell in love, Roger found out God wanted him here, but He worked it out so Raylyn could move here. I wish I'd been here to see it all happen."

Carolyn was quiet for several minutes. "I guess God works in ways we don't understand sometimes. This that I'm going through sure is one of them. I still marvel at how quickly He answered your prayer for my safety!"

Eric nodded and looked up at the open garage door. "I guess you're home, Carolyn. Thanks for going and I'll see you again, I'm sure." He grinned. "Oh, by the way, when we got back to DeLord's after dinner, there were two messages on their machine both hiking groups had called to cancel."

Carolyn grinned. "Great! You won't melt in this rain."

Eric also grinned. "Isabel says I wouldn't anyway. She says there are too many minerals in our rain for it to affect the salt I'm made of."

Carolyn laughed. "Oh, that's a good one! I've heard boys are made of snails and stuff, but salt…!" Carolyn looked puzzled for a minute. "Isabel doesn't go to your church, does she? At least I didn't see her either last Sunday or today."

"No, she's gone to a church in Blairsville for a long time, but she's a wonderful Christian lady, believe me." He shook his head and continued, "Last evening I got home just as the rain started. I'd barely gotten inside and my phone rang. I knew it had to be Isabel she has a chair in her living room where she sits and can see everything going on on her parking lot and even out to the street. It's really funny everyone knows she sits there to watch the action. She invited me for supper and that's when she told me I wouldn't melt. She's quite a tease, but I love the lady, she's like a grandmother."

"She sounds great and it's because of her I'm here."

"Yes, I know and I'm really glad. You should have seen her there at the hospital getting those nurses and the doctor to tell her where you were going! She was like a pit-bull!"

Carolyn nodded. "I could kind of see that when she visited. I wonder how she saw the resemblance between me and Derek. Angie, at the rehab center said she knew him, but even when she admitted me she didn't put us together."

"Yes, I wondered about that, too. She seems very intuitive."

*She opened her door to get back in her car at the gas station, but before she could step in a strong arm pushed her so she fell over the console, making her hit her head on something hard. Before she could right herself two strong hands roughly tumbled her into the passenger seat and before she could get her hands down to push up, those same hands yanked her by her hair into a sitting position and slapped a piece of duct tape across her mouth. The tears poured from her eyes, she couldn't stop them, he'd really yanked her hair so hard she couldn't help it and her face hurt from where she'd hit something on the console. Even as she pulled a breath in through her nose the man grabbed her hands and wrapped a long stretch of duct tape around her wrists several times. In the confined space of the front seat of her small car, he'd effectively made her immobile. She turned her head to see who her abductor was. She'd never seen him before.*

*He made himself comfortable in the driver's seat, but he must have been watching her from when she left the car to go in to pay for her gas, because he immediately reached across to her right side and not very carefully reached in the pocket of her skirt and found her keys. She heard fabric rip both before and after he pulled her keys from her pocket. It was one of her favorite skirts, but now there was a huge rip in it. She realized at this point, that was the least of her worries! A ripped skirt could be mended, but right now, she was at the mercy of a man! Obviously a man with no conscience.*

*He started up, yanked the stick into drive and left rubber on the pavement of the parking lot. She watched helplessly as he careened onto the city street, what could she do? How could she get away? They were barely out of the gas station lot before he hit the door lock, but she couldn't have reached the door handle anyway. He'd wrapped her wrists in such a way she couldn't lift them from in front of her without feeling excruciating pain shoot up her arms and* even into her neck. Because she'd hit her head on something on the console she could feel a headache starting, her scalp was also tender.

The minute the man knew he wasn't being followed he eased off on the gas, not wanting to call attention to himself or his passenger. He quickly drove onto the interstate that was only a few miles from the convenience store then drove for many miles, as if he had a certain destination in mind, but he didn't speak. Tears slid down her face, but the man didn't seem to notice he just kept driving. However, he only drove with one hand. With his right hand he began ripping her clothes and dragging his fingernails down her body. When he'd have a huge handful of cloth he'd throw the pieces of her skirt and top onto the floor at her feet. It seemed every time they were on a straightaway he'd look over and take a bigger handful of her clothes. Soon she had nothing but shreds covering her body. With her arms immobile she couldn't cover herself and felt terribly exposed. If only he'd get stopped for speeding!

Finally, at an exit that didn't have any buildings within sight he left the interstate. Her heart sank the farther he went from the highway. He had definitely found an isolated place to leave the highway. This was just a spot where the interstate encountered another smaller highway and the highway department had made an interchange. The road they turned onto was definitely deserted. It was several miles from the interstate before another car approached from the other direction and none had overtaken them.

It was late afternoon, but the sun was still several hours from setting when he slowed, pulled her car off onto a path that led into a cornfield, it was one a farmer would use to bring his machines in to work the field. Right now, all that was in the field was a growth of tall weeds the field hadn't been prepared for planting yet. He drove on the rutted path almost to the row of trees at the back of the field. She knew no one would see them, even if someone was looking for them. She knew no one would be looking for her she'd only started her new job last week. She was far from her brother. They had agreed she'd settle in to her job for a while before she'd call him. They couldn't just drop by any more.

Her heart thudded wildly, beating hard against her chest. What would this man do to her? She groaned, but that brought his hand up and he smacked her hard across her face. She bit her tongue to keep from making any other sound. He shut off the engine, left the keys in the ignition and continued ripping her clothes. All that was left on her body were tiny shreds of what had been a lovely *skirt and top. Also while he ripped her clothes he moved his fingers in such a way that his fairly long fingernails dug long scratches in her skin.*

*Tears slid down her cheeks, it wasn't hard to figure out his intent. Soon he wasn't satisfied he couldn't do what he wanted to do in a bucket seat with the console between them. For good measure, he slammed his fist into her jaw so that her head bounced against the side window, then he exited the car, but took the keys with him, like she could have started up and driven away!*

*While her brain still seemed to bounce from the impact of his fist, he came around the side, yanked open her door. Sometime after he stopped he had hit the mechanism to unlock the doors again, but that had slipped by her. With the pain he had inflicted since they'd left Atlanta, it was making her senses less acute. As soon as he had the door open he grabbed a huge handful of her hair and dragged her from the car. Now the tears fell and she couldn't control them, it felt like he was pulling her hair out by the roots. Now her headache was nearly blinding. Her body bounced, hitting the car frame then thudded onto the unforgiving ground. The jarring sent tingling down her legs, but she still had her tongue between her teeth to keep the groan in.*

*Now that she was out of the car, she started kicking, but that infuriated him. He had such large hands and he began using them anywhere he felt like it on her body. He was not only ripping her clothes but he used her body as a punching bag. When he had her clothes in shreds, he yanked her panties off and threw them into the field, then stood up, shed his own clothes and raped her, leaving her in even more pain. She had never felt such agony in her life. The tears were streaming down her cheeks, but no noise left her body.*

*When she was too weak to even think of moving, he opened the trunk and pulled out the tire iron. She saw it coming, but couldn't move. The last she knew before she passed out he bashed it into her left arm, then drew back his arm and swung it into the side of her head. The blackness was a blessed relief.*

Screams and blood curdling noises sent Derek straight off his bed that night. He didn't even look at the clock to see the time. As he stood in the dark beside the bed, he knew they weren't the thunder and lightning noises from the fierce storm outside, but screams coming from the room only a few steps down the hall. His heart turned over! Carolyn was having a nightmare! Perhaps she was remembering. He pulled on the closest pair of pants he could find and raced from his bedroom. He must get to her!

He nearly broke down the door into Carolyn's room, thankfully the door wasn't locked and when he slowed down a fraction he was able to turn the knob and open the door. He flipped the switch on the wall, nothing happened. She had turned off the light beside her bed when she lay down. It was dark in her room, since his house was in the country and his security light was on the front of the garage, there was no light that came into the bedrooms and at that moment there were no lightning flashes outside.

The screams continued, in fact they were nearly constant, blood curdling sounds coming from the woman in the bed. He could hear the heavy cast thudding against anything solid. Groping toward the bed and finally finding the shade on the lamp, Derek switched on the light. Carolyn's top sheet and blanket were wrapped around her tightly. She was clawing at the bottom sheet and had it nearly off the mattress. Her pillow was on the floor. However, her eyes were closed and she was screaming so loudly she was making herself hoarse. She was thrashing so violently her cast hit against the headboard and the bedside table. It nearly hit Derek before he could get the light turned on.

The instant he clicked on the light he called above her screams, "Carolyn, Carolyn! Carolyn, wake up!"

He didn't dare touch her, he was sure she was having a nightmare about what had happened to her before she was thrown out in the woods and Eric had found her. It had to have been a man who had so violently abused her. When she didn't respond or wake up he called again, but this time he grabbed the cast which came at him. Momentarily she screamed louder, if it were possible. At that moment, there was also a horrendous crash of lightning and she surged to a sitting position, the bedclothes keeping her on the bed.

Holding onto the cast for all he was worth, he yelled again, "Carolyn, Carolyn! Stop! It's me, your dad!"

She gave one more scream, but when she couldn't get the cast free, her eyes popped open. She stared at Derek and finally recognition came into her eyes. Her hair was drenched and matted to her head. There was a huge rip in her nightie and it was soaked. Without a word she looked around her, then at the bed, then back at Derek.

"What happened?" she whispered, just as another lightning snap echoed outside, followed instantly by a deafening roar of thunder.

"You were having a nightmare, Sweetheart!"

Derek was breathing hard as he answered. He was also sweating. She'd had such strength he'd had all he could do to hold onto her arm in the cast. His eyes were scratchy he wanted to cry because of all she was going through. However, now that she was awake, he let go of her cast and sat down beside her on the bed.

"I was?" She shuddered as another bolt of lightning crashed and thunder roared. "What was I doing?" She looked from his eyes to her cast to the wrecked bed covers.

"Yes, you were screaming so loudly you woke me. I came as quickly as I could. You don't remember what you were dreaming?"

"No…" she shook her head, "no, I don't remember anything. All I remember was you saying …'your dad.' You were trying to wake me?"

"Yes. I was afraid you'd hurt yourself."

Looking down at the bed again, she shook her head. "I must really have been living whatever happened again, look at this bed!"

Now that she was totally awake, Derek put a hand on her shoulder and reached for the sheet and blanket that kept her tightly bound. Kissing her tenderly on her cheek, he asked, "Do you want to get up, Carolyn?"

"Yes! I think I need to take a shower, maybe stay up for a while." She shook her head and tears welled up in her eyes. "Oh, I wish I could remember what I was dreaming, maybe that would help, but there's still nothing in my brain!"

Derek nodded. "Maybe." He wasn't too sure he wanted her to remember something so bad it gave her such a terrible nightmare.

There was another lightning crack outside, it lit up the room almost like daylight, but the noise wasn't as loud and the roar of thunder wasn't instantaneous, but it was loud. The sound of the rain pelting against the window was so loud they couldn't hear themselves breathing. When the covers were out of the way, Derek looked at Carolyn and immediately took the young woman in his arms. He could easily see the fear still in her eyes. She went willingly into his arms and laid her head on his chest as he put his arms around her. As he used to do when she was small and needed comforting, he held her and slowly stroked his hands through her hair down onto her back.

After they were quiet for several minutes, he whispered, "It's okay, Carolyn, don't try to force it out. Your mind's not quite ready to let you know what happened. Besides, all that happened may never come, only what's been going on in your life."

"Yes, I guess that's so." With her head still on his chest, she wrapped her arms around him and murmured, "Thanks, Daddy, thanks for coming. It was like you always did. I think my brain is letting me know that you're really my dad."

Derek held her for several minutes, just stroking her back. He didn't say anything, but her words fell hard on his hungry soul. It brought tears to the back of his eyes. Yes, this was his Carolyn. Unconsciously she was remembering that time and many times after that when she'd come to him with tears sliding down her cheeks and he'd held her, comforting her and stroking her back. Right after her mama had died, she'd had nightmares and he'd gone to her just like he had moments ago to comfort her.

Obviously she realized what she'd said, because she asked, "Did I remember that?"

"Yes, Sweetheart. You came to me or you had nightmares and I went to you and I comforted you just as I am now," he whispered.

"Oh, maybe something's coming back!"

Still stroking her, he nodded and she felt his head bob on her crown. "Maybe, but don't try to push it. I'm sure it'll come in the proper time. Only God knows when that is, so let Him be the one to bring things back and only what He wants."

She sighed, "Yes, I'll wait." She snuggled back into his arms and let him rub her back. She was content to be quiet in his arms.

"That's my girl."

They sat that way for maybe fifteen minutes. The storm outside was ferocious, but inside they sat quietly together on her bed. Derek continued to stroke his hand slowly through her hair down onto her back. When her breathing evened out and she seemed able, Derek let her go. Slowly she left the bed and went in the bathroom, so Derek fixed her bed and went back to his suite. He slumped into his recliner, since he couldn't sleep now either, but he left the light off so he could think. The lightning flashes illuminated his room enough.

He waited to hear the shower turn off then he went in his own bathroom and took a long shower. While he stood under the water the thoughts marched through his mind. Wondering how she could have been so close for someone to drop her off here in Vansville. Did she still live in Louisiana or had she moved? Had she found him on the web? Being the president of the Blairsville bank didn't make him an obscure person by any means. Would she ever remember? He shook his head, when would things come to light?

After his shower, he pulled on a warm sweatsuit and sank into his recliner. Reluctantly he turned on the light. On the table beside the chair was his Bible. He picked it up, but didn't open it immediately; instead his mind went back to times more than a decade earlier. He would never forget that time just after Carolyn graduated; it was printed in living color on his gray matter. He wondered, even today, if Carolyn had really wanted him to leave or if Lance had forced her to say the words. Whatever the reason, they had hurt him deeply. He had shed many silent tears over his children.

He had written, he had called. His letters were returned unopened and his calls had always been answered by a machine. Each time he'd pled into the phone to speak with one of them or that they return his calls. Even after he moved to Vansville, he'd left a phone number, but nothing had ever happened, no one had called. He hadn't been right with the Lord back then, but he still continued to lift their names up to God in his heart day after day. He pushed out a long sigh, it was entirely possible if he'd been right with his Lord back then he wouldn't have even given Millie a second look. He shook his head the Devil took every advantage to do damage in the lives of human beings.

Finally, as the rain outside seemed to taper off just a bit, the lightning and thunder had definitely passed over. He let out a long sigh, placed his hand gently on the Bible and opened it to the book of Psalms to read for a while. King David had written many that Derek could easily relate to. He read Psalm after Psalm until finally the dark of night turned to the grayness of morning. Still the rain poured down.

He read for a while longer, since he'd already taken a shower, but he needed to get ready for work soon. The room on the other side of the wall was quiet, perhaps Carolyn had been able to go back to sleep. He could only hope so. The nightmare must have been a terrible experience, well, if it reflected the abuse she'd endured, that was a terrible experience also. He hadn't seen her at the worst, but what he had seen that first time made him shudder.

Finally, the aroma of Mrs. Beecham's baking sweet rolls seeped under his door. His stomach growled, reminding him it was Monday morning. He set his Bible down, went in his bathroom and immediately started shaving. Duty called, the bank opened at nine o'clock. His time to start was eight thirty and it took a half hour to get there. No one ever knew him to be late for work and this Monday morning wouldn't be that time.

Carolyn took a long shower, even washed her hair, since it was wet with sweat and it seemed that every strand was cemented to her head. Her body was also covered with sweat; she couldn't remember ever sweating like that before. She lingered under the water for several minutes. It felt like the water was washing away the remnants of the horrible experience she endured in her nightmare, even though she couldn't remember even one scene of it.

She sighed, maybe that was good; maybe it wasn't. When would she ever remember her life before? If the results of the nightmare were what she'd seen in her bed, maybe she'd like not to remember that awful time, only what took place in her life before that. When she shut off the water, she lingered even longer in the warm cocoon behind the curtain and let herself drip for a few minutes. Finally, she reached for the big, fluffy towel, dried her hair, then her body and finally stepped out into the cooler room.

The instant her body registered the cooler air an awful tasting liquid welled up in her mouth. She rushed to the toilet and vomited. Making herself stay on her feet, she quickly cleaned herself again then ran to her bedroom, the light was still on beside the bed, so she could see to open a drawer of her dresser and pull out a warm sweatsuit and put it on. It wasn't cold in the house, but she'd been covered in sweat and took a warm shower, so there were goosebumps on her arms and she shivered.

Derek had left a Bible on a table beside a comfortable chair in her room, so she turned on the light beside the chair, then went back and turned out the light by the bed. When she returned to the chair she sank into it, pulled the Bible into her lap and opened the front cover. At the Bible study she'd attended with Eric last evening, she'd felt a kinship with those in the room, but also seemed to know her way around the Bible she'd held. Now, without looking in the index, she opened the Bible to the book of Psalms and began to read. She read Psalm after Psalm it was like balm to her soul.

About a half hour later she became so sleepy she couldn't hold her eyes open any longer. She closed the Bible, turned off the light and felt her way back to the bed. She barely had the sheet and blanket over her before she was sound asleep. What woke her was the sound of running water coming from the bathroom on the other side of the wall. Derek was up and getting ready for work. After last night she was convinced Derek was her dad, he'd comforted her perfectly. She had felt the kinship in her body.

Carolyn turned to her back and stared at the ceiling. Today was Monday again. Sandy hadn't volunteered to take her anywhere. It was still raining, so the men wouldn't come to work on the swimming pool. Derek would be gone for the workday and Mrs. Beecham would be busy cleaning the house and cooking dinner. That left Carolyn with nothing to do and a whole lot of time to do it in. She'd never been in Derek's den or his office, maybe he had some books she could read. Had she done much reading in her old life? She sighed, that was something else hidden behind that steel door.

She left the bed. She had on the sweatsuit, it was warm, but she went in the bathroom to splash her face with warm water. While she brushed her teeth she saw the nightie she'd worn to bed laying on the sink counter, still damp. She picked it up, ah, there was something she could do today! The nightie was only days old, she liked it and didn't want to get rid of it. She could surely mend the huge rip it had in it. Surely, she could thread a needle, pull the two sides of the tear together and run the stitches to close the hole! Surely, life 'before' was more complicated than that? She could only hope!

Holding the nightie, she returned to her bed and sank onto it. She stared at the pretty cotton garment, but whispered, "God in heaven, must I go through life not knowing anything? There are so many things I wish I could remember. Derek is really good to me, but I need to know what was going on in my life. Please, God, help me remember." She pushed her feet into some tennis shoes and stepped to her mirror to comb her hair.

Another Monday rolled around. It had stopped raining. All the guides for DeLord's, including Eric, were back on a trail and the ground had dried up enough that Sam and his helper were back at Derek's house working on the nearly dried out back yard trying to repair what the several days of rain had done to their first attempt at making a swimming pool. Sam and his helper had taken a look at the hole and decided they could shovel out the dirt that had caved in. Actually, Sam was surprised how well the sides had held up. Since there had been no forms in the hole, he'd thought the worst.

Carolyn sat in the great room reading a book from Derek's library, but also looking up every so often to see how the men were progressing in the back yard. Carolyn realized, as another shovelful cleared the top of the hole, she was excited for the men to get finished with their work. Maybe Derek was right, maybe she had been a swimmer in her other life. She shook her head obviously she was older than just finishing four years of college. What had she been doing with her time, did she have a job? What was it? That dead air space between her ears seemed to laugh at her.

She let out a long sigh she was alone in the great room, after all and laid her book down open and upside down on the arm of the comfortable sofa, intending to come back to it eventually. She sat staring out through the glass wall of the great room looking across the green into the far trees. Why could she not remember anything? Perhaps she wouldn't mind never remembering the awful happening she'd lived through only weeks ago, but it was like a barricade across her brain keeping her life before from coming through.

Derek had told her something about her young life, until she graduated from high school, but what on earth had she done since then? How long had it been since then? Had she used that swimming scholarship just to go to college or had her education centered on her swimming ability? She sighed, who knew? Somebody knew, she was sure of it, but it wasn't anyone on this side of her amnesia.

The sun was peeking through the far trees. The roof over the patio wouldn't let her see much of the sky, but what she saw was a deep blue. She watched another shovel full arc over the top of the pile already there, then another joined it momentarily, it seemed both men were now in the hole. She guessed once they had the hole put back to rights Sam would call a cement truck to make the pool walls. She wasn't about to go out there to see, but she wondered how much dirt had collapsed into the hole from the rain they'd had. It surely had been a deluge!

# Ten

The men had come at eight o'clock, now it was ten and they were both in the hole shoveling. Right now there was a huge pile on the ground. However, it must be manageable because Sam hadn't gone back for his backhoe to dig it out. Rain was good. They needed it for growing things, but sometimes it came at a bad time or was too much.

Carolyn had her fill of coffee and orange juice at breakfast, so it needed to come out. When she left the bathroom, she went upstairs, she could use another drink. It was cool in the house, Derek had the best climate control available, but she was still thirsty. Mrs. Beecham was cleaning somewhere she wasn't in the kitchen, so Carolyn found her favorite glass and filled it with the housekeeper's tea. It was the best she'd ever tasted. Moments later, she was back on the sofa in the great room, the glass stood on the end table and the book rested on her lap. Still more dirt had built the pile taller while she'd been gone. This time, instead of watching out the window at the men working, she turned her head and looked at Sandy's huge picture. The scene was an autumn scene from somewhere here in the county. It hung on the rocks that formed the massive fireplace and accented all the colors in the room. It was awesome!

Both Ramon and Eric were leading shorter hikes this time. For this hike Eric's group had come on Friday and today was their last day. For a change this was not a youth group, but a group of three unrelated couples from Atlanta. They were exactly the same age as Eric. One of the men, when he found out that Eric had been in the Marines, had claimed to have been in the military for seven years, but he'd only mustered out four months before. He'd even boasted about some exploits he'd done. However Eric felt no kinship with him, in fact, he made Eric feel very uncomfortable. He didn't seem to have any characteristics of one who'd been in the military at all, let alone seven years of his life. He certainly hadn't been in the Marines his hair was much too long to have left that branch only four months before.

Usually, if someone had been in a branch of the service and only left it four months ago, they were eager to talk about their time, but Ron never spoke about his time, except to make that one boast. Ever since that first evening when they'd introduced themselves around the campfire, Eric had wondered at Ron's story. It almost sounded like a fabrication. At the time, he'd shaken his head. Why would anyone make up something about such a time in their lives? Being in the military, overseas in a war zone wasn't something he'd make up stories about!

As usual, Eric was up early for his devotions. He had his Bible and was sitting with his back against a tree close to the stream where they were camped. He was never loud when he read and prayed, but he never liked to be inside the circle of tents while he read, especially when the group were not from a church and Eric had seen no evidence that any of this group were church-goers or even had any desire to belong to a church. They were from Atlanta and Eric found out over the days of their hike that each one worked a different job. So much so Eric couldn't see how they had even gotten together for a hike. Another thing, Ron didn't seem to know the lady he was teamed up with nearly as well as Eric would have thought a couple should know each other to go on a hike together. Since the group was made up of only unattached people, they all stayed in one-man tents and as far as Eric knew, none of them had gone in anyone else's tent. That was just fine with Eric he wasn't much on being morality police when he was a guide for a group of adults on a hike.

Eric looked at his watch as Ron crawled from his tent. His watch alarm would go off in eight minutes for him to get the group up and on the move. Eric watched Ron, as he went to the trees on the other side of the camp site, but that was to be expected first thing in the morning. That was part of his morning routine. However, he obviously didn't see Eric.

Something in his brain told Eric to watch Ron very carefully. When he came back a few minutes later he had a short, but very thick branch. Maybe he'd picked it up for the morning fire. However, he walked closely beside the tent of the woman whom he claimed to be partners with. Eric couldn't hear any talking, but obviously Ron had said something, because Emily's tent started to move. The hairs on Eric's neck and arms stood on end when Ron stopped beside the zipper opening to her tent, waiting for Emily to come out, holding the branch like a club! A person exiting a one man tent would be crawling on hands and knees, the way Ron stood, he could bash Emily's head before she could do anything to defend herself!

Eric's skin crawled. He slammed his Bible closed, then jumped to his feet, there were still a couple of minutes before his watch alarm was to go off, but he determined nothing strange was going to happen on his watch. He had his Bible in his hand as he quickly jogged toward the group of tents and called out, "Hey, everybody, it's time to get up and on the move! We leave in an hour and a half!"

Ron was the only other person outside a tent, but he obviously hadn't seen Eric sitting away from the tent circle until he called out. Eric had a moment to observe Ron's face as he ran, that also made him shudder. When he heard Eric he quickly threw the branch toward the dead fire and started to laugh. "Great! I was a bit early, but I found that really great log back in the woods, so we're one ahead of the game for heating the water for coffee."

"Sure, that's great! I'll get the fire going right away," Eric said, as he headed for his tent to put his Bible away. He noticed the branch as he walked to his tent, it was big, all right, but it was also green, it wouldn't burn worth a hoot! Noticing the condition of the log, he had every reason to watch Ron very closely!

Emily emerged from her tent and immediately headed for the woods. Ron watched her go, but since Eric was so close by, he didn't follow her as his look said he wanted to. The hairs on Eric's arms were still standing up and the look on Ron's face gave Eric a very bad feeling, but nothing had happened, so Eric let it pass. However, he determined to keep a close eye on Ron through the day. He was glad this was their last day, they would get back to DeLord's this afternoon and Eric could say goodbye to the group. He realized that if he hadn't been part of Carolyn's rescue last month that

Ron's actions would have passed and he wouldn't have thought a thing about them. Maybe he was becoming paranoid.

Eric put his Bible in his backpack and pulled it outside so that someone could take down his tent. He stepped back, but Ron had moved from Emily's tent and stood very close behind Eric, so close, in fact that Eric nearly stepped on him when he turned around. "Oh, I didn't know you were so close, Ron. Can I do something for you?"

Ron nonchalantly stepped away, saying, "No, no, just wondered what that was you were holding. You seem to get up early each morning, before anyone else does."

*Was that an angry tone in Ron's voice?* "Yes, I meet with God early. I found when I was in the Marines that having morning devotions really started my day off right and I've just kept up the habit since then. It seemed like you were up a bit early, too."

Ron chuckled. "Yeah, I felt the need pretty strong this morning, maybe too much of that spring water last night for supper. Actually, I am an early riser, sunrises are my thing." The man hadn't looked at the sky since he left his tent! However, Eric let that pass he could only hope the hours would go quickly until they arrived at DeLord's.

By now, the other two men had joined Eric and Ron and John said, "I guess it's our job to get these tents down while Eric gets the fire up and going and the ladies fix breakfast. Come on, Ron, Eric's gotta get the fire going so we can have coffee pretty soon."

Ron spun around, gave the man a pathetic excuse for a smile and said, "I'm with you guys, shall we start with Eric's?"

"Sure, mine's all ready to go."

Eric walked to the pile of ashes, but soon he had a good fire going and only moments later Emily brought a kettle full of water to the fire to hang on the spit Eric produced each morning. On the trail this group used instant coffee there was no good brewing coffee smell to entice the hikers to bring their cups. Some groups brewed their coffee and Eric missed the smell, even though he didn't drink it.

By eight thirty Derek was sitting at his desk at the bank for his normal workday. It had been another good weekend with his family. He loved fixing steaks on the grill for Carolyn and Ramon's family. He really loved how little Jon had immediately taken to his new 'Japa'. He loved that darling baby to pieces! He sat and reminisced for several minutes. If Lance were married now what he'd missed in knowing his daughter-in-law and any children they might have had in twelve years! He wondered if Lance had married Linda. He'd liked her and he'd felt that she liked him, although she couldn't show it much with Lance's attitude.

Only moments after he sat down, his secretary brought in the Atlanta paper and without comment set it on his desk. At the moment, Derek had nothing pressing, so he picked it up, unfolded it and absently scanned the headlines. However, on the bottom half of the front page a headline caught his eye:

## TEENS FIND WOMAN'S BODY BY STREAM

"The partially decomposed body of a young woman was found on the banks of a small stream last evening about a hundred miles southwest of Atlanta, by several young teens who were planning a fun evening of fishing and swimming. They quickly abandoned their planned activities and called the local Sheriff's Department who responded to their call.

It is believed that the young woman had been brutally abused and raped. She was found with duct tape binding her wrists and covering her mouth, making it impossible for her to call for help. It is also possible the blow to her head was so severe that she was rendered unconscious. It is believed she died from exposure and such severe injuries, then being abandoned in such a remote area.

There were no identifying belongings found with the young woman and what clothes she might have had on were only in tatters. Some cloth and underwear were found close by. This, along with other evidence, caused the officers to believe the victim had been raped. An autopsy is being conducted in hopes of identifying the young woman and also determining time of death. They are hoping there will be something to identify the man who had done the criminal act. Authorities are not holding out much hope that the abuser will be identified.

As the sheriff and several deputies were responding to the call they found a car abandoned along the road in a very remote area with the interior completely gutted by fire, including the contents of the trunk. It is speculated that the car might have belonged to the young woman. The car was so completely gutted inside there was no way to discover even the VIN number."

Derek reread the short article. His hands were shaking as he laid the paper down on the desk. Sweat broke out and he could feel a trickle slide down his back. The longer he thought about what was said about the young woman the more he was convinced that she had suffered from the same hands that had abused his dear Carolyn, only thanks to Eric's quick intervention she was alive and was now doing well. He bowed his head he couldn't check the tears that came to his eyes. He pulled a handkerchief from his back pocket, wiped his eyes and blew his nose, but still the tears flowed. He felt terrible for the family of this victim, wishing there was some way to find this terrible abuser before he did anything more. Maybe they'd find some skin or hair from the man, he would pray to that end.

Tears choked him and he had to swallow hard to get his next breath. As soon as he felt in control enough he called the local sheriff's private phone number and said, "Sheriff, this is Derek Casbah, have you by any chance seen a copy of today's Atlanta paper?"

Knowing that he spoke to the president of the local bank, he said, "No Sir, we get the paper delivered, but I haven't had a chance to pick it up. Monday mornings are a bit hectic around here. What's on your mind, Mr. Casbah?"

"On the front page, the lower section, there's a short article about a young woman who was found dead, but with the same characteristics as the young woman discovered in Vansville last month. Thankfully, there's no picture."

"Really! Mr. Casbah, I'm getting the paper out right now." There was silence on the line for several minutes then the sheriff blurted out, "You are absolutely right! Sir, could I ask why you would know about the young woman found here… well, in Vansville? We worked very hard at keeping her where-abouts very secret."

"Several circumstances… well, perhaps you know Isabel Isaacson, she visited 'Jane' before she was discharged to the rehab center, then contacted me because she was convinced we had to be related. She was convinced 'Jane' and I looked very much alike. When 'Jane' was discharged to the rehab center I also visited her. Because of our looks, but other things I noticed about her, I was also convinced that the young lady that was found in Vansville was undoubtedly my daughter. Of course, she is still suffering from amnesia, so she doesn't know her own name or any other things that would help identify her. Because I was so convinced about her identity she is now living at my home and instead of calling her Jane Doe we are calling her the name my wife and I gave our daughter, 'Carolyn'."

"You say she's still suffering from amnesia?"

"Yes, that's correct, but her injuries have healed except her left arm is still in the cast."

"She still has no recollection of her abduction or assailant?"

"No, that's true, but one night last week she had a nightmare, but when I woke her she couldn't remember anything about the dream at all."

The sheriff let out a long sigh, "We could only hope!"

"Yes, that's true."

Obviously reading the article again, the sheriff said, "They found an abandoned car that had been burned inside beyond recognition… Sounds exactly like what happened there in Vansville! At the time, I couldn't find a connection, but when Mr. Thomas came in the next day and described the car that left the scene I wondered. Thank goodness for that young man and his quick response at finding her! She could have ended up like this young woman. Thank you, Mr. Casbah, for bringing this to my attention. I think I need to contact that Sheriff's Department and if possible find out anything they know besides what's been printed in this article. This is too close to what happened to our Jane Doe to be a coincidence!"

"Yes, you're welcome, I for one, don't believe any of this is a coincidence, Sheriff. It sounds like the criminal is still on the loose! I'm glad my place can be locked at all times and we have never left Carolyn alone."

"I'll agree with you on that, but it appears the criminal is also fairly well traveled. Of course, until our Jane Doe can tell us where she came from we have no way of knowing, but this woman is nearly at the other end of the state!"

"I'll have to agree with you."

"Thank you, Mr. Casbah, may I keep in touch with you about this?"

"Yes, that would be fine. In fact, I would be very relieved if you can find out about the criminal being behind bars!"

"Yes, wouldn't we all!"

About three o'clock, Eric led his group out of the woods onto DeLord's parking lot. He planned on going in the house when the group had left, so he only leaned his backpack against his car and turned to say goodbye. He had watched Ron quite closely all day, but the man hadn't done anything that Eric could question, still the man made him feel uncomfortable. Why that was he couldn't be sure. After all, youth group kids were always coming up with pranks that were harmless, but Ron didn't seem harmless. However, he was glad he'd see the last of him in the next few minutes. This group of hikers hadn't been his favorite.

As the hikers moved toward their cars, he noticed that Emily took keys from her backpack, but Ron only went with her to her car. For the other two couples, it was the man who opened his trunk. Still, that wasn't all that strange men rode with women all the time. They all said their goodbyes, the women smiling and two of the three hugged him. The three men shook his hand. Only moments later, Eric stood alone on the parking lot, as the three cars drove away. Emily was between the other two cars.

Eric could see that Sandy and Jon were in the office, so he decided it would be a good opportunity to get his next assignment while he was here and Sandy had the computer up and running. He tapped on the door, but then opened it before Sandy could speak. "Hi, guys, I'm back. What's the scoop? Anything new in this booming metropolis?"

Sandy hit a few keys on her keyboard and the printer started spitting out paper, when she said, "I heard you come back and I was sure you'd want your next assignment, so it's spitting out now. So how was your hike?"

Eric was looking out the door at the place on the parking lot where Emily's car had been. He scowled and said, contemplatively, "A bit strange, Sandy."

"Really? How do you mean?"

"I can't really put my finger on it and maybe I'm just paranoid, but two of the couples I had seemed to know each other like they were going together and had been dating for some time, but the other couple, didn't seem to know each other well at all. In fact, the man seemed a little strange. When he found out I'd been in the Marines, right away he said he'd also been in the military and even boasted about some act he'd done, but from then on he never acted as if he had even been in the service at all. Other things he did made me wonder about him. None of his actions convinced me he'd been in the military."

He shook his head. "This morning was the strangest of all. I was having my devotions by the stream, but I could see the campsite. Those are two things I try for each morning. Ron came from his tent not long after me and went into the woods. That didn't seem strange, of course, but when he came back he had this huge branch from a tree that looked really heavy. He walked beside his partner's tent and obviously called to her, but then he stood right by her tent door holding that branch like a club! It spooked me a bit, because when someone leaves a one man tent they must crawl out on their hands and knees... well you get the picture. I wasn't about to let anything happen on my hike, so I yelled for everybody to get up. Ron laughed and threw his branch toward the firepit and said he'd found a good one. The only thing, it was so green, I couldn't use it for this morning's fire."

Sandy scowled a bit, but then she said, "Yes, that is strange, Eric, but you got them all back here safe and sound, so you're off the hook. Get your papers and get out of here! Have a good day off. Hey, why don't you take Carolyn for the day tomorrow? As far as I know, she's just sitting there at Derek's house watching out the window as those men dig out the dried mud from the swimming pool hole."

Instantly uncomfortable, Eric wagged his head back and forth, as he said, "Oh, I wouldn't want to take up her time, Sandy. I have some errands to run. I'll need to go into Blairsville for most of the day tomorrow. She wouldn't want to follow me around as I do my banking!" He shuddered a bit for emphasis. "I'd hate to have to take her shopping! If there's anything I'm allergic to it's shopping!"

Sandy looked up at the uncomfortable young man and grinned. "Eric, you're a nice guy, you could use the company of a very nice young lady.

Besides, who knows, she may not like to go shopping!" Sandy added, her eyes dancing.

He cleared his throat. "Thanks, Sandy." He wasn't sure if he was thanking her for the compliment or for the papers she'd printed out that he was reaching for.

Jon chose that minute to say, "Ick!"

Eric glanced down at the little guy hanging on the corner of his shorts. "Hi, there, little man, how's life?"

Now that Jon had Eric's attention, he let go of his shorts and held up his arms. "Up, Ick, up!" He gave Eric a bright smile. "Up, Ick!" He bounced up and down, as if he planned to jump into Eric's arms if he didn't reach for him immediately.

Eric laughed, glad for the diversion from Sandy's words and squatted down then held out his arms to the tiny child. "So how's my favorite little man?"

"Ja good!" With Eric's thigh so close, Jon put his hands on it and started climbing.

Eric's arms circled the little boy and he stood up. Jon put his hands on Eric's bearded face and smoothed down his short beard. "Ja no like."

"What, you don't like my beard?"

Solemnly, Jon shook his head. "Na, uh."

"Well, I'll go home and shave it off just for you! Doesn't your daddy have one when he comes home sometimes?"

Jon nodded. "Ja no like."

Eric chuckled. "No wonder I never see Ramon with a beard either."

Sandy grinned. "Jon and I are kinda alike that way."

"Well, I'll be!" Eric exclaimed, as Jon bent over and gave Eric one of his trademark slobbery kisses. Eric's eyes were moist, as he leaned over and set Jon back on the floor. The more he was around this child, the more he wished for his own. "I guess I'm out of here. I got laundry to do and my supply of Alex's dinners is rather low, so I better get there before he closes for the night. I'll see you folks on Wednesday for breakfast." He looked down at the little boy. "Keep your mommy in line there, fella."

"Bye, bye, Ick!" He waved his little fingers.

Eric smiled down at the toddler and said, "Bye, little guy." With his papers in his hand he headed for the door to the parking lot.

"Oh, by the way," Sandy said. "I had a call today from a man from Blairsville who wants to start as a hiking guide. Of course, Ramon'll have to do an interview and okay that, but perhaps you guys won't be so swamped with work."

Eric scowled. "How would that work, Sandy? I remember I had to go with Ramon and Duncan as a guide-in-training. Would the guy go with us like that?"

"That's the policy, but Ramon'll have to see to it."

"Well, I'll be interested to know about it. Keep me posted." Becoming thoughtful for a moment, he added, "That first hike I went on with Ramon was when Natt accepted Christ."

"Yes, you're right, I remember that."

Eric reached again for the doorknob. Before he could close the door, Sandy said, "Remember, Eric, Carolyn could probably use a breath of fresh air outside the house she's living in and you're just the man to do it!" She grinned and watched as the door closed quickly behind the young man. "Have a good day off, Eric!" she called.

Eric pulled in a deep breath. "You're wrong on that note, Sandy," he whispered. "Believe me, I'm too attracted to her and when she's well…." He shook his head and hurried to his car, grabbed up his backpack and pulled out his keys. Remembering the time he'd walked from here home, he knew he'd never subject himself to that again. He was just too tired. He shook his head. If they hired another guide would there be enough work for four fulltime men? He didn't know if the phone was still ringing off the hook with requests. Who would ever guess that this little town would boast such a business?

That afternoon Derek considered telling Carolyn about the article in the paper, but then decided against it. There seemed to be nothing to gain by telling her and probably she'd only dwell on what had happened to the other woman. He certainly didn't want that to happen! He did ask Sam when he would have his machines out of his back yard; he intended to enclose the whole area in a board fence that could also be locked. Carolyn shouldn't have to be a prisoner inside the house now that the weather was warm. If there was no fence, the pool wouldn't be secure. In light of that article, the man was definitely still doing his heinous activities, so she wasn't safe until he was caught. Actually, no woman in the state of Georgia was safe! That woman had been found south west of Atlanta, Vansville was almost due north.

Just before the work day was over, Derek stuffed the newspaper article in his briefcase. Then before he left the bank Derek pulled out his phonebook to check the yellow pages for someone to build a fence for him, but nothing sparked his interest. Of course, there was no one in Vansville who could do the job.

Emily pulled between her two friends' cars as they left DeLord's parking lot. She'd had a good time, but not because of the man sitting in her passenger seat. She wondered why she'd even invited him to go along. The longer the hike the more uncomfortable she felt with him. They had quite a ways to go back to Atlanta from the little town in the foothills of the Appalachians. It was mid-afternoon, but it would probably be suppertime before they arrived back in the city and Emily was scheduled to work at eight o'clock in the morning, so she was anxious to get home. If nothing else, a good hot shower and shampoo were in order. She had to admit, their food had been better than the convenience store take out or the frozen dinners she stocked, but to eat at home, sitting on a chair, at her table, was something she'd missed.

She remembered she had laundry to do. She swallowed a sigh, she hadn't done any before she left for this outing and her hamper would be glaring at her when she walked in her bathroom. However, it had been a great experience to hike in the hills that led up to the higher mountains. There had been some really spectacular views and she had some great pictures to show around the office as proof.

To break the silence in the car, Emily said, "So, Ron, what's on your mind for tomorrow? You have a job to get to?"

The man sighed and turned his head toward the side window, "Work, of course! Didn't you say you'll be back on the job tomorrow?"

"Oh, yes, it's the bane of a single girl's existence! I've tried to find that rich man to marry and take me out of this mundane ratrace, but I just haven't found him yet. Not that you qualify, but what do you do for a living, Ron?"

"Oh, this and that." The woman was getting too close for comfort! How to answer that? "My latest job was at the Med Center there in Atlanta, but I got laid off and because of that I had to leave my apartment."

*You worked in a hospital and got laid off? Why would anybody get laid off from working in a hospital? Medicine was big business, from what I know!* "I'm sorry to hear that, Ron. Surely you aren't homeless are you? Goodness, that's terrible! So where do I drop you off when we get back there?"

"You'll have to stop for gas before that, won't you? I'll get out there and make my way to a buddy's of mine. I'll shack up with him for a few days see if I can't find something." He flashed her a grin, hoping it would put her off. "After all, we've been sleeping in a tent, on the ground, it's no big deal."

"No, no!" Emily exclaimed, "I'll be glad to take you to your friend's place!"

"Oh, no! I couldn't ask you to do that! I mean, after all, you've given me a ride up there and back for that hike. I'll be okay."

"If you're sure?"

"It's not a problem, Emily." Goosebumps raised on her arms. The man almost sounded like he was angry she'd been considerate!

"Whatever you say, Ron." They lapsed into another silence as Emily drove. Ron didn't give Emily any warm, fuzzy feelings, but she was determined to reach Atlanta where people knew her. Hopefully, he'd leave her alone until then. She was beginning to wonder.

Ron kept watching Emily's gas gauge. In fact, he looked at it several times, enough that Emily noticed. "Ron, give me credit! I can see my gas gauge! I know how far my gas goes and I have plenty to get back to Atlanta. I have a favorite convenience store back there where I get gas. I'll fill up there. It's close to home and the guys know me there. Besides, it's a good place to drop you off. The city bus stops real close, so if you need to get someplace you can catch that bus to the terminal. Say, it's the place where we met two weeks ago! You know the place."

"Good idea, I'll take you up on that. Sure! I'll catch the bus to get to my buddy's place. I'll get a transfer to the other line." Ron sat back in his seat, determined not to call attention to any suspicious behavior.

Emily however, couldn't wait to get to her favorite store. The man in her passenger seat was giving her the willies. She'd seen him holding that huge branch this morning she could see his shadow through her tent wall.

She'd wondered about him when he'd called her to wake up then stood by her tent door! She knew the only way out of her tent was to crawl, but she wasn't going to do it until Eric's shout. Had he really planned to bash her head with that branch? The thought now crossed her mind.

She knew Eric had seen him, because he called them early and Ron had made a big deal of throwing his log at the firepit, but he'd been right outside her tent! She'd be glad to get back to civilization and wished there weren't so many miles of wide open spaces between the little town they'd left and the city. Yes, there were plenty of cars on the interstate and her four friends were in cars very close to hers, but there wasn't another person in this car. She didn't know Ron very well; in fact, she'd only met him a few times at that convenience store. He'd been friendly enough, but still…

Finally, she saw the exit and swallowed a sigh of relief. She only had a few city streets until she could stop for gas and Ron would get out. It couldn't be too soon for her. She'd noticed him glance a few more times at her gas gauge, but it wasn't as obvious as before. What was so all-fire fascinating about her infernal gas gauge? A chill went down her back. Leaning over to see her gas gauge put the man really close to her body! Thank goodness he wasn't doing that any more!

She quickly threaded the needle between cars going by on the street and pulled up to a gas pump at the convenience store. Before she got out to go inside to pay for the gas she pushed the trunk release and said, "I opened the trunk for you, Ron. You can get your backpack. Actually, I see a bus down the street. If you hurry you can catch this one."

He gave her what might pass for a smile and said, "I'll just do that! Thanks for the lift and I really had a good time on the hike."

"Yup, so did I." Emily grabbed her purse and opened her door at the same time as Ron opened his. She nearly ran for the convenience store, as Ron headed for the back of the car. Before she reached the door she heard her trunk lid slam. She breathed a sigh of relief maybe she wouldn't have to deal with the likes of him again.

Before she reached the door, however, a picture in the store window grabbed her attention. The caption under the man's headshot said, **Anyone with any leads to the whereabouts of this man call 911 immediately.** Her heart beating like it would come out of her chest, Emily reached to the side pocket of her purse for her phone, whirled around to look at her car, then scanned the gas pump area, but Ron was not there. She looked toward the bus stop and saw him disappear behind the crowd of people preparing to board the bus, because he had his huge backpack on his back, but he didn't act like that's what he would do. Even so, Emily stood in the entryway and hit the numbers.

"State your emergency!"

"I'm here at this convenience store…" she gave the address, "…and saw the picture of Ralph Wever in the window. He just crossed the street close to that bus stop! Maybe somebody could catch him!" she exclaimed, breathlessly then ran inside.

"Thank you, Ma'am, we're on it now!"

"Great!" Emily breathed a sigh of relief. From reading the wanted caption underneath the picture, Ron was not someone she wanted to be around. He'd called himself Ron while they hiked, but there was no mistake, it was his face, but his name was Ralph! Her quick glance at the poster said he'd been in prison and had violated his parole.

She stood in line to pay her money and before she finished paying there was a police cruiser in the parking lot with his lights flashing. She saw two officers scramble from the car and head for the bus stop. However, the bus had pulled away and no one was there beside the sign. Emily shook her head disappointed. The man had gotten away! Maybe he'd gotten on that bus or maybe he'd just disappeared. She really hoped he wouldn't come back to this convenience store any time soon. As she pumped her gas she wondered why he was so interested and almost insisted that she needed to stop at a gas station before reaching Atlanta. Could it be that he knew his face was on posters around Atlanta?

Tuesday morning, Eric was up early, if the sun was shining, he couldn't sleep much past sunrise, so he took his Bible out to the wicker chair on the porch and started reading. The sun shone in his bedroom window, which was on the back of the cabin, so his porch faced west and was still nice and cool. Since it also faced the big meadow, he could hear the birds twitter their wakeup sounds and that big bullfrog off by the brook doing his deep-throated 'garumps'.

He hadn't made it to Alex's store last night, so after breakfast he had to make that stop before going in to Blairsville for his business. He wished

Derek would open a bank branch here in Vansville. If there was one here, he wouldn't have to make the trip so often. Of course, he must wait until nine o'clock for the store to open, so he finished reading another chapter and offered his morning prayer before he left his chair to go inside to fix his breakfast. As he opened the door, the air conditioning unit kicked on. It would be a warm day, but then, June was the first month of summer.

After breakfast, he cleaned up the kitchen, then went in the bedroom and made his bed, after all, any good Marine kept his quarters spotless. Of course, he was an ex-Marine, but he still felt the need to keep his quarters as neat and clean as possible. After all, Isabel and Ruth were not spring chickens by any means and he never wanted them to clean a messy cabin on his account. That was one reason he kept his dirty clothes well hidden in his hamper. When his watch beeped, telling him it was nine o'clock, he headed out the door and crossed the street, then turned and walked down the block to Alex's store on the far corner. Along with the TV dinners, he must get more tea and a box of laundry detergent. He was glad the life of a single man was so simple. Men with families had it rough!

He barely made the turn to reach for the door handle and looked at the poster Alex had posted in the window. His hand fell from the handle and he stared at the picture. Below Ron's face was the statement: **Anyone with any leads to the whereabouts of this man call 911 immediately.** Eric nearly lost his breakfast there on the sidewalk.

Around the bile in his mouth, he whispered, "God in heaven! That's Ron! The man from my hike! Oh, God! May they have caught him when he got back to Atlanta! Oh, God my Father! May Emily still be safe!"

The poster didn't give any details about the man, other than to say he'd been in prison and violated his parole, but Carolyn was never far from his mind. It made him wonder if Ron-Ralph was the man they were looking for. Could he have been the one who did those horrible things to her? How would they know? Had she finally remembered? Sandy hadn't said anything yesterday, maybe it wasn't common knowledge. Even so, chills made tracks up and down his back.

He pulled in a long breath to settle his roiling stomach, yanked open Alex's door and nearly ran to the counter where Alex stood. "Alex!" he blurted out, his thumb pointing over his shoulder. "That man on that poster in your window! He was on my hike that I brought back yesterday! He's from Atlanta!"

Alex immediately pulled out his cell phone from his waist carrier and handed it to Eric. "Here, call 911 and tell them! I'm sure any leads would help!"

Eric did and the voice said, "State your emergency!"

"Sir, this is Eric Thomas from Vansville! I just saw the poster in the store window of that man... um... Rrrr... it said to call 911! I had that man on a hike over the weekend, but he went back to Atlanta yesterday afternoon! He was with a young woman...!"

"That's the last you know about him?"

"Yes, he and the young woman left together in her car."

"Do you know the woman's name?"

"It was Emily... something. But I don't know her address. Sorry."

"But they were definitely going back to Atlanta."

"Yes, all of my hikers on that hike were from Atlanta."

"Even that Ralph guy?"

"Yes, but he called himself 'Ron' to us."

"We'll pass this on and thanks for your help, Mr. Thomas."

Eric closed the phone and handed it back to Alex. "Thanks, Alex, I don't know if I was much help, but as least they know he's from Atlanta! I wonder if that's the man who beat up Carolyn and left her for dead back in those woods." He looked back at the door. "It didn't say on the poster, but he's a wanted criminal!"

"I don't know, Eric. It's possible. The deputy didn't tell me anything when he brought that by, just asked me to post it in the window. Of course I did. I never want a criminal on the loose! Any honest citizen could be in danger."

"Oh, my! If it was him I surely pray Emily got back to Atlanta safely! He got in her car and they left together! Do you know? Has Carolyn remembered?"

Alex shook his head. "No, I don't know that. Maybe something else turned up or it could be this isn't at all related to her."

"Yes, I guess that's true. Well, you know my list..."

Alex smiled at the young man. "Fella, what you need is a lady. I know those TV dinners leave a lot to be desired. What you need is a good home-cooked meal!"

"Um, Alex, let's leave that one alone! Okay? I think I'm doing just fine on your TV dinners and your gallon jugs of tea. I fix a home cooked meal every time I have breakfast in my cabin. You know I buy my eggs and cereal here."

"Yup, that's a fact!" Alex agreed.

Giving the older man a grin, he said, "Besides, you know the ladies that go on my hikes usually fix the meals. Aren't they considered 'home' cooking?"

Incredulously, Alex said, "You'd consider a meal on the trail a home-cooked meal?"

"Well, sure!"

Alex shook his head. "You really need a wife, man!"

Tuesday morning Derek's secretary came to his office door even before the bank opened holding something in her hands in front of her. Derek looked up from his papers and Marlene said, "Mr. Casbah, a policeman came by just now and asked us to post this in the window. I decided I needed to check with you first before I did that."

"That's fine, Marlene. You know I want any criminal caught as quickly as possible. Who is the person? What's he wanted for?"

"It doesn't say what he's wanted for, just that he was in prison for eight years and violated his parole, but it says to call 911 if we know where the man is," she said, as she turned the poster around so Derek could see the man's face.

Derek shrugged. "He looks like most other criminals who had a mug shot when they went to prison. I sure don't recognize him, but go ahead and post it in the front window. It can't hurt to get his face out there. Maybe he escaped from being detained or maybe they can't find him at all. Who's to know?"

"I'll do that, Mr. Casbah. How's that young lady at your house?"

"She's doing quite well. We're getting along famously, thanks."

"Better than you and Millie?"

Shaking his head, Derek said, "Oh, Marlene, there is no comparison! Millie and I hadn't spoken ten civil words to each other in many days, believe me. She had no use for me and now that she's gone, I can do so much more!"

"So you don't really miss her?"

Derek shook his head. "No, Marlene, I truly don't. I've done many things I felt I couldn't do when she was with me. In fact, when I learned she'd left I called my lawyer to write up divorce papers. It really was a relief to do it." He grinned at his secretary. "And I got to cancel her credit cards!"

Marlene wasn't as old as Mrs. Beecham, but she was a lady of the south and had very strict standards. With a bit of censure in her voice, she said, "Well, if you're okay with it, it's okay with me, Mr. Casbah."

"Thanks, Marlene."

Wednesday afternoon, Derek's desk phone at the bank rang. It was nearly time for the bank to close for the day. Expecting to have one of his employees on the other end he was surprised when he answered, when the sheriff identified himself and said, "Mr. Casbah, I'm glad you haven't left for the day, but I knew you'd be interested to know what I found out when I was finally able to talk with that Sheriff's Department that was talked about in the article you called to my attention. It took some digging, since the county wasn't named in the article. I guess that was intentional, but it made for a bit of digging on my part. I was finally able to reach someone who knew the scoop."

"Oh, yes! What can you tell me?"

"Because the young woman was dead, they were able to do many more tests during the autopsy than they were able to on our Jane Doe. They found cells and hair from the man on her body and were able to trace the DNA. The man was in the system."

Derek couldn't keep quiet, he didn't like to interrupt, but he exclaimed, "Oh, my! What did they discover?"

"The man was a known criminal! He'd been in prison for eight years for doing similar deeds before, but had been released on parole around the first of the year on good behavior...."

"Good behavior!" Derek exclaimed. "He must have kept his true behavior well hidden while he was in prison!"

"Absolutely! That was my feeling exactly!" the sheriff exclaimed. "He had been living in the Atlanta area for several months and the girl found dead had been living fairly close to where the man's apartment was located.

This leads me to believe that our Jane Doe might also have been living close by."

"Oh, my! Yes, it would seem that way, wouldn't it?" Derek said, around the huge lump in his throat. Carolyn had moved a long way from her childhood home, if she'd been living in Atlanta. "Is he in custody?"

It took the sheriff several seconds to answer, but when he did, he said, "Unfortunately not. As soon as the information came into the Atlanta Police Department, officers were dispatched to his residence. However, when they reached his apartment it appeared that he had cleared out. There was nothing belonging to the man in the apartment. In fact, he may have been gone for a while painters were in the apartment refurbishing it. The landlord said he hadn't paid the rent for the month, so he was glad he'd left. It also looks like he had no car, there was none registered in his name at the license branch."

# Eleven

Derek had to swallow before he blurted out, "Oh-h-h my! So even though they know who it is, my Carolyn still isn't safe!" Derek could feel his hands become clammy and start to tremble. "Sheriff, this is just awful! It sets me on pins and needles!"

"That's about the size of it, Mr. Casbah. Of course, they have warrants and bulletins out statewide for his apprehension, but it hasn't happened yet. Still, it makes you wonder how far he got without his own vehicle unless he took some kind of public transportation. It also seems that he's working even harder to cover his tracts, since that young woman was found in such a remote place, as was her car that she wasn't found until she'd died. Obviously, he realized he'd been careless with our Jane Doe, he'd dumped her in a small town."

Derek pulled in a deep breath. "Oh, my! If both that young woman and Carolyn were from Atlanta, probably he drove the car away! He must have overpowered them. Perhaps that's why the duct tape."

The sheriff cleared his throat. "It does appear that way, doesn't it?"

Finally, after another breath, Derek said, "Thanks, Sheriff. All this you've told me makes me shudder! I am putting a swimming pool in my backyard, but I will definitely enclose the backyard with a locked fence immediately. Carolyn isn't safe until this man is caught. I'm sure he remembers where he dropped her off. By the way, was he employed?"

The sheriff cleared his throat. "Yes, he was, actually. This also may narrow down where to find the man or even where our Jane Doe worked.

He was employed as a male attendant in the largest medical center in Atlanta! However, as I understand it, he hasn't showed up for work recently. Not that that's surprising."

Around the cotton in his throat, Derek said, "Yes, it might give us some leads as to Carolyn's life before this happened to her."

"Yes, that's true. I'm wishing more and more that your Carolyn would regain her memory, not to remember her horrible attack, but anything would help us in this investigation."

"I know, I agree a hundred percent. Thank you, Sheriff. I'll be sure to take more precautions in Carolyn's behalf."

"My strong sentiments exactly!"

When Derek hung up from talking with the sheriff, he realized his hand was shaking. Atlanta, the largest medical center, an apartment complex, all of this made his skin crawl! As soon as he got himself under control, he called Sam's cell phone. He was in Derek's backyard and Carolyn saw him answer his phone. Derek barely let him speak before he blurted out, "Carolyn's not outside with you, is she?"

"No, Derek, she's never come out when we've been here, why?"

Sam heard a long sigh come over the line. "Oh, thank God! I just got off the phone with the sheriff. Did you see the article in Monday's paper about that woman who was found dead south of Atlanta over the weekend?"

"Didn't you tell me about that?"

"Yes, I guess I did. Anyway, by doing some tests on the body, they've been able to find out who the man is that did the deed. At least we're pretty sure it's the same man, since he did the same things that happened to Carolyn to that other woman south of Atlanta. Even though Carolyn still can't remember, that article in Monday's Atlanta paper described Carolyn's injuries exactly. The bad part is, he's still on the loose and has disappeared!"

"Wow!"

Derek's hand was so sweaty the phone nearly slipped from his hand. "Yes, that's exactly my feelings! Do you do anything besides installing pools? I'm wanting immediately to install a fence around the back yard that can be locked. I can't imagine that Carolyn is safe if she uses the pool until I can secure the back yard."

"I'm sure that's true, Derek, but no, I haven't expanded my operation to include fencing."

Derek chuckled a bit. "You wouldn't want to expand your operation, say this afternoon, with a fence to my back yard, would you?"

"Well, now, you know, it'd be a sure job for us!"

"Absolutely! And the compensation would be just as available as for the pool. Give it some more thought, Sam. I really want my Carolyn safe!"

"Derek, I'll give it some thought. Will you be home before I leave like you were on Friday? I'll talk with Ernest and have you an answer when you get here."

"Yes, I was planning on leaving as soon as the bank closes, but in light of what I've learned today, it's a good probability I'll be home in minutes. What the sheriff told me has me on pins and needles!"

"I can believe that! See you later."

"Yes, banking isn't holding too much of my interest right now! I'm not sure I can do anything until I see Carolyn with my own eyes!"

"I hear that!"

Derek hung up and found his hands were shaking again. *God! Keep her safe!* Sam and Ernest were in the back yard. Mrs. Beecham was inside somewhere and Carolyn was also inside, but until he saw her with his own eyes, he couldn't stop worrying. He looked at the clock on the wall then glanced out his open door. Marlene was at that moment walking toward the front door to lock it and close down for the day. Well, that was good enough for him! His brain was working overtime with the sheriff's words!

Quickly, he pulled all the papers he'd been working on when the sheriff called together into a pile in front of him. He gathered them up and nearly threw them into his in-box. There were some letters he knew Marlene had typed that needed his signature, but that could wait until in the morning, he was too distraught to worry with them now. How could he even think about it? The man was out there somewhere and Carolyn wasn't safe! Perhaps he wasn't thinking rationally, with two men in the back yard surely she was safe! He wasn't the only one who could protect her, but then again, she was vulnerable.

"I'm out of here!" he muttered. He slammed his laptop closed, clicked the locks on his briefcase, grabbed them up and reached for his suit coat. All of this before Marlene came back to her desk. She smiled at him as he reached his office door, but Derek was too preoccupied. He slammed that door and turned the lock, then headed for his private entrance at the back. The big clock across the square had barely finished striking the hour when he jerked his car door open and scrambled in. Normally, he had another half hour before he left for the day, but today that thought never crossed his mind. His clammy hands slipped on the metal doorknob, but on the second try he yanked it open. He was gone!

Lance came home from another day at the office, glad the sun was still shining. Sometimes, on days like this it would be long gone before he could pull away. He pulled in his garage, but sat for several minutes after shutting the car off, just enjoying the quietness. Probably it wouldn't be this quiet inside; it certainly hadn't been this quiet at his work place today! Finally, he pulled in a long breath, left his car, pushed the kitchen door open, walked in and slumped into his chair at the table he was exhausted. If his usual workday was like today he'd find another line of work!

In the week or so since they'd been in Birmingham, he and Linda had decided to try another avenue to find his sister Carolyn. After Lance's little family sat down for dinner, he asked, "So, did you find out anything?" He picked up the large spoon and put a small serving on the brightly decorated plate and handed it to Linda.

"Yes, something very disturbing, really!"

"Oh? What did you find out? Was it from her employer or her landlord?"

Very seriously, Linda put some vegetables on Brenda's plate and set it in front of her. The little girl wasn't interested in her mommy and daddy's conversation, so she started eating. "Honey, I contacted both places. Carolyn worked that first week, but hasn't showed up since. She hasn't been in her apartment according to the landlord in that same length of time. He lives in the building, but her neighbors have reported to him that they hadn't seen or heard her in that long. Also he said her mailbox is full. Honey, I'm worried about her!"

Lance scowled. "Really! That's not like her at all! She's so conscientious and I know this was a job she was really looking forward to. She was ecstatic when she landed it. Something must have happened to her!"

Lance finished putting Linda's serving of the casserole on her plate and contemplatively set the spoon back in the dish.

Tears came to Linda's eyes she brushed them away immediately so Brenda wouldn't see them. "I know, but what? And how could we find out?"

Lance scowled and looked at the nearly empty casserole dish. "I don't know, I guess we'd have to file a missing person's report with the police."

Linda accepted her own plate from her husband, automatically dished up some vegetables onto her plate and shook her head. She picked up her fork and slid it under some noodles, but then the fork stayed suspended in midair. She scowled and said, "Honey, Atlanta's a huge place! I'm sure people disappear from there all the time."

A large dollop of food landed on the last plate, as Lance said, "I know, but that's the only thing I can think of. She'd be so new there that she probably hasn't made any solid friendships as yet. If she'd only been at work for a week or even in her apartment, she wouldn't know a soul! I know she's a likeable woman, but still...."

"I know, but we need to do something!"

Hesitating only for a moment, Linda asked, "How about your dad, have you hunted for him? Could he be in Atlanta?"

Lance let out a long sigh and looked at the mound of food he'd put on his own plate. It didn't look nearly as appetizing now that they were on this topic. He hated talking about his dad. He felt conflicted about him every time he thought about him. For a long time he'd hated the man, but as he grew older he realized that was his own mental image of him, not what the man really was. He knew he couldn't go back for a do over, but could he move on? He pulled in a long breath, realizing he really hadn't moved on.

"No, every time I think about it, something seems to come up and it gets put on the back burner. Besides, it's been twelve years since... well, if we count all the time he tried to reach us, maybe only ten, but still..."

"Honey," Linda chastised him, "You have a computer on your desk at work. You have your laptop in your office here at home. It isn't hard to pull up the internet, put his name in and find something if he's still alive."

"Yes, you're right, I must do that..."

Linda reached across the space, put her hand on Lance's arm and said, "Honey, you keep saying that. You need to do it."

"Yes, I'll do it. I'll put it on my pocket calendar to do first thing in the morning. I can't put it off any longer. He may be our key." He scowled at his wife. "Still, he wasn't a criminal, why would she have disappeared, her phone not work, she not go to work, all those things if she found Dad and went to see him?"

"That's right, Honey, I don't know."

Thursday morning when Lance turned on his office computer, it had barely warmed up when it chimed, 'You've got mail!' He quickly shed his suit jacket and sat down at his desk, scooted his chair around to face his computer and went through the process to activate his Email. The only message that he hadn't seen the day before read:

> "You were given as a reference by Carolyn Casbah for a supervisory position here at the Med Center in the Physical Therapy Department. As of this date, she has been absent from her place of employment with no explanation or call indicating she is ill for over a month. We have tried to contact her on numerous occasions with no success. Please be advised that her employment with us will be terminated unless we hear from her or you with an explanation immediately. Thank you for your prompt attention to this important matter.
>
> Dean Martin, Physical Therapy Department."

Lance sat staring at the words for several minutes. He'd only recently realized himself that his sister was somehow missing. How was he supposed to advise her place of employment where she was or why she hadn't appeared for work in over a month? He wasn't even in the same state she was in! This whole thing with Carolyn was a total mystery. Carolyn was not like this at all, that was another way she was like their dad! She rarely became ill and if she wasn't sick she never missed a day of work. Besides, he or Linda was always the first to know when things were going on with his sister, but it hadn't happened this time. The question Linda had asked last night: '*How can we find out?*' slid into his mind. "How indeed?" he whispered.

He hit 'Respond.' Thoughtfully, he typed: "I only recently became aware my sister is missing. I have no idea what has happened." and hit 'send'. Sitting, looking again at the short message Lance pulled his hand through his hair. He couldn't remember when he'd prayed last, but the words slipped from his mouth. *"God in heaven, where can my sister be?"*

As soon as his secretary knew he was in, she tapped on his door and brought in a short stack of papers. Lance sighed, "Holly, you have been busy! You've got things for me to sign all ready?" He smiled at her. "You're sure you haven't been here all night working?" He picked up the top letter, then looked up and grinned. "This is impressive!"

"Oh, no, Lance, I came in at my regular time, but you've been working so hard lately I got behind, but I'm caught up for the time being."

Holly turned to go back to her desk in the next office and Lance pulled his pen from his utensils holder to start reading the first letter when his cell phone rang. He barely had it activated and his mouth open to speak when Linda's frantic voice said, "Lance! I just got a text from Sis! She'd just put Mom and Dad on a plane headed for Los Angeles for their vacation. She was still watching it taxi down the runway. The plane never made it off the ground! It exploded near the end of the runway and everybody on the plane and close by were killed!"

"Oh, man! I'll be right home! We'll go as soon as I get there! Pack some things!"

"Yes, oh, yes! Oh, Lance, this is so horrible!"

"Yes, Darling, get things ready. I'll be home on a few minutes!"

Lance looked back at what was lying on his desk. Quickly he scribbled his signature on the page, shoved it aside and signed the next letter. By the time he'd sent his office computer through the shut-down process, he'd signed four more sheets and his short stack was ready for mailing. Holly could do that. Quickly, he pulled his briefcase from the floor and his suit jacket from the hook and ran into Holly's office.

"Holly! That was Linda! Her parents were just killed in a plane crash! I signed all those things, can you mail them? I'm gone!"

"Of course, Lance! See you sometime!" she called to his back. There were tears in her eyes, the man worked hard, but he was so unhappy. She'd rarely seen him smile it made her wonder what in his life made him so perpetually unhappy. Of course, as his secretary, she didn't pry. Now his in-laws had been killed tragically. What more could happen to the poor man?

Lance rushed from the huge office building to his car. The fact that his sister was missing and that he needed to find his dad had totally left his mind. Right now, he needed to be with his wife, her tragedy, the death of her parents much more important than anything else making his heart shatter for her. He couldn't imagine her grief right now. He beeped his car unlocked, threw his briefcase and laptop in ahead of him, then dove in himself and raced off.

When he arrived at home, Linda had just placed two suitcases beside the door. Her eyes were puffy when Lance entered, so he took her immediately into his arms. Without saying a word, he tucked her into his chest and stroked her back. Very soon his shirt was wet from Linda's tears. Only moments later, Brenda came up beside them, tears also rolling down her cheeks. Lance wondered if her tears were falling because of her mommy's tears or if, at her young age, she really knew what had happened only moments before. He took one arm away from Linda's back and scooped his daughter up in his arm. The little girl laid her head down on her daddy's shoulder, sniffled and let out a shuddering sob.

Linda hiccoughed and whispered, "Sis said there won't even be a funeral service, only a memorial. There wasn't enough left of anything to identify."

"Wow! That's awful!" He looked down at the two suitcases. "Are we ready?"

"Yes. Brenda, what are you taking?"

"My dolly, my horsy and my blanky," the child answered, shakily. Both Linda and Brenda pulled in a deep breath. Linda took a step away from Lance and he put the little girl down on the floor. This was hard.

Lance also pulled in a deep breath, this wasn't something he ever wanted to do, but of course it had to be done. He had been forced to deal with the death of a parent at a very early age. He realized now he hadn't done a good job of that. It had made him a bitter teen and he realized he was still harboring bitterness. An unscheduled trip to Louisiana wasn't something he was crazy about. He and Linda were both from Baton Rouge. Lance's memories from his early life were what he had tried to bury for years. However, going there automatically resurrected them. It didn't matter; this trip was all about Linda and her loss. He needed to bury his bad feelings and be the support she and Alli needed from him. Alli's husband had left her for no apparent reason only a year ago.

Lance's in-laws were good people and didn't deserve to die so young. They'd never see their granddaughter grow up or if he and Linda had more children they'd never know. They loaded the car, fastened Brenda into her car seat and left. It was several hundred miles away, but they'd talk with Linda's sister when they arrived as to where they'd lay their heads that night. Linda had a box of tissues on the console, but she wanted to be brave. Brenda didn't need to see her crying all the way to Aunt Alli's house.

When the little Casbah family arrived in the Baton Rouge suburb, Lance drove directly to her parents' home. Her sister had texted her again and told her that's where they'd meet. Even though Linda had tried not to cry on the trip, her eyes were puffy. She had silently whimpered much of the trip. Lance felt her anguish and for most of the way he drove one handed and held her hand between them. Brenda sat in her seat and soon after they left places where she and Linda went a lot, she fell sleep and slept most of the way. Lance was very glad of that, since she had to sit in a car seat, there was no way her parents could console her during their long trip. Besides, Linda was in no shape to console her daughter.

As Lance pulled up the drive for the large house, he said, "There's Alli waiting for us."

Linda hiccoughed and whispered, "I bet she's devastated! Sis has lived with them since Mike left. I wonder if she'll sell the house, since it's so big."

"Yeah, that's a good question. I'd think she'd want to."

"Yes, with all the memories, I know I'd want to. Brenda, wake up, Honey, we're here."

Sleepily, she said, "I'm awake, Mommy. We're at Gramma's house?"

"Yes, Sweetheart," Lance said, "but it's only Aunt Alli who's here."

In a weak little voice, Brenda whispered, "Oh, yeah…"

Lance also pulled in a deep breath, this wasn't something he ever wanted to do, but of course it had to be done. He put his hand on the door latch his sister-in-law was coming toward them. He needed to be strong both for Linda and Alli. While Linda helped Brenda from the car seat, Lance unloaded the trunk. When they closed the car up, Alli ushered them into the house. It had been a long trip, so Linda took Brenda immediately to the bathroom.

Alli looked up at her brother-in-law and said, "I guess we'll all stay here. It's big enough, there's no reason for you guys to get a room somewhere else."

"That's good. This is all terrible for you!"

"Yes, I saw the plane explode! It was the worst thing I've ever seen or done!"

"I'm sure! So what happens?"

"Other family will arrive from now on. We'll have the memorial tomorrow afternoon. Like I told Sis, there's not enough of anything to bury. But there's this house to empty out."

"I can't stay long, Sis, but surely Linda can stay indefinitely and I can come back."

"That's good of you, Lance. I appreciate all you're doing."

Lance put his arm around his sister-in-law and squeezed her shoulders. "We needed to come, Sis. You'll both need each other, I'm sure. Will you sell the house?"

Alli nodded slowly. "I think it's the only thing to do, Lance. Their wills said that if they go together that the property must be divided equally between Sis and me. That can't happen unless we sell it. Besides, I don't want it, it would be too hard."

Lance pulled in a deep breath and looked compassionately at his sister-in-law. He had to swallow before he said, "I understand how you feel, Alli. I'll stay until Sunday and help all I can. If you need Linda longer than that, it's all right if she stays."

Brushing at the tears leaking from her eyes, Alli said, "Thanks, Lance, I know just being here in Baton Rouge is hard for you, I know you have some memories you have to deal with, so it means a lot for you to stay."

Lance blew out a long breath and said, "I've realized recently that I haven't dealt with things very well. I'm going to have to do that, maybe being here for several days will help me do that. I'm hoping so, anyway."

Very early Thursday morning Duncan and Nancy left their home and descended on DeLord's house. Duncan had a hike going out at eight o'clock, but Ramon was out leading his own group and wouldn't be back until Friday afternoon. Sandy, with her little helper, was busy in the kitchen getting breakfast ready for two of her favorite people. She was glad Nancy had the day off, the two of them, along with Jon, planned to do something together.

When Duncan had a hike going out, Nancy always came with her husband for breakfast, whether she had to work or not, but when she came she brought sugary treats to go with the eggs and bacon that Sandy always fixed. It was a treat and Jon loved his sugar high. Coming up the walk they smelled the aroma of Sandy's delicious coffee. As far as Duncan was concerned, Sandy fixed the best coffee. Of course, his wife's was a close second.

Duncan had driven, knowing that Sandy would drop Nancy off at home that afternoon, but Duncan's hike started at a trailhead down the road. When they met in front of his SUV, Nancy said, "Honey, your group doesn't go from here today, does it?"

Before he answered, Duncan took a long sniff of the sweet rolls his wife was carrying and said, "Nope. Mine leaves from the trailhead down the road."

"Do you have to meet them there?"

"No, they come here, but we'll take my SUV and another vehicle to park down there. That way there aren't as many vehicles to clog up the place. It's not like this parking lot, it's much smaller, but it is on a public road. I like that trail for a diversion once in a while. Actually, that's the trail we took my first hike from here when I went with Ramon when he hired me. I guess this group has been with us enough times they want to see something new."

"Maybe, but I've heard Ramon say that's a more rugged course, so he doesn't want to send a greenie bunch on it unless they ask for a challenge."

"Yeah, that's true, but we'll do fine."

Duncan had his arm raised to knock when they heard Sandy call, "Come on in!"

Duncan opened the door and said, "We're about to!"

Soon, Nancy was moving around the kitchen while Duncan stayed in the dining room and Jon came in to be with the 'man'. Sandy's kitchen was big, it had to be because of her chair, but Duncan knew to keep out of it when two women were busy there. Nancy was about to ask Sandy a question when the phone rang. Sandy picked up the hand set, but Nancy began taking things to the table so Duncan could start eating and be ready for his hike on time. Of course, he'd already taken a large mouthful of Nancy's confection he only waited for her to bring him a cup of Sandy's coffee.

"Honey," Nancy scolded quietly, "you need to wait for Sandy so we can pray! Besides, you're like a little kid! You eat dessert before the regular meal."

Giving her a sheepish grin, he said, "I already did… in my heart," he added, when Nancy looked at him quizzically. "Yeah, really, I did, didn't I Jon?"

Jon dutifully nodded his head, but Nancy said, "Mmm, I believe that!"

Taking the large mug from his wife's hand, he took a good sized swallow and grinned. "See," he nodded at Jon, "he says I did."

Nancy shook her head. "What's a fifteen month old know!"

"Besides, if Sandy doesn't come real soon, I'll be late, so I need to get on with it."

Nancy looked at the table and saw that she'd brought everything in, so she slid into her chair and bowed her head. Without waiting for Duncan to speak, she said, "Father, God, bless this food to our bodies. Bless Duncan as he goes on this hike, keep him and all the hikers he takes safe." She sighed, "And help us all to always speak the truth, amen."

"Well," He muttered, "this'll be a long hike."

Sandy had the phone to her ear as she wheeled herself into the dining room. Raylyn said, when she answered, "Sandy, hi! Roger has a meeting starting at ten that's to last most of the day in Blairsville. Want to meet for a day of fun?"

"Love to! Nancy's off today and could I ask Carolyn if she wants to come?"

"Sure! That'll be great! The more the merrier! How about we meet at the bank?"

"Good idea. Maybe we can get Derek to join us for lunch. He absolutely adores Jon."

"Go for it!" Raylyn said, on a chuckle.

Sandy laughed, "You know I will! If he knows Jon is part of the equation, he'll submit to anything Ramon or I suggest."

Derek was swigging down his last few mouthfuls of coffee when his landline phone rang. He grabbed up the handset and answered, "Derek Casbah…"

"Hi, Dad! Called to see if it was okay to take Carolyn for an outing today. Seems us girls are going to Blairsville for an all day."

"Sandy, Carolyn's fine, but I have a problem. It seems the Sheriff's Department and the Atlanta Police Department have determined who Carolyn's abductor was, but he's still on the loose. That's my only concern."

Cheerfully, Sandy said, "Derek, between us three girls and three children, we will not let her out of our sight. Surely she'll be safe in numbers!"

Derek chuckled, as he looked at his lovely daughter. "I guess there's enough strength there to hold off the bogey man."

"Great! Is she available or did I call too early?"

"No, she's right here and smiling like a Cheshire cat, knowing it's you on the phone."

Derek handed Carolyn the phone, looked at the clock and picked up his mug. After depositing it in the sink, he grabbed his suit coat and briefcase. As he walked toward the door into the garage, Carolyn said, "Hi, Sandy, we're going someplace?"

"If you're up to a day with Nancy, Raylyn, Heidi, Lenny, Jon and me, then I guess we'll be going someplace with you along."

Listening to the door close behind her dad, but excited for the diversion from another long day in the great room, Carolyn exclaimed, "I'm all for it! I'll be ready when you get here. Can I bring anything?"

Conspiratorially, Sandy said, "No, actually, we're thinking about enticing Derek to go for lunch with us since his grandson'll be going."

Carolyn laughed. "Great! Two boy toddlers and a man, with five females, he'll love it."

Sandy laughed with her. "Yes, we're counting on it. I'll be by sometime after nine. Oh, be sure you're dressed for a day on the town!"

"I'll be watching."

"Terrific!"

She hung up, a huge smile on her face. Sam's truck pulled onto the grass in the back yard and stopped beside the big hole. Thank goodness it hadn't rained since those few days of deluge and the men had made great progress. Carolyn sighed at least today she wouldn't have to sit in the great room holding a book she didn't really want to read while she watched the men work outside. Of course, she hadn't been outside to watch, but she thought they were close to having the cement truck come. She'd seen them taking different things down into the hole and assumed they were building forms the past two days.

Carolyn dressed in comfortable clothes, glad that the only thing still visible from her ordeal was the aircast on her left arm. Her hair was growing and Derek had taken her to a hair dresser who had given her a different style, which was cooler for summer and made the really short hairs over her scar much less obvious. Of course, the bruises and swelling had disappeared days ago. She felt nearly human, except for her empty brain. Everyone, including Dr. Simon who'd seen her over a week ago, had assured her it would fill up real fast in time. She sighed, she could only hope!

Just as she promised, Sandy pulled up on the driveway close to the garage only minutes after nine and Carolyn was watching from the foyer. Sam and Ernest had been on the job for an hour, but Carolyn didn't worry about them. She never went out to bother them. She guessed they were nice enough, Ernest looked like he could be just shy of her dad's age and Sam might be old enough to be an older brother or cousin, but they were men and right now, men in general, with only a few exceptions were not on her get-friendly-with list.

When Sandy touched the horn, Carolyn pulled her purse up on her shoulder, opened the massive front door and hurried out to the van. It clicked behind her and she knew it had automatically locked. Sandy was letting down the lift as Carolyn walked up. As she waited for it to reach the ground, Carolyn pulled in a big breath of fresh air. She realized it was a beautiful day, the sun was out, there were only a few fleecy clouds in an otherwise deep blue sky, but she knew she didn't get much fresh air being inside all the time. Hopefully that could change one day soon. How could she swim in the pool if she must stay behind locked doors all the time?

From inside the van, Sandy called to her, "Climb on, girl! You get the dubious honor of sitting beside your nephew!"

Carolyn returned Sandy's smile as she stepped on the lift and pressed the button to take it up. "Terrific! Jon and I get along just great." When she had closed the door, she said, "Hi, Nancy! So where do we go today?"

"Raylyn and the kids are riding in with Roger, but he's dropping them off at the bank. We'll meet them there. Not that we'll need much money, but maybe we can storm the president's office and force him into accepting a lunch date." Both Nancy and Carolyn laughed. Sandy had such a great sense of humor.

When Carolyn turned to the bench seat one little boy gave her his best grin, held up his arms and crowed, "AnTEECar!"

Carolyn grinned at the little guy, sat down and kissed the child in the carseat beside her, who would not be ignored and said, "I think with this guy along the president'll go for anything. He sure does love this little guy."

"We're counting on it."

Sandy drove to the Blairsville bank. Raylyn, Heidi and Lenny were waiting beside the main door, Heidi saw them and started waving and started running at the same time. Sandy pulled around into the parking lot and parked in the handicapped space where she usually did. When they were all out and the van secured, Jon sat on Sandy's lap, clapping his hands, he loved an outing. 'People watching' was his favorite thing to do. He and his mama were two of the friendliest people and many in Blairsville knew them. Nancy and Carolyn walked on either side of Sandy's chair. They rounded the corner and headed for the Clemens family. By all indications, it would be a great day!

Heidi was the first to reach them. She was still waving as she came around the corner of the big building. She never stopped racing toward the little group. Sandy stopped her chair when Heidi came close, knowing where Heidi was headed. Without even looking, she jumped up on Sandy's footrest as if it was the natural thing to do. "Hi, Jon!" she exclaimed.

"HiDEE!" he exclaimed and held out his arms.

"Don't much like each other, do they?" Nancy commented as Heidi's arms went around the little boy. With Jon in her arms, Heidi stepped back off the footrest and led the three ladies toward her mommy and little brother.

Carolyn chuckled. "You could say that."

A few yards from the door, Sandy called out, "Hi, guys! It's a great day for an outing!"

"Oh, it's great!" Raylyn agreed. "Hi, Nancy and Carolyn."

They all reached the front door, but Carolyn didn't look at Raylyn, instead, her eyes zeroed in on the poster in the front window. Instantly a scream broke from her mouth, she started shaking and her purse fell from her arm and plopped forgotten to the pavement. She slapped her hand over her mouth, but that didn't keep in the great gasps anyone around could hear and the tears that gushed from her eyes and streamed down her cheeks. Carolyn's whole body started shaking.

Horrified, Sandy said, "What is it, Carolyn? What's the matter!"

The color draining from her face, Carolyn slumped against the wall away from the picture in the window, but she couldn't seem to pull her eyes away from it. She pulled in a great gasp of air, then another. "That picture..." she whispered, "...that's him!" She covered her face with both hands, not wanting to look at the horrible face.

Immediately the other three women glanced at the picture and knew that was her abductor. Nancy quickly grabbed up Carolyn's purse from in front of her and opened the front door of the bank, but Sandy grabbed Carolyn's hand and pulled her inside so she couldn't see the face any longer. Sandy could feel Carolyn's hand shaking and it was ice cold, but her tears kept streaming down her face. Her whole body shook from her sobs.

Raylyn and Heidi came in last with the two toddlers and found chairs in the waiting area right away, then made sure the toddlers were around them. Of course, Heidi still held Jon, but Lenny was easily distracted and didn't always stay with his mommy and sister. Raylyn always had things for the little ones to play with in her large bag, so she quickly dug them out. They made quite a gathering in the lobby

Nancy took Carolyn's arm that was in the cast and the three of them headed for Derek's office, which was across the large waiting area. His door was partially open, but they couldn't see him. Derek's secretary, Marlene, had seen the action through the glass doors, but knew Sandy, so she didn't say anything as the three young women barreled across the open area, passed her desk and reached Derek's office. She did look at Carolyn, concerned. She hadn't seen her before, only heard Derek talk about her several times. But just like everyone else, she could easily see the family resemblance. Immediately, her heart went out to the young woman and tears made her eyes glisten.

His door was open, so the trio continued into the room. Marlene stood up and followed them to Derek's door. Derek, of course, heard the whine of Sandy's chair before he saw them, so he knew she was coming. With all the noise in the bank he didn't hear Carolyn's crying, in fact, she had subsided just a bit, since both Sandy and Nancy were holding her hands. Still tears were streaming down her cheeks and she was shaking like a leaf. She still didn't have any color in her cheeks she looked like Elmer's glue!

Surprised when all three barreled through the doorway, he asked, as he threw his pen down on top of the pages in front of him, "What's up, girls?" Of course his eyes zeroed in on Carolyn. He took one look at her and knew something traumatic had happened. She'd cried and screamed from her nightmare, but this was quite different. In fact, the sobs made her body shake even more. She was truly distressed.

Derek was out of his chair, but hadn't even reached her, before the word exploded from Carolyn's mouth, "Dad!" Carolyn pulled in a gasp of air. After another swallow, she blurted out, "That picture in the front window! That's him! Dad, it's that awful man! Is he… is he someplace close? Why is his picture in the window?"

"Oh, my!" Derek exclaimed.

"What…?" Nancy whispered.

When Derek jumped from his chair, it crashed into the wall behind the desk, but he paid it no attention. He rushed around the desk, his arms out and grabbed Carolyn into a fierce hug. "Carolyn! Oh, I'm so sorry you had to see that! That's a picture of the man who hurt you?" Of course, Sandy and Nancy let go of Carolyn so Derek could have her.

"Yes! Oh, yes!" she wailed through her gasps. The tears still streamed down her cheeks.

Derek looked at Sandy and Nancy and shook his head. "Girls, on my! What do I say?" He looked at Carolyn again and said, "I'd better call the sheriff!"

Sandy nodded. "That'd be good!"

Derek pulled Carolyn with him closer to the phone. He wouldn't have let her go for anything. Of course, Sandy and Nancy had already let go of her, she needed her dad's comfort and she had just acknowledged that he was. It seemed he couldn't get her close enough to him, so he hugged her tightly. Sandy realized that this might be a break through, so she asked, as Derek dialed, "Carolyn? Are you remembering?"

Carolyn stood in the circle of Derek's arm, her arms tightly around him and looked out the window beyond his desk, the tears still flooding her face. Finally she looked at Sandy and slowly shook her head. "No, I guess all I remember was the man's face. I still can't remember what he did or what happened before."

"Oh, my!" Sandy murmured.

The sheriff had obviously answered, because Derek said, "Sheriff, my daughter came to the bank just now and saw the poster we put in our window Tuesday morning. She has definitely identified that man as the man who did the act against her!"

Obviously, the man swallowed before he asked, "Does she remember anything else?"

Derek sighed, "She's just told her friend that she doesn't remember anything else. It was the face on the poster that triggered this memory."

His frustration easily came through, as he said, "Well, I'm glad for that much, Mr. Casbah. We still haven't located the man, which is truly a frustration, but the Atlanta Police and also the state police have a bulletin out on him. We know now that he's wanted not only for murdering that young woman down south, but also attempted murder against your daughter. I'll be sure to pass this information on. It'll make his capture top priority!"

"I will be praying earnestly for that to happen!"

"Yes, I'll add mine to that!"

By the time Derek hung up, Carolyn had stepped out of his arm. All three of the other women had noticed that Carolyn appeared very weak and urged her to sit down. Her whole body shaking, she collapsed into Derek's desk chair. Marlene had found some paper towels, had wet some and brought them to Carolyn who was now only whimpering and was wiping her face. A tear only escaped occasionally and Carolyn was dabbing at them. However, Sandy and Nancy still hovered around her.

"Have they found him?" Sandy whispered to Derek.

"Unfortunately not."

"Oh, my!" Marlene said.

Nancy also heard him and shook her head. "When will this ever stop? Criminals seem to have such a knack of disappearing! Any of us non-criminals – if we get a speeding ticket they come after us if we don't get it paid!"

"Yes, they do. Sometimes when criminals are on parole I wish they'd put bells on them or something that would alert the average population to watch out!" Derek came to Carolyn and put his arm around her, then looked from Sandy to Nancy and asked, "Um, girls, was there a reason, since you didn't know about that poster, why you're here?"

"Roger dropped Raylyn and the children off here, so this was where we were to meet them." Sandy grinned at Derek. "Actually, we wondered if you'd like to join us for lunch later on. You know Jon's with us, Japa."

Trying to act put upon, but failing because of the wide grin on his face, Derek said, "You will always turn my day on its ear when you come to town, young lady! Of course I'll meet you for lunch!" He made a face. "Um, it's you three, Raylyn and Heidi, plus the two boys?"

"Yup! You'll love it, won't you?"

Derek chuckled. "That I will, that I will. It will make my day!"

After everyone left Derek's office and things returned to normal, Derek had just picked up his pen when his phone rang. He let out a sigh, lifted the receiver and said, "Derek Casbah, could I help you?"

"Mr. Casbah, Sheriff Winslow."

"Hello, Sheriff, what can I do for you? We only talked a few minutes ago."

"Yes, actually, that's why I'm calling, you triggered a thought."

Derek chuckled. "By all means, let's hear it!"

"What do you know about Eric Thomas? What can you tell me about him or his time in the service?"

Derek sat thinking for several minutes, before he said, "He doesn't talk too much about his enlistment, actually, he not too talkative at all. He seems to be a good listener, but I do know that he was in the Marines and did at least one tour of duty in Afghanistan. I really don't know anything about his life before that, however. What I know of him personally is very positive. He lives simply in one of Isabel Isaacson's cabins, is very conscientious, very helpful and is a fine Christian man."

"So you don't know if he did any kind of police work?"

"No, I don't, Sheriff. Why do you ask?"

"A very surprising development has happened in the state law enforcement office! It seems that those gentlemen have done something I've never known to happen in all my time in law enforcement and that's been a good twenty years! Believe it or not, they have authorized me to hire another individual through my office, a new position, but to be stationed in the Vansville area. As we spoke just now it made me think of Mr. Thomas and wondered if he'd be a good candidate for the position."

"Sheriff, I think he would be a good choice. Of course you know he's now employed by DeLord's Hiking Service. I know for a fact that they are covered up and Eric only gets one day off between each hike he leads."

The sheriff's sigh came over the phone. "I'm aware of that and I know it's not a good time to contact him, but the man at headquarters has given me some time to fill this position. I'll try to reach him soon and see what he has to say. Thanks for your input, Mr. Casbah."

"Not a problem, Sheriff. Thanks for calling."

# Twelve

"By the way, I'll be sure to keep you posted about any developments I hear," the sheriff added before he hung up.

"I'd appreciate that a lot, Sheriff." Derek sighed, "It will not be too soon to get that man behind bars!"

The sheriff cleared his throat. "You know, I think it was a breakthrough that Carolyn recognized that face. At least we know and can pin her ordeal on this man."

Derek put down the receiver and picked up his pen again, but didn't do more than twirl it between his fingers. He wondered what Eric would think of being a sheriff's deputy. Derek knew he was a good hiking guide, but he also knew he was working well below his potential and since he'd been in the Marines, he would be an excellent choice to be a deputy sheriff. In the Marines he'd handled weapons, but would he be opposed to that now? He would work out of Vansville; that was interesting. Had one criminal incident triggered that decision? It made him wonder how soon the sheriff would contact the young man. Should he, Derek, add his encouragement? Perhaps he'd better wait until Eric brought it up, if he ever did. He sighed, took the pen deliberately in his hand and looked down at the first letter in front of him. It didn't take much brain power to scratch his signature at the end of a letter!

After he hung up from talking with the bank president, Sheriff Winslow picked up his own pen and twirled it between his fingers. He'd spoken the truth to Mr. Casbah, he could never remember the Department of Corrections and Law Enforcement ever hiring someone to a new position, not since he'd been with the department and that had been for twenty years! If anything, jobs had been cut and manpower spread thinner. What could have gotten into the man from headquarters to do something so out of character? Didn't he remember that another man meant another salary and therefore more money? Something he claimed not to have! Well, he had contacted him and the slot was within his jurisdiction, he would fill it!

When the department head had contacted him he was so shocked he'd sputtered for several minutes, but then told the man he'd get right on that. His boss reminded him that the position was a new one he didn't have to fill it tomorrow, but as soon as he came up with a name to pass it on to him. The sheriff said he would and he'd mulled it over for several days. When Mr. Casbah had called only minutes ago it had triggered a thought and made the sheriff wonder about Eric Thomas's abilities. He'd liked the man from the moment he'd met him in the woods. He seemed quite professional, even in that terrible situation. When he'd come in the next day he seemed genuinely concerned for the young woman.

Looking at the pen in his hand that he was worrying to death, he muttered, "Well, I know Isabel Isaacson pretty well. Since he lives in one of her cabins, maybe she can give me some thoughts on the man." Before he heaved himself from his chair, he said, "I'd better call the lady before I pull in her driveway, though. Don't want that curmudgeon to have a heart attack before I talk with her." He pulled out his phone book and looked her up.

He lifted the receiver and dialed her number. On the second ring, she said, "Hello?"

"Ms Isaacson, Sheriff Winslow."

"Ah, yes, Willie, what's on your mind?"

The sheriff had to swallow, he hadn't been called Willie in twenty-five years or more! He grinned, that lady was something else! She'd always been a character. He cleared his throat and said, "Good to talk to you, Ms. Isaacson! Would you be home in say half an hour? I'd like to run something by you if you'll be home."

Sounding a bit put-upon, she said, "Sonny, I'll be here unless I'm not, so come ahead. Is Ruth in trouble?"

Sheriff Winslow laughed. "As I remember Ruth, she was a quiet soul and never in trouble. So you think she might be?"

With a deep sigh the sheriff could hear easily, she said, "Well, I was hoping not, since I'd have to come all the way to Blairsville to bail her out."

Still chuckling, the sheriff said, "No, this has nothing to do with Ruth and nobody's in trouble. I'll see you in a bit."

"Yes, Willie, that'll be fine. I'll be here, don't need any groceries yet today."

When Isabel hung up, Ruth stuck her head around the archway into the living room and said, "Mother! Why did you bring my name up?"

"It's fun to get you riled, girl, that's all." Ruth huffed and went back to the kitchen.

The sheriff left his office chuckling and grinned all the way to Vansville. He remembered that Isabel was good for a chuckle years ago, it didn't seem like she'd changed. He pulled his white sheriff's car, with the one word emblazoned on the sides, onto her parking lot and as he stepped from the car, Isabel opened her door.

Looking significantly at the car, she said, "Ah, gotta show off, is that it, Willie?"

The sheriff looked down at his car then grinned at Isabel. "No, Ma'am, but I couldn't have gotten here in a half hour if I'd gone home for a car."

"Well, fine, come on in." She showed him to a seat in the living room and she sat down in her favorite recliner. "So what's on your mind?" She sighed, "I been on pins and needles wondering what you have to talk about with me for that half hour."

"You have a tenant I'm interested in."

Indignantly she said, "Eric? He's not in trouble! I won't have him be in trouble!"

The sheriff chuckled. "Why do you think he'd be in trouble?"

Not answering his question at all, she said, "Because he's the perfect renter! Right behind my all time favorite, Sandy."

"That's good to know. Actually, I want to hire him."

Isabel scowled and slapped her hand down on her armrest. "He's already got a job! Why, he's as busy as a cat on a hot tin roof!"

"Oh, I know he's a hiking guide right now, but don't you think he could work as a sheriff's deputy after the season?"

She was only quiet a minute, before she exclaimed, "Well, yes! He'd be the best."

"See, that's what I wanted to know."

"Well, why didn't you say!" she huffed.

"I did, actually."

Nodding thoughtfully, Isabel said, "Yeah, I guess you did in a way. Sorta like you used to talk when you raked my yard."

Sheriff Winslow grinned. "It's the way they train you in police academy."

"Ah, it's good you already knew how back when you were just out of diapers." She shook her head. "That mama of yours... why I could see bald spots where she'd pulled out her hair. Told me it was that boy of hers."

"Now, Ms. Isabel, no telling secrets out of class."

"Wouldn't think of it. You got all you want to know? Oh, by the way, I had Ruth package up a couple of cinnamon buns, you wouldn't want any, would you?"

"Ms. Isabel! You still make those delicious buns? Of course, I'll take one!"

"Good, good. Why, what do you know! Here, she left them on my table. You got all your information?"

He reached for the bag of buns. "Yup, pretty much. You have a good day."

"I'll do that once you pull that snazzy car out of my yard." She grinned. "You have a good day and hire Eric real quick."

"Thought you said he's all tied up."

"Sonny, get on outta here before I take those buns back!"

The impressive man, with a belt load of paraphernalia around his waist, heaved himself from the chair, grinned at Isabel, kept the cinnamon buns securely in his left hand, saluted Isabel and walked out. *Yes, Isabel was good for a laugh.* From beside the sheriff's car he grinned and waved, since he could see Isabel in her chair watching him.

The four ladies and three children did up the mall royally all morning! As Sandy had predicted, they didn't spend much money, but they did some serious window shopping. Since Heidi was home schooled and Lenny was barely out of diapers, no school clothes for fall were on the list. However, both boys were growing like weeds as little boys were known to do and Heidi wasn't far behind, so there were a few packages that both Sandy and Raylyn carried after a visit to the children's department of several stores. Even so, there were a few trinkets purchased along the way as well.

Not too strangely, the girls ended up at the food-court close to noon. They had barely pushed two large tables together and found two high chairs and a booster seat when Derek came puffing in. As he zeroed in on the mostly female group, his eyes sparkled and his grin spread across his face. It looked like there'd be an empty seat beside Jon.

Carolyn placed Jon in one of the high chairs, but when she stepped away, his eyes found Derek and he yelled, "JAPA!" and tried to climb out of the chair.

Derek dashed the last few steps with his arms out. Keeping the little boy in his seat, he hugged him and said, "How's my little guy?"

"Japa, I good!" He looked around the tables and pointed. "Mama, AnTEECar, Na, Ra, Len, HiDEE, Japa!" Mournfully, he added, "Dada gone."

Derek patted Jon's back and nodded. "Goodness, Jon, you got them all! You are really super!" Jon grinned at Derek and nodded proudly.

Derek looked from Sandy to Carolyn and said, "Well, girls, order up!"

The food court had several shops, but they all had counters facing the dining area and people made their choice then went to the counters to order. As soon as everyone found a seat and Carolyn and Sandy said their preference, Nancy, Raylyn and Derek left the rest of the group at the tables to make their orders. Nancy would help carry food for whoever needed help to get the meals back to the tables. They were several minutes at the counter, Raylyn had three to order for and Derek had four.

The three with the food barely made it back to the tables when Carolyn let out an agonized, "Oh-h-h.", turned as white as a sheet, her eyes became glassy and she slumped over, nearly toppling from the chair, but hitting her head on the table. Quickly, Nancy put her tray down on the table. Raylyn was turned toward her children, so she didn't see Carolyn, but Derek's tray nearly clattered onto the table forgotten.

"Carolyn!" he cried. Absently, he gave the tray of food a shove, since it teetered precariously against his leg.

She moaned again and her body slid against the chair back, her arms limp at her sides and her head flopped to one side.

Derek quickly stepped around Jon and Sandy to reach Carolyn before she fell to the floor. Nancy had chosen the seat beside her, so she was already reaching for her hand to find a pulse. As soon as she found it, she was relieved, it was strong and normal. Derek looked from Carolyn to Nancy and whispered, "What's wrong? Should I call an ambulance?"

Carolyn slid further down in the chair, as if she were stretching out on a bed, another groan left her throat and her mouth dropped open. Nancy nodded and looked around. The food court was full of people, all staring at their table. "Yeah, I think you'd better, Derek!"

Derek yanked his cell phone from his waist carrier and hit three numbers. Immediately, the voice said, "State your emergency!"

"I'm here at the food court at the mall! A young woman has fainted, we don't know why!" Derek called into the phone.

"Be right there!"

Someone else in the food court, probably someone behind a counter, had called the mall security, so a man in a uniform rushed up just then, "What's happened?" he asked.

"My daughter's collapsed!" a frantic Derek answered. "I called nine-eleven!"

As soon as he heard that, the man started motioning other diners to move their chairs so there was a clear aisle from Carolyn's chair to the closest exit. Just as the last person moved her chair, the running feet of the emergency crew were heard above the normal noise of the mall. A man, carrying a stretcher and a woman paramedic appeared and raced toward them. All eyes in the court were glued on the group.

"What happened?" the woman asked. Even while she spoke the man placed the stretcher on the floor and both of them started to lift Carolyn carefully from the chair.

Sandy spoke up, because she'd been sitting at the table with Carolyn and saw it all. "She let out a moan which sounded like she was in great pain! She turned as white as a sheet, her eyes glazed over and her head hit the table. Only a second later she flopped back against the chair and her arms fell to her sides."

Agony in his voice, Derek asked, "You'll take her to the ER?"

"Of course!" The man hit the trigger on the stretcher, which made the legs with the wheels open up and raise the bed into position so it could be pushed. Carolyn groaned again, but didn't wake up. They hurried from the table area, through the aisle the people had made and started down the corridor toward the door.

Together, both Nancy and Derek said, "I'll come along!"

"Only one can fit in the ambulance!" the man said.

Nancy ran with the stretcher, but she said, "Derek, I'll ride with her, you drive. You'll probably need your car."

"Yes, fine!" There was no time to waste, nor any need to argue. Nancy was a nurse, if her services were needed it was better that she be close to Carolyn. In fact, he was glad for her calm, it helped him stay focused.

The little group ran down the corridor, Nancy was holding onto the stretcher and Derek following only two steps behind. People close by scurried out of the way. Before they reached the outside door, the paramedic in front had his arm out to push the door open. Derek's car was parked close to the same entrance where the ambulance had stopped. He had his keys in his hand and sprinted past the rest of them, he had several more strides to cover from where they would load Carolyn and he intended to be on the move when the ambulance moved. He swiped at his eyes, dampness was blurring his vision. Could anything else happen to his beloved daughter? It seemed so!

He beeped his car unlocked and with another beep the car started. Derek dove in and slammed his door, just as the driver of the ambulance slammed the back doors. He and the woman climbed into the front and Derek pulled up to the end of the parking aisle. The ambulance siren started and the truck started to move, but Derek pulled in behind it. His emergency flashers were already going.

Inside at the food court, Jon watched his Japa run from the table. He looked at Sandy and said, mournfully, "Japa go way?"

Sandy put her arm around the little boy and squeezed his shoulders. "Yes, Honey, Auntie Carolyn got sick real fast. They took her to the hospital and Japa went with her."

"Oh. Mama go? Ja go?"

"Not right away, Honey, we have lunch here."

Sandy and Raylyn looked at each other. There were two women, one of them in a wheelchair, and three children still at the table. The two toddlers were reaching for their food. They were fussy after all it was lunch time. Their little tummies were empty and didn't understand why they weren't being fed.

The boys wouldn't understand and certainly wouldn't be content in a hospital waiting room for very long, especially of they were hungry. Raylyn had no car she and her two children had crowded into Sandy's van to come the short distance from the bank to the mall earlier. They were in Blairsville, more than twenty miles from home.

Raylyn took a deep breath and said, "Sandy, as I see it, these kids need to be fed."

"Yes, I think that's the most pressing thing right now. We can go to the hospital once they've finished."

"Yes, of course."

As they sat feeding their little ones and eating themselves, one of the servers from the food store where they'd made their purchases came to their table with several to-go boxes and a bag. She smiled at the women and said, "I saw what happened. It surely was a sudden thing! I thought maybe it would help if you boxed up the other meals and took them with you. Would that work?"

Sandy immediately smiled and said, "Oh, thank you, that's super! We really appreciate you being so thoughtful and especially when you're so busy."

"It's not a problem! What happened?"

"My sister-in-law has had some health problems recently. We aren't sure why she passed out, but she did and it all happened so fast!"

"I'm truly sorry!"

"Thank you, we'll finish up here then go to the hospital."

"Of course!"

It didn't take the children long to finish eating, so as soon as their meal was finished, the extra food packaged and in a bag, the mommies cleaned up their little boys. Sandy put Jon on her lap and set several things on her footrest and her armrest. Raylyn hefted her bags on her shoulder, helped Lenny from his seat and handed Heidi the bag with the food in it. They left by the same door as the others and went to Sandy's van. Now that Nancy and Carolyn weren't there the van wouldn't be so crowded.

When everyone was secure in a seat, Raylyn pulled out her phone and sent a text to Roger. *Honey, they rushed Carolyn to the hospital. Meet us there.*

Only moments after they loaded Carolyn into the ambulance and Nancy scrambled in, the truck raced from the mall parking lot with its siren screeching and a car following with his flashers going. As soon as the driver left the parking lot, he radioed ahead to the hospital to alert them of their arrival and the woman paramedic took vital signs and started an IV. Nancy watched and held Carolyn's hand.

The paramedic looked up from taping down the IV and said, "Don't I know you? For some reason you look familiar."

Nancy nodded. "Actually, I was thinking you looked a bit familiar. I'm Nancy, used to be Southerland when I worked at the rehab center a few years ago. I left there when the clinic in Vansville opened and got married."

Nodding, the young woman said, "Ah, yes, now I remember. I'm Katie Baxter. When you worked here I was a CNA, but I took the paramedic training, so now I race around town instead of on the wards."

Nancy chuckled. "Yes, it is about the same speed, isn't it?" Looking down at the still person between them, Nancy added, "Would be good if she'd wake up! Maybe we could get some clue what's wrong."

Katie nodded. "I agree."

The driver pulled into the emergency entrance at the hospital and while the emergency crew opened the doors, Derek found a place to park close by. Katie and her counterpart unloaded the stretcher, sent the wheels to the asphalt and quickly wheeled her inside. Nancy followed and Derek came running up. "Is she still out, Nancy?" he asked.

"Yes, not a peep, Derek!"

"Goodness, what could be wrong?"

Katie was following the stretcher and added, "My feelings exactly! We haven't heard a sound from her since we loaded her."

As the stretcher entered the ER area, the staff clicked into high gear and helped the paramedics move Carolyn onto their table. Carolyn groaned as she reached the table. "Oh!" Derek exclaimed, tears clouding his vision.

He reached for her hand, but his hand fell short and he touched her thigh. "Carolyn! Are you waking up?"

Still with her eyes closed, Carolyn whispered, "Oh, hurts bad!" and brought her hands up to rest on her abdomen.

The nurse looked at Derek. "Carolyn?" he nodded. "What hurts, Honey?" She reached and took her hand.

"Inside," she groaned again, "… cramps," she said the words only in a whisper.

Dr. Simon entered the crowded room, looked around, then at Carolyn and exclaimed, "It's Jane Doe! What's going on?"

Derek spoke up and said, "Doctor, we don't know anything, other than Carolyn turned pale and fainted a few minutes ago."

The doctor scowled. "Are you her dad?"

He looked sheepish and gave the man a slight smile. "Well, we think so. That's why we're calling her Carolyn and now she lives at my house. Since she's been there from the rehab center she's been sick and vomited twice, kind of like morning sickness. She's still not remembering what happened or her life before, except this morning she recognized the face on the poster as the man."

"Hmm, and you are?"

"Derek Casbah."

Dr. Simon's head had been going back and forth while Derek spoke, so he nodded. "Yes, I'd say there's a definite family resemblance, but she's still amnesic?"

"That's right. A while ago she had a nightmare, but she remembered nothing after she woke up. Today she saw the poster in the bank window and knew the face was of the man who did the deed, but she remembered nothing else."

Dr. Simon nodded, stepped closer, then turned to Carolyn who was holding her hands over her abdomen, but she was groaning, tossing her head and rolling from side to side. "Carolyn? You're having cramps?"

"Awful!" was the only word she spit out between groans.

Immediately, he turned to the ER nurse and said, "Get Dr. Rosen down here STAT! I think she's aborting! She needs a D & C!"

Derek was still in the room. "You say she's losing the baby, Doctor?"

"I believe so!"

While Carolyn was having emergency surgery in Blairsville Hospital, Natt Thomas was experiencing an emergency of his own in his store in Vansville. He had just taken someone's picture card and placed it in one of the mailers to send away for processing. As the door closed behind the customer, he looked up toward the front of the store and saw his granddad silently topple from his favorite chair behind the counter. Of course, Natt was on the move instantly. Brad gave out one long sigh and stretched out on the floor. Natt rushed over to him and saw that his chest continued to rise and fall, he was relieved at that.

The man didn't seem to be in any distress, but Natt unbuttoned his top button anyway and said, "Grandad, can you hear me?"

When there was no response, he continued to watch him, but he left the man's side and picked up the handset from the counter and punched in 911. As soon as he gave the details, he also called his gramma's house. She answered on the second ring and Natt said, "Gramma Joyce, Grandad just toppled from his chair to the floor. I've called emergency and the ambulance is on its way. Just thought you'd want to know since you'll probably want to go with him to the hospital."

"Oh, yes! Natt, of course! I'll be there in a jiffy!"

"I figured that, Gramma."

On Thursdays there was no doctor at the clinic down the street, so any medical emergency had to go to Blairsville anyway. Natt wondered if his granddad was having another stroke or if it was something more life-threatening such as a heart attack. However, if he remembered his first aid class, the man would be in pain and probably fighting for his life if he was having a heart attack. He knew, however, that whatever would happen in Brad's life, any new emergency would probably take him out of the store permanently. Natt felt badly about that, the store had been his life for so many years.

Something like this couldn't be anticipated, but he wondered how soon his cousin Matt would be able to leave his present job. They had decided when Matt came from Orlando for the wedding that he'd be prepared to leave there and come to Vansville to help Natt in the store. As he waited for the ambulance and for Joyce, he debated calling Matt. Should he call him immediately or wait until they found out what had happened to Brad? He hadn't decided when the back door of the store crashed against the back wall.

Joyce burst through the door and faintly, in the distance, while the door was open, Natt could hear the siren as the ambulance approached. "Oh!" Joyce exclaimed, "I barely got here in time! I can hear the ambulance coming. Did you call Roger?"

"No, Gramma, just you and the ambulance."

"Well, call him now! He can't get here before the ambulance, but he'll need to know Brad's gone to the hospital."

"I'll do that as soon as they have him loaded, Gramma."

"Yes, yes! That's good."

The ambulance backed up to the front door, Natt hurried over and opened it for them. The paramedics opened the back of the ambulance and pulled out the stretcher, then came in. Joyce stood over Brad and was frantically gesturing them toward the counter. "Oh, he's over here on the floor! Come on, please hurry!"

Natt didn't say anything, the man was on the floor, but he was breathing and didn't seem to be in any pain or distress. "Yes, Ma'am, we're coming!" one of the paramedics said.

Fearfully, Joyce looked from Brad to the paramedic and asked, "What's the matter with him? Why would he fall down like that? He was sitting on that chair, why did he fall off? He sits there all day and drinks coffee, why should he fall to the floor?"

Smiling at the distressed woman, the paramedic said, "Ma'am, we'll let the docs at the hospital figure that one out. Will you be coming?"

"Oh, yes, of course! My grandson'll call our pastor he'll meet us there soon."

"That's fine. Any other family?"

"Oh, he'll call his dad, too. Won't you, Natt?"

"Of course, Gramma. I'll take care of everything don't worry about anything but Grandad. Dad and Mom will probably be up in a few hours. I'll have them meet you at the hospital when they arrive. I'll need to stay to keep the store open."

From the doorway, she called back. "You're a good boy, Natt."

Natt had to chuckle about that as he watched the paramedic slam the back door of the ambulance. He figured as a store owner and a business man in town, with a wife and a house of their own, he was a bit more than just a boy. But then, grammas remembered when their grandchildren were born, she'd probably helped his mom change his diapers a few times. He'd chalk that one up to experience.

Finally, he'd had to text Roger about his granddad, but he'd reached his dad at his office at the newspaper in Atlanta. He assured his son that he'd contact Natt's mom and they'd do everything they could to arrive at the Blairsville Hospital as soon as possible. When he hung up from that phone call, Natt still debated calling his cousin.

However, before he could decide his phone rang. Marcy was calling and asked, "Honey, do you know why the ambulance just left town?"

"Yes, Sweetheart. Grandad just collapsed on the floor. I called them and they've taken him and Gramma to the hospital. I called Dad they'll come as soon as they can."

"Oh, I'm sorry! I guess you'll call Matt to come?"

"You don't think I should wait to find out about Grandad?"

"Why wait? You two decided if anything happened major in his life he'd be out of the store even if he lived."

"Yes, you're right. I'll give him a call."

"Good, I'll see you at five o'clock, Honey. Love you."

"Back acha, Girl!"

Natt disconnected and looked up another number. He called and was surprised when the man himself answered. "Matt! Surprised to hear your voice in the middle of the day like this."

"I was taking a break. What's on your mind? Is it Uncle Brad?"

"Yes, I just sent him and Gramma to the hospital in the ambulance."

"Got any clues?"

"No, I'm guessing it's another stroke, but worse than the mini-strokes he's had. He toppled off his chair here at the store. If I hadn't been watching him I'd never heard him, he never let out a peep, but he didn't respond when I spoke to him."

"Sounds likely. Say, I'll wrap up my interests here. It'll take me a few days, but with loading stuff and stopping everything it'll take, say a week. How about we plan on me being there a week from Monday to start with you? Can you make it till then?"

Natt chuckled. "I don't see much other choice, do you?"

"Well, no not really. Brother's too wrapped up in his life, he couldn't help you out. Actually, he's not cut out for a job like that."

"That's the truth! Okay, I'll see you in a week."

"Oh, could you rent me, or at least enquire from Ms Isabel about a cabin?"

"Sure, not a problem. It'll be all set for you."

"Great!"

Natt hung up and a customer walked in the front door. "What happened? Where's Brad? Did you have to call the ambulance for him?"

"Yes. I think maybe he had another stroke."

The man shook his head. "Such a shame. Will miss him in the store."

"Yes, I think the whole town will."

"I know that! He's been in this store a very long time. Achally, it was him got those gas pumps in out there. Hadda go to Blairsville for gas before that."

"Wow! I didn't know that."

"Yep, take care, fella." Obviously, the man wanted to start the grapevine, but didn't need anything from the store. Natt sighed; life was like that in a small town. The local grapevine was more than a live, growing thing. As Natt sat in his silent store he wondered what other excitement people from a small town had to do but get on a grapevine.

Friday afternoon Ramon brought his hikers back to DeLord's place. As his people packed their backpacks in their trunks, a car pulled on the lot with just one man in it. He found a parking place, then looked at all the bedraggled hikers and watched them store their things, then get in the cars and leave the lot. One man remained, his backpack leaning against his leg. The young man shut off his car, then stepped from it as Ramon turned toward him.

Holding out his hand, he walked toward Ramon and said, "Hi, I'm Jerry Monahan. I'm here for that interview you promised me."

Ramon took the young man's hand and shook it warmly. Grinning he said, "Good to meet you, Jerry, I'm Ramon DeLord, come on inside. Couldn't have timed that better if we'd tried. As you can tell I just brought a group back." He gave the young man a grin. They turned toward the office door and Ramon said, "You'll meet my wife and son inside. As sweaty as I am, you'll need to excuse me for a few minutes while I take a shower. Five days on a trail leaves a lot to be desired in the cleanliness department. Mind you, there are creeks and pools along the way, but it's nothing like a hot shower in your own bathroom!"

"Oh, I understand completely!"

Ramon opened the office door and ushered Jerry in. Sandy, with Jon on her lap was at the desk and smiled at the young man. "Hi, glad you could make it, Jerry. I'm Sandy."

Jerry looked briefly at Sandy's chair, then looked up at her again and grinned. "Now I know why your name sounded familiar! You used to go to my church in Blairsville. Sandy, you played the piano sometimes and gave some concerts."

"Yes! So that's who you are! We both wondered why your name rang bells but we couldn't place you." Ramon answered. "So you want to be a hiking guide?"

"I sure do! Can I start right away?"

Ramon slapped the young man on the back and said, "We can get you on as guide-in-training on Monday, if that's soon enough."

"Oh, that'll be great! How long must I train?"

"We send you out with at least two of our guides so you get the feel of how we work then we'll go from there."

"Great!"

Ramon picked up some papers from the desk that Sandy had pulled from a file cabinet, handed them to him and said, "Jerry, read these through carefully. Fill out what needs filling out and bring that part back. The rest of it tells what you need to know about our operation, what we expect and what you'll need for your pack. Surely you can get that by Monday."

Enthusiastically, Jerry reached for the papers and grinned at Ramon. "I will! When should I be here?"

"You'll go out with me on Monday. After that hike we'll have to figure out who to send you with for the next hike. All our hikes leave the parking lot out here at eight o'clock, but we always feed our guides breakfast on the day they leave, so be here around seven. We'll see you then and have a good weekend, Jerry."

Jerry grabbed the stack of papers Ramon held out. "I will, thanks!" With a spring in his steps, Jerry walked out of the office and nearly danced into his car. He waved jauntily to the people still in the office before he left.

"That was a short interview, Honey!"

"Yup! I figured since we knew him we could trust him to do it right. Besides, I want to take a shower real soon."

Jerry had barely left the parking lot and Ramon still stood at the window, when a white sheriff's car drove in and parked in the same space as Jerry had. Ramon looked out the window and scowled. "Love, did you know the sheriff was coming by? He came without his siren, so it can't be an emergency."

"No, I had no idea!"

Ramon muttered, "Well, so much for that shower...."

Sandy grinned and pointedly sniffed the air. "It doesn't smell too bad in here, Honey."

"Mmm, thanks a lot, Love."

The big man left his car and started for the front door, but Ramon opened the office door and said, "Sheriff? We're here in the office, what can I do for you?"

Sheriff Winslow looked at Ramon's hiking clothes and said, "Did I catch you at a bad time? I guess I could come back, but it's hard to catch you when you're home, Ramon. Anyway, I only had a few questions for you."

Ramon stepped back from the door then motioned the sheriff to a chair. "I got back from a hike a bit ago, but a new man came by who wants to be a guide. We just got done with a short interview. I'd planned to take a shower, but..." he shrugged.

The sheriff grinned at the young man. "I only have a couple of questions then I'll leave you alone for a good long shower. And a good long evening with your wife."

"Okay... what's on your mind?"

The sheriff slouched into the chair facing Ramon and started out by saying, "I'm looking for a few good men..."

Ramon scowled. "Umm, that's the motto for the Marines, Sheriff. I never was in the military, let alone the Marines."

"Yup, you got one?"

"Well, I have an ex-Marine who's one of my guides."

Grinning, Sheriff Winslow said, "Yup, he's the man I'm thinking about. Tell me what you know about him."

Ramon grinned back and asked, "Why should I do that?"

"Well, it's like this. I need you to give him up and let me have him."

"Hmm, I'd have to think about that!"

Jon had been quiet, just sitting on Sandy's lap and looking the big man over, but now he pointed to the sheriff and said, "Man, gun!"

"Hi, there, little guy! You okay?"

"Uh huh, gun!"

"Yeah, but I don't use it much, little fella." He turned a little in the chair so Jon couldn't see the gun quite so well then raised his leg to cross it over his knee. He looked back at Ramon and said, "So, what can you tell me about your ex-Marine?"

Ramon sank back in his desk chair, acting very relaxed and said, "And you still haven't told me why I should do that, Sheriff."

The older man sighed, "I haven't? Here I thought it was all out there..."

"Nope. Out with it!" Ramon's eyes twinkled. "I can be just as cagey as you. I didn't go to school with you, but I know you aren't much older than me."

"Well, it seems as though the powers-that-be at the state capitol have told me to hire a new man and have his base of operations be the Vansville area. Mr. Thomas's name came to mind and I'm wondering if he'd be a good man for the job."

"Oh, wow!" Sandy exclaimed.

Acting stunned, Ramon scowled and asked, "You were told to hire a new man? The state has money for another deputy?"

"Is kind of surprising, isn't it?" Sheriff Winslow swallowed and added, "I was sort of speechless when the bossman told me."

Acting very dramatic, Ramon exclaimed, "Sheriff, he's one of my three best guides. How could I give him up?"

"One of your three best guides. How many do you have?"

"Three."

"I see. Care to tell me more?"

Acting as if he was really contemplating his words, he rested his elbows on the armrests and held up his chin, but worked very hard to show the sheriff how serious he was. However, his eyes twinkling, he finally said, "He's very conscientious, reliable, goes the extra mile, intelligent, never shirks his duty, goes to church whenever he can… he'd look great in a deputy's uniform… any other words you need to hear?"

Grinning, the sheriff said, "So how soon could I have him?"

"Well, see, it's like this… we've been so busy this season that our men only get one day off between hikes. That's our fulltime men then there's me. I take the short hikes so I'm always home on Sundays."

The sheriff scratched his jaw. "Thought you said you just gave an interview."

"Yeah, but he'll have to go out on at least three hikes with our present guides and then we'll have to evaluate. Oh, you have Mr. Thomas's okay on this?"

"No, I'm on a fact-finding quest first."

"I see. You got all your facts?"

"I have all I need."

"Good, no sooner than August first."

"Perfect! Thanks, Ramon. Good to talk to you. By the way, when would I be able to speak with Mr. Thomas, when's his next day off?"

"Ah, that would be Monday afternoon starting around four o'clock."

"Great, I'll sit in Ms Isabel's driveway until he shows."

Ramon chuckled. "I'm sure she'd love to have your shiny, white, sheriff's car stationed in her driveway until then."

"Oh, I know she would! I was only there a day or two ago. She pointed out to me how snazzy my car was. After I asked a few questions she ushered me out pretty quick!"

Ramon and Sandy both laughed. "I believe that!" Sandy exclaimed.

"Ms Sandy?" the sheriff looked at the lady in the chair, "Isabel told me you were her all time favorite renter; but I'm sure she's told you that, too."

"Yes, I love her to death!"

Putting his hands on the armrests, he looked at Jon and grinned at the little boy. "Little guy, you keep your daddy in line, okay?"

"Dada good. Wuv Dada."

Sheriff Winslow stood up and walked over to Jon. Ruffling his hair, he said, "Yup, your daddy's a good man, so's your mommy."

Jon grinned and put his arm around Sandy's neck. Laying his head on her chest, he said, "Mama good. Wuv Mama."

"How precious," he whispered. "Keep up the good work, guys. See you again."

"We're too busy to do anything else, Sheriff."

Sheriff Winslow touched his hat, walked out and closed the door behind him. As he stepped into the sparkly sheriff's car, Ramon pushed himself from his chair and said, "Well, I think I'll try and get that shower now. Now that I've seen all the important people, I think I'll wash off all this trail grime."

Sandy giggled. "It's about time, Honey!"

Ramon grinned at his pretty wife. "Come help me?"

"Of course!"

Ramon touched Sandy's shoulder. "Come on, Love, let's go!" He grabbed his backpack and started down the hall. "You know we may need to hurry before someone else comes!"

"That is the absolute truth!" Sandy exclaimed.

# Thirteen

When he'd arrived back at the convenience store from the hike he'd noticed the poster in the window and decided that his first and foremost action had to be to put plenty of empty space between himself and the woman he'd ridden back to the city with. Of course, they'd been quite close in the past few days, she'd recognize the picture. He grabbed out his backpack from her trunk, slammed the lid closed and high-tailed it from the lot. Thankfully, there was a huge crowd at the bus stop, so he moved quickly across the street, weaving his way through the crowd with his head down, but didn't stop. He wouldn't take the bus anywhere. Someone in that crowd could have seen the picture Emily had seen.

By the time the bus came and the crowd all got on he'd moved far enough down the sidewalk that he'd reached an alley and ducked in. He was pretty sure the woman would do as the poster said and call 911. Cops would be swarming in only minutes and he wasn't going to be anywhere close by for them to find him! In fact, as his stride lengthened, he heard sirens nearby. His stomach growled, but he'd have to find some other way to fill it. Buying food in a store was not an option, not with posters in the windows! He walked on, zigzagging down streets and alleys. He needed to disappear - fast!

As the day turned to dusk he plopped down beside a huge dumpster that was behind a large restaurant. Pulling off his huge backpack he sighed, the weight off his back was a relief. He leaned back against the dumpster to rest. The aromas coming from the restaurant drew out the grumbles from his stomach again. He was really hungry! Lunch on the trail was a long time ago and it hadn't been much. Too bad he didn't have one granola bar in his pack. Only moments later the back door of the restaurant opened. He grabbed the straps of his pack and scooted behind the big bin out of sight.

Two people came from the restaurant toward the dumpster, chatting about their busy shift. Dinner time on Monday wasn't usually so busy, but it had been today. They each threw a huge garbage bag in the dumpster and both of them landed with a dull plop. The people were glad the restaurant was emptying out, their shift was about to end. They hurried back into the restaurant and closed the door.

The man with the pack waited in the silence that followed the door slamming for several minutes. No need to call attention and get caught. He left his pack on the ground and hurried up the outside of the dumpster and saw the bags still steaming. The aromas coming from them made his stomach growl again. He leaped into the big bin and frantically worked on the first bag to get it open. Scraps were good when you were as hungry as he was!

Most of what he found in the garbage bag were loose scraps. He started filling his mouth immediately, but while he dug through them, he found several boxes. The scraps were most likely table scraps, but the boxes might be leftovers the kitchen was getting rid of. He continued to eat, but he pulled out all the boxes he could find, there were quite a few. He even opened the second bag and found more. Maybe he'd find an empty warehouse where he could hole up for a while until the craze to find him had worn off. He could use the food any time, as long as it wasn't bad. By the smells coming from the bags it was far from bad.

When he couldn't eat any more, he found a way to make all the boxes into one good sized package. After searching around in the dimly lit dumpster, he found some twine and tied his package so he could carry it when his backpack was on his back. Carefully, he climbed out of the dumpster. It was full dark now the only light was the streetlights on the alley and the even dimmer lights from the buildings. Those lights were few and far between, since they were on the back of the buildings and the windows were small. With a groan, he shouldered his backpack and adjusted it, then picked up his food package and started off again. He yawned, he'd gotten up a long time ago and the day hadn't turned out like he'd hoped.

Eventually, he heard a large clock somewhere in the city bong out the time. It was ten o'clock, but he'd finally reached the warehouse district of the city. He began looking for one of the huge buildings that didn't have trucks backed up to the loading docks or had a swarm of men either on the docks or coming from the building ready to go home. He desperately needed one that was quiet and empty. He needed to get this pack off his back. Hiking a trail with it was one thing, but city streets were a whole new ballgame. City streets with a huge backpack on your back was rather obvious and not what he wanted.

Finally, the last building before the open lot was dark and quiet. Now to find a door into the place that wasn't locked. He started with the door that was closest to him. As he moved around the building he began to wonder if he'd have to pitch his tent in the field. He shook his head that would be too obvious, any patrols would see the tent and pull him in.

He was nearly back to the first door when he found a very small door. He nearly missed it in the dark, but he wearily put his hand on the knob. Not expecting it to turn, he was surprised to feel it move when he turned his hand. He pushed the door open and encountered darkness so profound it was like a blanket hanging two inches from his face.

Undaunted, because he was so tired, he took two steps through the doorway and closed the door behind him. He would find his sleeping bag and stretch out right here. Morning was soon enough to explore the place for a better hiding place. In the darkness he fumbled with the straps keeping the pack on his back and shrugged the straps off. Before he let go of the pack he found the clips holding his sleeping bag in place and quickly unrolled it. He stretched out and let out a long sigh. He was exhausted. Sleep enveloped him instantly.

His growling stomach woke him in the morning. It took a few minutes to orient himself, since the room he was in only had small windows high up in the room, normally where a second story would be and not much light came in. Still with his legs inside his sleeping bag, he grabbed his food package and dug in to quiet his noisy stomach. After it was quiet, he found a place to relieve himself then started through the building to find a good hiding place to live for a while. That didn't take long. Toward the back of the building there was a staircase that led up to a small second floor. It was big enough he could hide there easily. However the major problem he found was there was no water in the warehouse and none close by outside. He'd have to watch the working warehouses for a time to sneak in to wash and fill his canteen.

After he'd found his place and made himself as comfortable as he could, he sat on his sleeping bag to assess the situation. He liked the woman he'd gone on the hike with well enough, but that wasn't his usual habit. He didn't like using a woman he knew. However, he'd been without for a while. He knew there were lots of young women who shopped and got their gas at that convenience store. The woman in the spring had been the prettiest he'd ever seen, but the woman by the quiet stream had been the last and his body was screaming for release. *Boy, it was hard getting back from there! Maybe next time I'll keep the car, just burn up the evidence.*

He had to remember his face was on a poster, probably in every store in Atlanta. He had to lay low, prison life was the pits! Of course, that face on the poster was clean shaven his beard had started on the four day hike, now it was five days old. He'd wait a few more days for it to grow more and cover his face better. He had enough food in his package, he could wait that long. Besides, he needed duct tape.

Emily worked at her job. With a four day weekend she'd gotten a bit behind, but working instead of taking breaks for the next four days, she caught up and by Friday afternoon left for another weekend with an empty in-box. She was downright proud of herself! With all the extra work, she'd put Ron out of her mind. After all, she'd only met him briefly at the convenience store those few times when she'd stopped for gas or a quick snack in the weeks before she and her friends had scheduled their hike. They had urged her to find someone to go with her. Ron had certainly not been a boyfriend!

She didn't look for him at the convenience store when she stopped in, but she remembered him when she saw his face on the poster. She kept looking at the headlines on the papers in the dispensers to see if he'd been captured. He must have really moved fast that afternoon and with a pack on his back! The cops had come almost before she'd hung up and searched for quite a while before they finally left. Without their quarry.

She sighed it seemed criminals could hide better than the average citizen. Perhaps that's why they were criminals. Did they have special schools for potential criminals to teach them how to disappear? Perhaps when he was in prison he and other prisoners had bragged on staying out so long and how they'd done it. She wondered if perhaps hiding had been one of the reasons Ron had been so willing to go on that hike. Surely a man with a backpack as big as the one Ron had carried would stick out in a city as big as Atlanta! Someone would surely spot him and turn him in soon. That was one reason the police put up those posters all over so that people were aware that a criminal was in the area.

She looked at her gas gauge as she left the office building parking lot on Friday. She hadn't used much gas, but she was tired and hot, the last of June was hot in Atlanta. She punched the control to send the air conditioner higher and let the cool air blow on her face. She could use some snacks and the convenience store was on her way home. A grilled cheese from the deli would make a good supper. She'd make that stop.

A disheveled man with a beard walked onto the parking lot as a car with a woman alone pulled up into the last slot in front of the convenience store late Friday afternoon. The man's heart sped up as the woman stepped from her car. He swallowed a grin and kept his face blank. It wouldn't do for anyone to notice him. He loitered around the pumps, perhaps people would think he was an attendant who monitored the pumps. He forgot how much like a tramp he looked in four days without changing clothes or bathing.

As he expected, the woman went inside. He walked around and around moving from one pump to another, trying to stay out of sight. After all, his face was still on the poster in the window. Cars came to the pumps, some drivers went inside first; others swiped their cards and pumped their gas. Still the woman didn't come out. Other people came outside and went to other cars parked in front of the store. He watched the door, his hand in his pocket fingering the small roll of duct tape he had at the ready.

He quickly moved to the bushes around the store that were closer to the parked cars. It had to be fifteen minutes later the woman he'd had his eye on came from the store. Her purse strap was on her shoulder. One hand was full with a large Styrofoam cup and the other held a large take-out box. She took a long sip through the straw then walked to her car. With her back to him, she set the take-out box on the roof top and reached for the door handle. The man made his move. He was at her back as the car door opened.

Emily felt his heat, even before he touched her and let out a loud scream. She whirled around; the large cup hit the man in the chest. The top flew off and fell to the ground between them, but the contents splashed all over the man and in his eyes. A man inside was watching one of his favorite customers as she made her way to her car. He didn't hear her scream but he saw the man and pushed a button on his side of the counter, twice.

Ralph Ronald Wever had no place to hide or run to when the sirens and the police cruiser entered the convenience store parking lot that Friday afternoon. He was still trying to wipe the sticky liquid from his eyes.

It was five o'clock Friday afternoon. Derek waved to Marlene, then closed his office door and headed out the back door. After her D & C yesterday, Dr. Simon had admitted Carolyn for observation for twenty-four hours. He told Derek he could collect her and take her home after five. She had indeed had a miscarriage, now she was free of any long term problems that her abductor had created. She still had the aircast on her arm, but that would come off next week. Both of the sutured places had healed well. Derek was most happy that they hadn't had to decide what to do with the baby she had carried.

He hurried from his parking place at the bank to the hospital and went to the floor where the room was to which she had been moved. Since no one knew if her abductor had been caught, Derek had insisted, once her surgery was over and it was determined she must stay over night that the sheriff supply some protection for Carolyn while she was at the hospital. His request had been quickly fulfilled after all, he was a bank president. As he hurried onto the ward, the deputy stood up, watching for him.

"Mr. Casbah, she's already for you to sign out. You just need to stop at the desk. They have papers there for you to sign."

Derek turned toward the desk and the nurse stood up with the papers. Quickly, he signed what needed to be signed and a CNA produced a wheelchair to follow Derek to Carolyn's room. "So, everything's all right?" he asked the nurse.

While she ripped duplicates apart and made two stacks, she said, "It seems so, Mr. Casbah, once she woke up, she hasn't had any pain. Since it's Friday and Dr. Simon wanted her in to see him on Monday for the cast, he took it off this morning and everything checks out on X-ray, so she doesn't even have that any more." Holding out one of the stacks, she added, "Here are your copies, Mr. Casbah. Your daughter was a model patient."

"Wow! That's great! Now if they'd just find that criminal we could breath easy."

"We're all rooting for that, Mr. Casbah!"

Derek sighed, "Maybe it'll happen one day soon. Since Carolyn's injuries have all healed completely, maybe it's time to find the criminal."

"Yes, maybe so."

He turned from the desk and the CNA followed him down the hall to the room where the deputy waited for him. While Derek stood and watched Carolyn settle into the chair, the deputy's phone rang and he pulled it from his waist carrier. "Sheriff?" he said softly.

Derek took a step back to be close to the man, but he couldn't hear what the sheriff said. Instead, the deputy said, "Sheriff, he's right here. Want me to put you on speaker phone?"

The sheriff must have agreed, because the deputy pushed a button and the sheriff's voice said, "Mr. Casbah, I understand you're there. Just thought I'd tell you the news I just now received via a wire from Atlanta. Ralph Wever was apprehended moments ago. He hasn't confessed anything, but the man fits all the evidence and definitely is the man in the picture that has been posted around. I believe your Carolyn is safe!"

"Sheriff," Derek said, after a sigh, "You can't know how relieved I am! This is wonderful news! Now I can take Carolyn home and we can enjoy the weekend. Thanks for thinking to call here with the news."

"You're welcome, Mr. Casbah. I'm glad I caught you."

"Yes, I am too."

As the deputy closed his phone the CNA brought Carolyn to the door and said, "After you, Mr. Casbah. I guess your car's at the entrance?"

"Yes, the guard gave me fifteen minutes to get it moved."

The deputy fell in behind the little group and said, "If he's still concerned, I'll set him straight, don't worry."

"Thanks, but it doesn't seem like we'll need that."

Once they were in the car, Derek turned to Carolyn and smiled. When she looked at him, he said, "So, you had a miscarriage, your arm's out of the cast, the man's been caught, now all we're up against is your memory."

Carolyn shook her head, put her hands around her head, covering her ears and sighed. "I know, but that's the worst of all! It seems like there's a rock-iron fortress around it and a six foot thick door guarding it! When will it open?"

"In God's time, my dear, in God's time. Actually, it probably wouldn't be bad if you never remembered what that man did to you, just so you could remember what was going on in your life before all this happened to you. I really think that's what we need to pray for." Derek touched her hand. "Of course, you know, I would be a happy man if you never left."

"Yes, I'd settle for that." She was quiet for several minutes, then pulled in a deep breath and said, "You know, if I had a job it's probably gone now. I've been away from wherever for over a month, isn't that it?"

"Yes, you were in the hospital for a week and you've been home with me for at least four more. I doubt, unless you were your own boss that someone held the job for you. It's too bad none of this was your fault."

"Yes, that's what I figured, too."

Derek squeezed Carolyn's hand and said, "Sweetheart, there's no rush for you to find a job. I'm very well placed. Your granddad left me a good sized estate, which I've invested with a very wise man. I, myself, have made very good money over my lifetime, so there is no rush for you to support yourself."

"Maybe so, Dad, but I want to feel productive. Now that I know I'm not pregnant and I feel well, I'd sure like to get a job, but how can I until I get my memory back? You've told me a lot about my early life, but who knows what's happened since then!"

"Perhaps we'll have to wait for that. Like I say, don't rush it, though."

As they turned on the road that led to Derek's house, he said, "Oh, Sam called me this morning. He said he'd called the cement plant and a truck was to come today and pour the walls for the pool. He said it'll cure until Wednesday next week then they'll come back and remove the forms.

Of course, they'll have a few things to do once it's cured, but it'll be ready for use a week from tomorrow, he said!"

Carolyn's eyes sparkled. "That'll be great, Dad!"

"I thought you might be happy about that."

Derek pulled in the garage, turned off the car and put down the door. He and Carolyn walked inside and Mrs. Beecham met them. "Mr. Casbah, you had a call. Sheriff Winslow left a message that you're to call him."

"Mrs. Beecham, how long ago was that?"

"Probably a half hour ago. Maybe it was forty-five minutes. I left a note at your place, but didn't write down the time."

"I think I already got the message he wanted me to have, but thank you."

All three of them went to the kitchen. Mrs. Beecham quickly fixed her own plate, put the dinner she'd fixed on the table then left for her apartment. Derek and Carolyn sat down to eat and Derek said the blessing. They'd barely raised their heads when the landline phone rang. Derek sighed, he hated interruptions at mealtimes. He plucked the handset from the wall phone and said, "Derek Casbah, can I help you?"

"What do you mean canceling my credit cards?" a voice shrieked into his ear.

"Millie," Derek said, calmly, "it seems that you left me no choice in the matter. You never said where you were going and that I shouldn't try to reach you. Those cards had your name on them of course, but I gave them to you. They were linked to my accounts. When you said you were leaving and not to contact you, I felt no obligation to pay your bills any longer. My lawyer has drawn up divorce papers. He will find you and they will be delivered. I won't say I'm sorry, only that you've brought this on yourself. You have a good life, Millie. Don't bother calling back or coming by again."

"Well, of all the nerve!" There was a crash and the dial tone buzzed in his ear.

Derek turned off the handset and replaced it. He shook his head and said, "I wondered if she'd ever call. The woman can't be too bright if she thought she could use those cards for a whole month and not realize they weren't any good."

"You won't try to reconcile?"

"Carolyn, I should never have hooked up with her at all! If I had stayed true to the Lord way back when you were in school, I'd never have looked at her twice. I guess I must say, since I did, that I was lonely for a companion and she came along. You had your own interests, your brother wanted nothing to do with me so I looked to Millie for company. I was not on speaking terms with the Lord by that time, so the fact that she wasn't a Christian didn't worry me. I have regretted my decision many times since I married her, believe me."

When they were finished with dinner clean-up, Carolyn looked at Derek and asked, "Dad, could we go out back and look at the pool? I'd really like to see it up close. I haven't dared go close enough to look in it."

"Of course, my dear! The last I took a look was after that storm we had. I'm sure it's changed a lot since then. Let's go see."

They walked out onto the deck, then across it to the stairs down to the backyard. Some ways away they came to the pile of dirt that Sam and Ernest hadn't moved yet then walked around it to look into the hole. There were wooden forms on all four sides filled with cement and the bottom had a layer of cement covering the ground. Around all four sides there was a walk bordering the walls in the ground. The job looked very professional and Derek was pleased with Sam's work.

"Well, it looks like they've done a find job and its ready to cure like Sam said. Are you ready for it to be filled?"

Looking up at him with sparkles in her eyes, she said, "Dad, if you say I'm a swimmer, I'm ready! Looking at it from the house it didn't look as big as it does from here." Noticing that one end was much deeper than the other end, she asked, "Will they put in a diving board? Was that part of it?"

"Oh, yes! They must wait for this to cure then he'll place the board and its apparatus in place. Looks like he's got a couple of steps at the shallow end. I think he's contracted with a water supplier to fill the pool when it's ready. We'll have to read up on all the things that must be done to an in-ground pool, though."

"That's great! I am excited."

Sunday was a beautiful day. It was nearly the end of June, but the temperature was pleasant. After church, the DeLords came to Derek's house for steak dinner on the patio and an afternoon to spend together as family. Japa and Jon loved their time together. After Carolyn cleared dishes and food away, Jon was asleep on Sandy's lap and all four of them were sitting around relaxing, Derek asked, "Did you two hear that the criminal has been caught?"

"Really?" Sandy exclaimed. "Oh, that's great! Did the sheriff tell you?"

"Yes, while I was at the hospital collecting Carolyn he called the deputy. With his new-fangled phone we were all able to hear what the sheriff said. It was so recent that all he could tell me was that the man was in custody, but that was his face on the posters. He even had some duct tape in his pocket! Still, that's enough for us!"

"I'd say!" Ramon agreed.

Carolyn added, "I hope they put him away for a good long time!"

"Oh, they should, my dear, you identified him as the man who abducted you and there was some of his hair and other evidence on the body of the girl down south, so he's in on charges of murder and attempted murder. He shouldn't be out in this lifetime!"

"Just to think he'd done what he did to two women is enough to make me sick!" Sandy said. "God can forgive all sin, but that man needs to be punished for his actions."

"I know and I'm so glad he's been caught."

Sometime later, Ramon asked, "Dad, did you hear that the sheriff was in town recently?"

"No, was there something else that's been below the radar?"

"Well, I guess you could call it that. I'm not sure it's something that needs to be kept quiet, only until the other person involved knows."

Derek was quiet for a minute then he said, "Sheriff Winslow did call me the other day at the bank. He asked me what I knew about Eric Thomas."

Ramon grinned at his step-father. "Yeah, that's it."

Carolyn could tell she was the only one who didn't know what the men were talking about, so she asked, "What about him? He's a nice guy surely he's not in trouble for anything, is he? I mean, he's a hiking guide!"

Ramon's eyes twinkled. "Carolyn, are you interested in Eric?"

Her cheeks turned a bright red. She cleared her throat. "Well, only because he's a nice guy. He's not in trouble, is he?"

Derek chuckled. "Not that we're aware of, but I was astonished that the department wants to hire another deputy for the Vansville area. Except for what happened to Carolyn I thought this little burg was pretty safe and quiet."

"Yes, that's true, but after he left our place I pulled a map up on the computer and the rural area around Vansville is pretty big. Because of that I'm not surprised."

"So he came to see you?"

"Yes, we had a good chat. He also went to see Isabel." Ramon grinned. "She gave him some of her cinnamon buns and told him to hire him quick."

Derek laughed. "Leave it to Isabel!"

"She also told him to get his snazzy car off her parking lot."

"She is one delightful lady!"

After a moment's thought, Derek asked, "Do you think he'll do it?"

"I don't know, really. He'd be the perfect one, with his military background, but he seems happy leading hikes."

"True, but he never told you he'd stay forever."

"No, just that at present he felt the Lord leading him in that direction." Glancing at Carolyn, he added, "Maybe he'd stick around for another reason."

Derek didn't comment about that, but said, "The sheriff asked if I knew anything about his background, but all I knew was that he'd been in Afghanistan for a tour of duty."

"Well, he was there for two tours and helped open up a pretty hot spot. After Sheriff left, Sandy pulled out his paperwork and he majored in criminal justice in college."

"Ah, sounds like the perfect candidate for the job! My goodness! Not to put down your industry, but the man surely isn't working at his potential!"

"Could be he wanted to take it easy a while after Afghanistan."

"That's what we wondered, especially when he didn't want to commit for a long time. We'll see what he says. He's bringing his group back tomorrow afternoon. Sheriff said he'd sit in Isabel's parking lot until he gets there."

Derek chuckled. "Think she'll let him?"

All three of the others laughed and Ramon said, "Don't know, I guess we'll see. That snazzy car can call quite a bit of attention."

In Baton Rouge, Lance put his suitcase in the car. Alli and Linda had decided she'd stay another week to help get the house ready for the realtor. As Lance sat down in the car, Linda stepped up beside it and kissed her husband, but she said, "Honey, remember, we've been gone a week. Unless things have changed, you need to try to find Carolyn. Maybe find your dad."

Lance sighed, "I know, it's on my calendar to check the internet. I still have no idea where Carolyn could be or what could have happened, but I'll do some calling around. Believe me, Sweetheart, I'll miss you, but it's important for you to be here for Alli. Take good care of each other and I'll see you next Saturday."

"Yes, Honey. I'll miss you, but I'll be waiting for you, believe me." Lance had kissed his little one, but she hadn't wakened when he and Linda walked out to his car.

Eric brought his hikers to his favorite place Sunday afternoon to camp. He decided that the high plateau with the spring fed, frigid pool was the favorite of all the guides, because they all seemed light hearted when they knew this camping spot was part of their hike. The air was always sweet-smelling and clear when the sky was blue. Even on a stormy day it wasn't a bad place to camp. The only drawback was that the meadow was quite large and anyone gathering wood had to go a ways to the woods.

However, he felt that was a minor thing compared to the advantages. In the spring the Mountain Laurels had been profuse around the meadow and had given a lovely aroma to the area. Even now, in the heat of summer, the cold pool seemed to temper the heat. The water of the pool was cold and sweet. Even now, the water was too cold to swim in. Campers usually only splashed the water on their faces and washed their hands. Sticking their toes in the water only brought squeals from their mouths.

Eric always looked forward to having his devotions on the rock that covered the spring. The only drawback, they had to have a big fire because it took a long time to heat the water for dishes and hot drinks. However, in light of all the blessings at this stop, having to have a big fire was hardly a problem.

While Eric started the fire, the three guys and their male leader set up tents, while his wife worked with the three girls to get their supper going and filter water for drinks. When the fire blazed, someone filled Eric's big pan with water to wash up dishes. By now, everyone knew what was expected of them. Usually after supper everyone sat around to either have devotions or sing songs and choruses. On Sunday especially a youth leader usually had devotions. Eric knew that's what this youth leader would do, he'd had a different teen help with devotions each evening all week. The longest day of the year had just passed, so the evening was long.

Monday morning at the bank Derek picked up the Sunday paper that Marlene had put on his desk as soon as she came in. He always read the Sunday paper it had much more news than any other day of the week. He knew the criminal had been apprehended and was in jail on murder and attempted murder charges. At least that's what Sheriff Winslow had told him, but at that time they'd only surmised those things.

Down in the same corner as the last article Derek found another article:

### CRIMINAL APPRENENDED IN ATLANTA, GEORGIA

> Convicted felon, Ralph Ronald Wever was apprehended at a convenience store as he attempted to take another victim. It is now known that Wever had abducted another young woman earlier in the spring. However, this young woman survived his attack due to the quick intervention of a resident of the town where Wever dropped her. Wever is now facing charges of murder and attempted murder and attempted kidnapping. As of this date, he is being transferred to the prison where he had already spent eight years on similar activity some ten years ago. His arraignment will be scheduled at a later time.

Derek had cut out the first article and now he cut out this second article. He wasn't sure why he'd done it, but two small pieces of newsprint didn't weigh down his desk drawer by much. No names had been given in either article for which he was glad, but it was obvious that this article was talking about the man whom Carolyn had identified last week from the poster at the bank. Derek couldn't have been happier to know for sure that Carolyn was safe from her abductor, even though she couldn't remember what he had done to her. Now, if only she could remember what had been happening in her life prior to that abduction. He didn't want to see her leave his life, but she was an adult and needed to gather up loose ends.

Monday morning came early on the trail, even earlier than when someone was at home in his bed. As usual, Eric was up with the first rays of sunrise. He took his Bible with him as he crawled out of his tent. He looked around at the peaceful campsite. No one else was awake, all the tents were still. However, not far away he noticed some of the grass had been trampled it looked like some animals had had a scuffle during the night. He thought nothing of it no animals were there now, so he made his way to his rock.

He had barely splashed his face with the cold water and opened his Bible when he heard a roar in the woods beyond the open meadow. The sound wasn't that far away from his spot and sent a cold chill up his spine that had nothing to do with the cold water he'd just splashed on his face. He quickly looked around to see if he could locate the animal. Before he could, the roar came again and this time sounded closer. Encountering a bear when there were ten sleeping people that he was in charge of didn't really sit too well.

Although he had never heard a bear at this stop, there was always a first time. He quickly left the rock and headed back to the tent circle. He stepped up to the closest tent and heard another roar. "Come on, everybody! There's a bear in the area, we need to get moving!" he called loudly, but was nearly drowned out by another roar.

All the tents immediately started moving and soon heads appeared. Although the sun was barely cresting the horizon, everybody rushed from their tents and soon the meadow became a beehive of activity. Another roar gave impetus to the activity. Even the boys were content with a cold breakfast and the lady youth leader didn't make coffee for the three adults. In record time, the tents were down, food cleared away and backpacks were in place. With loud roars accompanying them, the group headed for the trail that led them away from the meadow. So far, they hadn't seen the bear, but that didn't mean it wouldn't appear at any moment!

In a wee voice, one of the girls said, "Eric, are there usually bears there?" With tears on her cheeks, she added, "That noise scares me!"

"No, Alissa, that's the first time I've ever heard a bear at that place. With that lovely pool there, I'm not surprised that wildlife comes around, but usually the hikers make enough noise to keep them away. I don't know why that bear stayed around, since we were making noise as we took down our camp."

Before they reached the trees, Tom, the youth leader said, "Oh, look! There were some animals here during the night the grass is trampled over there. I wonder if something was hurt but not enough to still be out in the open. That would explain the bear close by, it might have been hoping for a meal."

"Yes, that could be," Eric agreed.

When they reached the trees, however, the hikers knew why the bear was roaring. Not far from the trail in the woods lay a young cub. It looked like a big cat had mauled it very badly. Perhaps the mother bear had come upon them before the cat had finished the cub off and had left the little creature to die. It was a good possibility. Eric didn't feel they needed to stick around to get in the middle of a wild animal encounter, especially with several frightened girls, so he kept going at a much faster clip than he usually took his group. The hikers were happy to leave the scene behind. One of the girls even whimpered when she saw the little bear, but she kept moving just the same.

"Whew!" one of the boys exclaimed, "That critter sounded like he'd pounce on us any minute! I'm glad we're out of there."

"Yeah, me too," the lady youth leader said.

Because of their early start in the morning, it was also early in the afternoon when the hikers tumbled onto the DeLord parking lot. The teens had been anxious to leave the woods even though once they left the high plateau they couldn't hear the bear any longer. The group would be taking food home with them they'd only taken time to pull out granola and power bars for their lunch. Filtered canteen water had quenched their thirst.

After he waved the group off, Eric realized the DeLord's weren't at home. Probably Ramon was out with his group, but he was surprised that Sandy was gone since she knew a group was coming back today. Usually she stayed home on days like that. But then, she had her own set of wheels, she could take off any time she wanted to. Little Jon was the best behaved child he knew, Sandy could take him anywhere. She did have her own cell phone that had all the guides' cell numbers on speed dial, so she could always reach them or they her.

As the hikers' taillights faded out of town, he looked at his watch and decided that his three granola bar lunch hadn't filled him up much. At the thought, his stomach growled. He had also emptied his canteen along the way, if he wanted something to fill his empty stomach he must go home. After his last hike, he'd gotten a fresh supply of TV dinners from Alex's store. He couldn't believe his stomach growled again at the thought of eating a TV dinner!

Since no one was home, he couldn't get his information for his next hike. Oh, he could if he wanted to take the time. All the guides knew how to get in the office, but he'd stop by another time when Sandy was home to get it, so he quickly went to his car to leave for his cabin. He sighed eating one of Alex's TV dinners would go a long way to fill up his empty cavern. The impetus put him in his car and he quickly left the parking lot for Isabel's parking lot and his delightful cabin. He was anxious to shed his backpack for more than a few overnight hours.

He dropped his backpack beside the door into his bathroom, but went immediately to the kitchen and pulled out a TV dinner. While it heated in the microwave, he dashed back to the bathroom, took a quick shower and then started his washer. He emptied both his hamper and his backpack of dirty clothes then dragged the pack to the kitchen to clean it out the rest of the way after he ate. His dinner was waiting for him when he came back to the kitchen. He pulled his tea jug from the refrigerator, pulled his trusty fork from his dish drainer and sat down to eat. He barely lowered his head to bless his food before he took a big mouthful. This meal tasted the best he'd ever tasted since he'd been using Alex as his main food supplier!

He wasn't finished eating when the phone rang. When he answered, Isabel said, "You're home early this time, Sonny! It's still daylight and you're here already. Come on over and eat dessert with us."

Around another mouthful, Eric said, "Super! I have two more mouthfuls to gobble up, then I'll be right there, Isabel."

"Fine, fine!"

Eric stuffed his mouth, then cleared his place and walked across the parking lot. Isabel called him in and as he closed the door, she said, "Now, it's nothing fancy, but Ruth made a big apple pie for dinner yesterday and we didn't eat much of it, so we'll have apple pie ala mode. Will that tickle your fancy, Sonny?"

The bachelor gave the old lady his best smile and said, "Isabel, we only ate cold stuff on the trail today because a bear woke us up this morning and the kids didn't want to stick around long for fear it would come out of the woods and attack. When they're that close one can't be sure what a bear will do. When I got to my cabin I gobbled down that TV dinner so fast I'm not sure which variety it was, so apple pie ala mode sounds like heavenly fare to me!" Grinning, he added, "Ruth! Bring it on!"

As Ruth came in the living room she gasped, "A bear! At your campsite? Wow!"

"Yeah, it must have been a mother bear. We didn't see her, but as we left there was a dead cub beside the trail. We didn't stick around to learn the details."

Ruth shivered. "I don't blame you!"

In a very practical voice, Isabel said dryly, "Sonny, unless you've learned 'bear speak' since you've been leading those hikes, I doubt you'd have learned any details."

Eric chuckled. "You don't think so?"

"Nope, not in this lifetime."

"Well, maybe you're right, Isabel."

Eric had just scraped the last of the melted ice cream off his plate when they heard a vehicle crunch onto the parking lot. Isabel sat in her favorite chair and sighed, "There's that snazzy white car again! I told him I didn't want that piece of equipment on my parking lot! Didn't he get what he wanted the other day?" After a minute's thought she answered her own question, "Well, no, he couldn't have, some of us weren't here."

Ruth collected their plates and headed for the kitchen, but Eric scowled and looked at the old lady. "Isabel, what are you saying?"

Isabel waved her hand toward the door and said, "Don't mind me, Sonny, but you better get out of here! He's headed for your cabin!"

He would have been worried, except Isabel had a huge grin on her face. "Yeah, Isabel, I'll go see what he wants."

Isabel made motions with her hands to move Eric out the door. "You do that, but he needs to get that snazzy thing off my lot!"

Eric wiped his own mouth and stood. He looked at Isabel again, she still had that mischievous grin on her face, but she wasn't saying anything. He shook his head. The woman perplexed him many times, but then women in general usually did. As he reached for the door handle, he turned and said, "Thanks for dessert, ladies. As usual, it was super!"

"Good enough, Sonny. Go help the sheriff out."

"Sure, I'll do that, Isabel. What could he want?" Eric closed Isabel's door and called, "Sheriff? You wanting something?"

The sheriff turned and said, "Mr. Thomas! Good to see you! You're a hard man to catch up with, you know that?"

Eric shrugged, as if it was a given. "Well, I am gone a lot. One can't lead a hike sitting in front of the tube."

"Yes, I'll give you that. Have you got a minute to talk?"

"Sure, I'm off tomorrow and I haven't gotten my next assignment. What's on your mind this lovely last day of June? Oh, you might as well come in where it's cool."

Sheriff Winslow pulled his hat from his head and said, "Whew! I won't turn you down on that! It has turned hot."

"Actually, it's almost July. I think it's supposed to be rather warm."

They entered Eric's cool cabin and found chairs. "So what's on your mind, Sheriff?"

After making himself comfortable, the sheriff said, "I don't know much about you, except in reference to our Jane Doe. Everyone I've talked to speaks highly of you. Care to tell me about yourself?"

Eric shrugged. "In reference to?"

The sheriff also shrugged. "Ms Isabel and Ramon and Sandy DeLord seem to think you'd make a good deputy sheriff."

Stunned, Eric's mouth dropped open as he stared at the sheriff. "WHAT!!!" The word finally exploded from his mouth.

The sheriff laid his hat on the table beside him, leaned back against the soft upholstered back and raised his arm to rest on the top of the couch. He said, "That's what I said, they think you'd make a good deputy sheriff."

"You think… what!... a deputy sheriff? But I…"

"Yes, Ms Isabel told me to hire you quick and Ramon said you'd look good in a deputy's uniform. What else is there?"

Eric was still so stunned the sheriff's humor completely flew over him. Finally, Eric had his thought pattern nearly back in place and said, "Sheriff, I've been a hiking guide since last year this time. I live in this tiny town in rural Georgia. The major industry is the hiking service! Why would you think I'd make a good deputy?"

# Fourteen

Looking at Eric in the eye and no smile on his face, he instantly countered, "And before you became a hiking guide you did two tours in Afghanistan as a Marine and were instrumental in getting one of the major hot places made safe. Not only that, you were able to get your team and another team safely out of harm's way while under major attack. Also, if my information is correct, you graduated from college in the upper part of your class with a degree in Criminal Science, am I right?"

Eric swallowed, the man had done his homework. "Yeah, you're right. So where would I be stationed? I'd be one of your deputies in Blairsville?"

"Yes, you'd be under my jurisdiction but your base of operations would be here in Vansville. We'd do most of our interaction by phone or text. Perhaps you'd need to check in with me about once a week there in Blairsville. As I understand what my boss has told me, except for that once a week trip to my office, you'd be here in these parts."

"Wow!"

"So what'll it be?"

Eric scowled, but gave the man his full attention. "Sheriff, I get one day off between hikes. It's never the same day each week. We're covered up until into October, tomorrow's July first. Don't think I could do your department much service for several months yet, really. I suspect you're offering me a full time position?"

The sheriff pulled one leg up and rested it on his knee, before he said, "Yep! Ramon tells me he's hired a new man as a guide. He said after he's trained that he could let you go by August first. So what'll it be?"

Eric leaned forward, put his elbows on his knees and dangled his hands between his legs. He pulled in a deep breath and looked at the sheriff. "Yeah, I did go to Clemson and I majored in Criminal Justice. I did two tours in Afghanistan and I helped open up several hot spots. I saw some really bad stuff over there and I was glad to come home to this quiet village." He looked Sheriff Winslow in the eye and asked, "You think this place warrants a deputy sheriff? A criminal dropping Carolyn here is the worst thing that's ever happened in Vansville."

"Eric, my superior laid me out cold a week and a half ago when he told me to hire a new man to a new position. All I'd ever heard from the man before was that he was strapped for finances. Now he says he wants the new man to be based in the Vansville area. He told me to check out a map, which I did. This is a big rural area. I didn't know you until you called about our Jane Doe, but you handled that situation very well, I was impressed. After I thought about his request I decided you were the man I wanted. Your friends agree with me."

Eric pulled in a deep breath and as he let it out, he leaned back in his chair. After another moment's thought he said, "Sheriff, I usually try to give some thought and prayer to a change of direction in my life. Could I call you tomorrow?"

"I will not deny you that. Could you come to my office tomorrow?"

"Yes, I'll be in perhaps in the early afternoon?"

"That'll be great!"

Both men stood up, the sheriff grabbed his hat and held out his hand. "It's been a pleasure, Eric. I'll add my prayers to yours, surely the answers will agree."

Eric chuckled. "Perhaps they will, Sheriff. Thanks for thinking of me and for your obvious confidence in my abilities."

Sheriff Winslow settled his hat on his head and took a step toward the door, before he said, "Oh, in case you hadn't heard, Carolyn identified her abductor. That man surfaced and was finally apprehended in Atlanta last Friday."

"Was it the man pictured on that poster?"

"Yes, it was. I understand you called in to report he'd been on your hike?"

"I did. He had acted strangely the last morning. Of course, I didn't know at the time that he was a criminal. Was Emily safe?"

Sheriff Winslow nodded. "It was Emily Landin who was the catalyst. She was at a convenience store when he made his move and she was still close enough to windows in the store. The clerk inside saw what happened. Ralph had duct tape in his pocket. We assume he planned to do his deeds on her just as he had on Jane Doe and another woman south of Atlanta."

"Wow! I'm glad he didn't get a chance! Carolyn identified the man? Has she regained her memory?"

"No, but she saw one of the posters and it triggered that memory. She was with her friends at the bank downtown and saw the picture in the window. Ralph Wever will rot in prison for a good long time. He's in on charges of attempted murder and also murder. Of course, that's only what he can be charged for now, that doesn't count why he was already in prison before he got parole." Sheriff Winslow gave Eric a sardonic grin. "Leave it to the justice system to let the man out when the charges against him were for the same behavior!"

"Wow! I can't imagine!"

"It's because of your quick intervention that our Jane Doe is alive. Since she was unconscious for so long, even in the hospital, if you hadn't seen what happened, I'm sure she would have died there in those woods." Sheriff Winslow held out his hand. "Do come up with a favorable answer, Eric. I'll be waiting for it tomorrow."

Eric took his hand and shook it. "Thank you, Sheriff. I'll give it much thought and prayer until I see you tomorrow."

"All I ask."

Eric watched from his window as the sheriff took longs strides to his car, he didn't even wave at Isabel's window, even though he must know she watched him from her chair. So Isabel thought the sheriff should hire him quick. He had to smile. That lady was a terrific friend! Actually, she was too feisty to remind him of a grandmother! Ramon told the sheriff he could have him after August first. It sounded like he had the sheriff's vote of confidence. He'd be based here in Vansville. That made him wonder what he'd do with his time. Did the law enforcement department know something that wasn't common knowledge? Did they think marijuana growers would be moving into the countryside in droves? Maybe that was it. Even that thought brought a smile to his face. In Vansville? Not a chance!

If he wasn't leading a hike day after day, he'd eat a lot of TV dinners and drink a lot of tea. He wouldn't need to go to Blairsville to take care of his business as the only reason to go. He'd have to go each week to check in with his boss. Some little critter who had just jumped on his shoulder whispered, *You could maybe have a relationship with a pretty lady with blond hair and blue eyes.* He swatted his shoulder. Where in the world had that thought come from? He hadn't thought about a pretty lady with blond hair and blue eyes in – hmm, maybe since pie ala mode? Besides, if she ever got her memory back she'd probably high-tail it out of Vansville, back to wherever she was from. Where would that leave him?

By now, the sun was definitely in the west, shining on his porch and making it quite uncomfortably warm. It didn't matter he picked up his Bible and left the cabin. The brook crossed the meadow, but there was a quiet spot back in the woods where he could sit beside the brook to read and pray. He had gone there often enough it was a place close to home that reminded him of the high plateau. He told the sheriff he would pray about taking this position. When he'd taken the hiking guide position he'd felt like God had led him. He wanted that same assurance this time and obviously the sheriff was giving him that option.

Not long after he left his cabin he reached the quiet woods and followed the brook back into the trees far enough he couldn't see any buildings. When he found the big rock he'd used before, he climbed up on it and opened his Bible. Come to think of it, he hadn't had his devotions this morning because of the bear. However, now it wasn't just to read for the sake of reading, it was to seek God's guidance on another change in his life.

Before he opened his Bible, he blended his voice with the gurgling brook and said, "Lord, God, what would You have me to do?"

Some time later Eric closed his Bible, ran his hand through the cool brook water and stood up. He sighed, looked through the branches of the trees all around him and took a deep breath. God did seem much closer here in this quiet place. Since he wasn't overseas, his brother was relatively close he'd call and see if they could talk for a few minutes. Maybe his twin could help him get this new development in his life into perspective and help him decide. He'd still be here in Vansville, but not guiding hikes any longer. He'd only been at that for a year it didn't seem like a very long commitment. However, if God was in it, that didn't matter.

As he entered his cabin his stomach growled again. He swatted the offender, he couldn't be hungry! He'd only had that pie ala mode a few hours ago! He set his Bible down and went to the kitchen. He'd make a sandwich and call his brother. However, he'd barely set the plate with his sandwich on the table when his phone rang. He grabbed it up, then went to the refrigerator for his tea and activated the phone.

When he answered, a voice very similar to his own said, "Hey, Bro, you're home!"

"Yup, I am. Will miracles never cease! I was just about to call you. So what's up?"

"So why were you about to call me?"

"More important, why'd you call me?"

"I'm moving to Vansville, be there to start in the store next Monday. Why'd you want to talk to me?"

"So Brad had another stroke? When'll you arrive here?"

"I'll finish out the week here, be there on Saturday. Ms Isabel says she'll have a cabin ready for me when I get there. Yes, Uncle Brad had a major stroke last Thursday. I guess he's still in the hospital. His speech was affected this time."

"Oh, I'm sorry to hear that. It'll be good to have you here. I did want to talk to you, just for some input. What would you think about me being a deputy sheriff?"

There was silence on the line for several minutes as Matt digested his brother's bombshell. Finally, he said, "Well,... you *did* major in Criminal Justice in college. You *were* in the Marines for years. You *were* in Afghanistan for most of those years and you *did do* most of the work to open up that whole area. I'm sure you've *prayed* about it. So what's the problem?"

"I'd be quitting my commitment to Ramon mid-season. Sheriff Winslow wants me August first, but everything else seems like a go."

"So Ramon's holding you back?"

"No, he told Sheriff he'd let me go as of August first."

Without any hesitation Matt exclaimed, "So go for it! If Ramon's not against it, I'd say, get on with it!"

"Thanks, Bro, I may do that."

"See you the end of the week!"

"Yup, travel safe."

He finished his sandwich, cleaned up his mess and activated his phone again. When she answered, Eric said, "Sandy, could I come talk with you a few minutes?"

"Sure! By the time you come I'll have Jon in bed so come quietly, but I'm free to talk."

"I'll come to your office it's the farthest from Jon's room."

"Perfect! See you in a few."

Eric decided he'd recuperated enough from the hike it would give him a few extra minutes of quiet thought and give Sandy a few extra minutes to get Jon quiet, so he'd walk. He turned on a light, it would be dark when he came back, then he left and walked slowly off Isabel's parking lot. It took about ten minutes to reach Sandy's house. The light was already on in the office, so he crossed their parking lot and tapped on the office door and went in.

As soon as she hung up, Sandy was sure she knew what Eric wanted to talk about. She smiled as Eric sat down. "So Sheriff came to see you?"

"Yes, not long after I got home this afternoon. Sandy, what do you think?"

Sandy continued to smile. "I think it'd be a great opportunity!"

"You and Ramon wouldn't be upset? You'd be short-handed, wouldn't you?"

"Ramon's hired a former acquaintance of ours, Jerry's out with Ramon now. He's going to send him out with another one or two of you next week or so, so he won't be short-handed once Jerry's trained. Like I say, I think it'd be great! I read in your paperwork that you have a degree in Criminal Justice; why not? You've prayed about it, right?"

Eric nodded and said, "Yes, I prayed about it and just before I called you, my brother called and we talked."

"You're to let Sheriff know?"

"Yes, I promised him I'd come by tomorrow."

Sandy reached for Eric's hands. "Come let's pray about it."

Eric eagerly took her hands, they bowed their heads and Sandy said, "Lord God, Eric's been offered a job here in Vansville as a deputy sheriff. Everyone so far feels this is a good thing. Please confirm it in Eric's mind. Give him peace about accepting this position. In Your Son's matchless Name, amen."

As Sandy raised her head, she said, "You'll accept, won't you?"

Eric chuckled. "Seems I'd better, huh?"

"I'd say! Oh, by the way, while you were gone, Carolyn identified the man, she had a miscarriage and they caught the criminal."

A smile spread across his face. "So she's regained her memory?"

"No, but his face on that poster triggered that memory. We girls spent the morning together on Thursday in Blairsville. We were there at the bank and she saw that poster, she had quite a reaction to it! After Derek called the sheriff about it, we went to the mall, but at noon she fainted from the pain. She was out for about half an hour so they transported her to the hospital. Dr. Simon decided she was miscarrying and she spent the night. On Friday when Derek went for her the sheriff called and told him they'd caught the man."

"Wonder what it'll take to bring her memory back?"

"That's what we're all wondering."

Eric stood up, but Sandy said, "Oh, I knew you'd gotten back this afternoon, so I printed out your next hike itinerary. You've got a short one, these folks want to go out Wednesday and be back Saturday. Think you can handle that?"

"Sure! I'll get to go to church on Sunday! That'll be great."

With a twinkle in her eyes, she said, "You can sit with Carolyn again and go with us to Derek's house for steak."

Eric's cheeks flamed, but to cover his discomfort, he reached for his papers and said, "Sandy, if Carolyn hasn't gotten her memory back, we don't know what she's qualified to do. Maybe her job's waiting for her wherever she lived. I'm obviously supposed to stay here in Vansville. Why should I pursue a relationship with Carolyn in view of all that?"

"Have you never heard how God directed Roger and Raylyn's romance?"

"Yes, I guess I have. I'd say nothing's too hard for the Lord."

"Excellent thought, Eric! Absolutely excellent!"

Eric grinned at his friend. "Thanks for your time, Sandy. I'll sleep on it then go to see the sheriff tomorrow."

"Great! Tell him I said hi."

Eric left DeLord's parking lot. He walked the quiet street, not a soul was out and only streetlights illuminated his walk. That was to his liking. Even yet he could sometimes hear the sounds of war so clearly in his head. So the criminal was in custody, Brad had had another major stroke, his brother was moving to Vansville. Carolyn had identified her abductor, but still didn't have her memory back. The sheriff wanted to hire him to a deputy sheriff position here in Vansville. He liked the little town it surely couldn't be a hard job.

He had to chuckle. Isabel thought the sheriff should hire him quick and Ramon thought he'd look good in a deputy sheriff's uniform! Neither one of those things did much for qualifying him, but everything seemed to be a go. Of course, the sheriff had done his homework he did know his qualifications for a deputy job.

He opened his door, the air conditioning hummed quietly. He walked in and saw his Bible on the table. "Well, Lord, seems it's all in Your hands and I'm willing."

Lance had gotten home so late Sunday night from Baton Rouge that he had only stripped down and took a shower before he fell into bed exhausted. Not only from the drive back, but dealing with such a loss as the death of two parents was exhausting. Monday morning he looked at the pile of mail that the letter carrier had left in his box, in fact, there was so much he'd laid some between his screen door and the main door. He couldn't ignore his suitcase sitting on the chair that he needed to empty of dirty clothes and realized he had enough work to keep him busy all day at home. He called his office and Holly told him to take all the time he needed, she could handle the phone calls. She was glad he was back safely.

He started a load of clothes immediately then after breakfast took a cup of coffee and the mail to his office to work on and found a letter from Carolyn's employer saying they were sorry but they'd replaced her because she hadn't come forward. The one from her apartment manager informed him that her rent for the new month was past due. Would he please take the responsibility. He sat staring at the papers for several minutes, wondering again what had happened to his dependable sister. What could he do? If she wasn't allowed to live in her apartment any longer, it would have to be cleared out or her things confiscated! He knew to go to Atlanta was more than a day's excursion for him. Already he was behind the eight ball!

She had a few very nice pieces from their home which they had broken up after their dad moved out. He didn't want to loose those pieces and he knew she definitely wanted them. He'd be covered up when he got back to the office and he was committed to go back to Baton Rouge on the weekend. This was truly a rock and a hard place situation!

He saw a phone number on the letterhead for the apartment complex, so he found his phone and called. When a woman identified the complex, Lance looked at the name on the letter and said, "Ma'am, could I please speak with Alfred Gordon?"

"Could I tell him whose calling?"

"Yes, this is Lance Casbah. I'm Carolyn Casbah's brother. She rented a unit from you folks and I have a letter from Mr. Gordon here."

Soon a man's voice said, "This is Alfred Gordon, Mr. Casbah?"

"Yes, I've been out of town and just opened your letter."

"Well, it seems Miss Casbah hasn't been in her apartment in over a month, the rent's due and it's not been paid. What'll it be Mr. Casbah?"

Still looking at the letter and just as mystified as he'd been for several weeks, he said, "Mr. Gordon, I have a real problem. It was only a little over a week ago that I realized that my sister was truly missing and no one knew where she was. I was about to make some contacts when my wife's parents were killed tragically in Baton Rouge. Everything about Carolyn slipped into second place and I only came back from my in-laws funerals last night. My wife and daughter are still out there and I'm to pick them up on Saturday. I know I'm behind at my office because of my absence there. If it's possible could the contents of my sister's apartment be allowed to stay there until mid-month perhaps?"

"Hey," the man said, "you pay the rent it'll stay there until the end of July."

Lance breathed out a sigh. "I guess that'll have to be the solution. I'll get that out in the mail this morning. I guess I could wire it to your account."

"Naw, send a check, that's fine. Say, I'm sorry for your wife's loss. That has to be one hard thing to put your mind around."

"Thanks. She and her sister are trying to hold each other up."

"I can believe that! Thanks for your quick response, Mr. Casbah."

"Yes, that's one thing our dad taught us was to be responsible. Expect that check in a day or two, Mr. Gordon."

In all the catching up Lance had to do at home, his day was interrupted many times with thoughts of Carolyn. The situation just felt so wrong! As he'd said to the apartment manager, their dad had brought them both up to be responsible. He couldn't think of a time when she hadn't been. For her to go missing, not let anyone know where she was, not pay the rent for the upcoming month, her phone not to work and not to appear at work or call to say she was sick or hurt was something he couldn't put his mind around. As the sun set his stomach growled. He finally finished his catch up and went to the kitchen. After spending a whole day looking at papers, he wasn't very imaginative he fixed a bologna and cheese sandwich.

"Where *could* she be?" he muttered. "She wanted that position so badly! I can't imagine where she went or what she's done!"

While Derek spent another day at the bank, Carolyn would spend another quiet Monday at the house. It was becoming a broken record. Mrs. Beecham would be around inside doing whatever she felt she needed to do as the housekeeper, but no one would be out back at the pool site. It still had to cure until Wednesday. With the sun out and the temperatures they'd been having, that shouldn't be a problem. Carolyn was a bit bored with reading books from Derek's library, not that she'd exhausted the supply, but you could only read books for so long until all the words ran together into a nonsensical blob. She was about there!

She still sat at the kitchen table. Derek had left only a few minutes ago, Mrs. Beecham still stood at the sink cleaning up from her early morning baking and breakfast dishes. Carolyn turned and looked at her. "You know, the man's been caught. I don't have to stay inside to be safe any more! I think I'll go for a walk. I won't go far, I promise."

The older lady's breath hitched, but she said, "You're sure it's all right to do that? Mr. Casbah never said it was all right."

"Mrs. Beecham, he's been concerned because the man who did those things was still free, but now we know he's been caught and he's behind bars. He's in Atlanta and that's a long ways away, so I'm sure I'm safe. Besides, I'm about bored out of my skull! I'll stay close, maybe go in the back yard and only step into the trees out there. Surely that's fine."

"All right, Miss Carolyn, I'll watch for you to come back for lunch."

"Thanks, Mrs. Beecham."

Carolyn stepped out onto the deck. It was quiet, only birds chirped. The sun was out, but there were patches of clouds dotting the blue sky. It would be hot later on in the afternoon, but right now, there was a gentle breeze that was refreshing and not too hot. With the breeze blowing, she took a deep breath, enjoying the fresh air.

After another deep breath, she skipped down the steps to the back yard and headed for the big hole in the ground. It hadn't rained since they'd built the forms and filled them with cement, so the cement should be curing nicely. Sam and Ernest should be back in two days to take their forms away and place the diving board. Perhaps they'd level out the mound they'd had to dig out of the hole because of the rain. On Friday they'd fill the pool and it would be ready for use.

As Carolyn walked all the way around the hole, she grinned. "I'm excited! It'll be great to dive into that pool, maybe I am a swimmer!"

She looked out across the quiet countryside. It wasn't too far into the summer, grass, trees and shrubs were still a lush green. With the house and everything she'd learned, probably Derek had a lawn service to keep it that way. She knew that there were many things she knew that seemed to come to her automatically, but for some reason, her life before the man had abducted her was a total mystery. It seemed like her whole life was on hold.

*Why? Why can't I remember? What will it take to bring my memory back?* Having the man caught hadn't done it. Having a miscarriage hadn't done it. Her over night stay in the hospital hadn't done it. Putting this pool in the backyard hadn't done it. All she knew was she hadn't lived in Vansville, she'd never been here. None of the people she'd met since Derek had brought her here knew her.

She turned away from the house to walk toward the trees. This was the farthest she'd been from the house since her dad had brought her here. That was one thing she was sure of. For some reason, she knew in her heart of hearts that Derek was her dad. It wasn't just that they looked so much alike, but her mind had given her that assurance. He was a kind man, she enjoyed his company, but there was no question, he was her dad. She walked all the way across the green turf. One day soon, the grounds keepers would come to mow.

Once she reached the trees she slowed her walk. She stepped into the shade and listened to the breeze rustle the leaves all around her. It was very relaxing. A realization came to her she hadn't lived in the country in a very long time, maybe never. The quiet rustling of leaves hadn't been something she'd experienced in a very long time. Where had she lived? At this point, it was still a deep, dark mystery.

Tuesday morning, Eric took his Bible again and went out to his porch. He sat down then looked out across the meadow, but Duncan's and Natt's houses were in his sights. Those men had both come to Vansville as single men. It hadn't been too long after they came that they were both married. Perhaps maybe a year for both of them. He grinned, he'd been here a year… he didn't let that thought go any further.

Now Natt was the owner of the hardware store and Duncan was one of his colleagues on the trails. The women they'd married had also come from out of town. When they came, neither man was a Christian, but the women were and because of some circumstances, the men had both accepted Christ. He'd helped his cousin strengthen his faith. They'd had many good Bible studies together. In fact, he missed them.

For some reason, his mind turned to Carolyn. Was she a Christian? Derek was, from what he knew about the man he hadn't always been living like a Christian. Had he raised his child as a believer? He didn't know enough about him to make a judgment. Carolyn went to church and it seemed she knew her way around in her Bible, but that didn't make her a Christian.

"Enough of this wool-gathering!" Eric grumbled. After a long sigh, he opened his Bible he must go see the sheriff this afternoon. All things pointed to him accepting the job of deputy sheriff that he offered.

When he opened his Bible he turned to the book of Romans where he had been reading for his devotions for several days. It was a deep book, rich in God's directions for life. Romans 8:28 seemed to pop out at him.

'And we know that in all things God works for the good of those who love him, who have been called according to his purpose.' He read it once again and let each word soak into his heart and soul. With his finger on that verse he looked out at the clear blue sky and said, "Okay, Lord, I'll take that as a 'yes, go for it!'"

Eric ate a sandwich for lunch, but he had been thinking deep, contemplative thoughts all morning. After washing his plate, he took another swig from his tea jug and put it back in the refrigerator and went out to his car. Just because, he looked toward Isabel's front window, grinned and waved. He was sure she sat in her chair. He had to chuckle, but he wondered how many years she'd had that chair in that place so she could see what happened on her end of town. He stepped into his car and left for Blairsville.

About a half hour later he found a place to park close to the Justice Building and walked in the lower level where the Sheriff's Department and the jail were. The man at the front desk looked up and said, "May I help you?"

"Yes, I'm here to see Sheriff Winslow."

"Have an appointment?"

"He's expecting me."

The sheriff recognized Eric's voice, so he called through his door, "Send the man in! I am expecting him."

The man at the desk shrugged. "Guess you'd better go on in."

Eric opened the door behind the front desk to see the big man smiling at him. "So, you've come to take the job?"

Eric shrugged and closed the door behind him. "If you're serious about offering it to me, I'm serious about taking it."

Chuckling, the sheriff scooped up a short pile of papers, held them out to Eric and said, "I just happen to have these forms here on my desk that need to be filled out by a prospective deputy. You'll do that, won't you?"

Eric grinned. "Mmm, yeah, guess I will."

"So you prayed about this and it's all clear?"

Eric pulled in a deep breath and smiled at the sheriff. "Well, I not only did that but I talked to my brother and to Sandy DeLord. Sheriff, they both agree with you that I should take the job. Sandy prayed with me and I've sent up a few prayers myself. It seems everything agrees, so here I am."

Sheriff Winslow grinned and said, "That's good, because I had a talk with the man at the State Office Building after I talked with you yesterday. He wanted to know if I'd hired anyone yet and I assured him that I had."

Eric laughed. "Pretty sure of yourself, aren't you?"

"Well, I went home and prayed about it, too. Seemed like a flag with your name on it jumped right out of my prayers."

"Oh, I'm sure!"

Eric clicked his pen and put it back in his pocket, gathered up his papers and leaned over to put them on the desk. Sheriff Winslow was on his feet with his hand out. "Welcome aboard, Eric. I believe you'll make a great deputy."

"Thanks, Sheriff."

"The first open day before the first come on in and we'll have a session on everything you'll need to know and all the other particulars that go with the job. I still have a few things I need to iron out with my boss as to what else needs to happen, so I can't do that yet. Also that day we'll take your measurements and get you all suited up."

"That's fine, I'll be in touch."

Tuesday morning Lance didn't feel ready to tackle his office, but he knew he must show up. Holly couldn't hold down the fort indefinitely. He missed his little family, the house was too quiet. He washed out his mug and set it by the sink, grabbed up his briefcase and laptop and headed out to his car. It had had one day of rest, he wished he'd had the same. Soon he pulled in his parking space behind the office building. Pulling in a deep breath, he locked the car and walked inside. Time to face the phone calls, the paperwork and hopefully no prospective clients.

Holly was at the mailboxes as Lance walked in. When she turned around and saw him, he said, "I see you've got an arm full. Is my desk that full?"

She smiled at him. "Pretty much, Lance. There're lots of sticky notes on your desk and several letters I typed. Since we didn't know when you'd be back, I did take the liberty of opening some of the mail that I recognized and wrote up replies, but I can't fake your signature. Your desk looks like a sidewalk after a tornado upset a full trashcan."

Lance sighed, "I'm so glad to know that!"

Again on Tuesday Lance played catch up. In fact, he had Holly order take out so he could keep working. Between phone calls he had to return and others that came in, the letters he had to sign and the correspondence he had to read and reply to, five o'clock came much too quickly and Holly was telling him goodbye at the end of her day. Lance looked at the clock on his side table and sighed. What was there to go home to but an empty house? He stayed behind his desk for another half hour, but he couldn't stand the silence inside the four walls, so he left.

On the way home he realized he'd let two days go by without trying to find Carolyn. Yesterday he'd rented her apartment for another month, but that hadn't found her. He knew putting her name into a search engine wouldn't reveal anything he didn't already know, but after another burger from a drive-thru he'd put his dad's name in and see what that told him.

He put his bag with his meal on the seat and the large beverage cup in the holder and pulled in a big sniff. He was only minutes from his garage when his phone rang. He pulled it from his waist carrier and saw it was Linda. He activated it and said, "Hi, Love, I'm almost home I'll call you right back. Good to hear from you."

When he was inside with a stiff coffee on the table he called Linda's cell phone. She said, "Honey, you won't have to come after me, Alli and I made our decisions about things. She's staying on at the house, she likes it and it's close to her work, but I've rented a small U-haul and bringing some things home from Mom and Dad's. It's things I've wanted and Alli didn't care about. It's too much for your car and the three of us, so it seemed sensible to rent a truck and drive it home, since I know you've been busy with catching up and all. I'll probably be there tomorrow afternoon or evening sometime. Have you found Carolyn?"

"No, but I was about to put Dad's name into a search engine this evening. It would be sort of useless to put her name in, really."

"Yes, I guess that's true."

"I have been doing catch up all day yesterday and today. Yesterday it was here, hey, I even did a washer load of clothes! Today I worked at the office. Holly's good, I wasn't so far behind by the end of today. Love, I'll be so glad for you to get home! It's like a morgue here, but drive carefully driving a truck is way different from a car."

"Oh, I know, but it's just a glorified pick-up with a roof on. Still, I'm hoping it doesn't rain. It's a long way to drive in bad weather with a four year old."

Lance chuckled. "I hear that! See you tomorrow."

He hung up, fixed another cup of coffee and opened his laptop on the kitchen table. He sat for a minute he'd never tried to search for anyone, so he had to think what essential questions he'd need to answer about his dad. He shrugged, other than his name and date of birth he wasn't very sure about anything else. He'd never memorized his SS number. He remembered that eleven years ago the man had moved out of state and had left a phone number on the answering machine. However, Lance hadn't bothered to listen to the message, when he'd heard his dad's voice he hadn't paid attention, only deleted the message as quickly as possible. He hadn't wanted Carolyn to hear any of it. He sighed, again tonight he wondered of there ever was such a thing as a do-over. He knew he could have used his dad's advice several times in the past decade or so. He'd been a very young man and thought he was so smart – what did he know?

It was nearly bedtime when he finally had put enough information into the machine that a blurb and a picture came on the screen. Astonished, he looked at the picture for many minutes. "I can't believe it!" he muttered staring. "He and Carolyn could pass for brother and sister, except his hair's white!" Finally, he looked at the words beside the picture.

"Derek Casbah, age 60, lives in rural Vansville, Georgia. President of Blairsville First Bank in Blairsville, Georgia."

"Vansville, Georgia! Where in heaven's name is that?" he exclaimed. Georgia had never been in his sights for his dad. He'd moved from Baton Rouge to Georgia? Unbelievable! Was that where the woman lived?

He'd never heard of either Vansville or Blairsville, so he googled a map, expecting the towns to be somewhere close to Atlanta. He searched in vain for Vansville. There wasn't such a place at least the map search told him there wasn't. Looking at the map of Atlanta then widening his search, it took him a long time to finally scale down his search to find the relatively small city of Blairsville and it wasn't anywhere close to Atlanta, but nearly out of Georgia into North Carolina. Hundreds of miles from where they'd lived when he was a boy. He'd just come from that place less than a week ago.

He looked at his watch, then his calendar. His watch told him it was after midnight, his calendar told him it was now the second of July. If he couldn't find Vansville, he must go to Derek's bank to find him. Linda and Brenda would be home tomorrow, well no, actually, today sometime. Maybe he'd better go to bed he was supposed to work in the morning.

He shouldn't be gone out of town somewhere he'd never been before when they arrived. The internet search didn't tell him anything more. Of course, it didn't say if Derek was still married, which he assumed he was. He wondered at age sixty if his dad still had the 'go-to-work-every-day' ethic that he'd had or if his wife expected him to take more time off than just the holiday. If he was still as well heeled now as back then he could do that easily. He looked again for a phone number, there was none. He sighed, he'd have to print out travel directions at work his laptop wasn't set up for anything other than what would show on his screen.

Wednesday morning, early, Sam and Ernest came even before Derek left for work. They started immediately removing the forms and filling the back of Sam's truck. Before they were totally finished the truck looked like it would drag when it left the backyard. Derek went out the patio door to talk with Sam before he went in the garage. Carolyn watched as the men smiled and shook hands before Derek left. That had to be a good sign. Removing all the wood from the big hole had to be a good sign, too.

Carolyn no longer felt afraid. In fact, she'd spent most of Tuesday in shorts and tank top on the back deck. Some of the time she'd sat and read her book, other times she lay in the sun and let herself bake. The sun actually felt good on her skin. Even as fair as she was, she found her skin turning bronze instead of red. Not even one freckle had appeared.

After Derek left, Carolyn wandered out toward the hole in the ground. She stayed well away from where the men were working, but she watched as the last form came out of the hole. As Sam came back from throwing that large piece of lumber in the truck, he smiled and said, "Hi, there, Carolyn! Come to see your pool? We'll have her done here in a bit and the guy with the water can come fill it up."

"Yes, if you don't mind. I don't want to be in the way."

"Hey, it's fine! Derek tells me you're a swimmer."

Carolyn made a face. "Yes, that's what he tells me, too. I still can't remember whether I am or not. Maybe if I dive into that water you'll get in there it'll all come clear."

"You'd be glad of that, wouldn't you?"

"Absolutely! I am tired of this empty brain."

"Today we're smoothing out the rough edges and then install the diving board. We'll let it sit tomorrow, then first thing on Friday the water tanker will be here and we'll fill 'er up! This first time, since its part of our agreement with Derek, we'll add all the things to get it ready for use. By Friday night when we quit it'll be all ready to use."

Carolyn gave him a megawatt smile. "That'll be great! When I went shopping the last time I bought a swim suit, so I'm ready for that first dive into the water."

"Great! Derek's waiting too. He said he'll pull out his swimsuit, too."

"Yes, we both bought swimsuits the other day."

The minute Lance entered his office on Wednesday he turned on his computer. After it went through its boot-up, he activated the site he'd used the night before and put in the addresses for the starting point and the destination. It felt strange to be preparing to see his dad. A dozen years was a long time. With regret he remembered it was he who had nearly kicked the man out. He had been the one to give him the ultimatum: 'either give the woman up or get out.' Sons didn't do that to their dads, did they? He wondered if he'd been more civil if his dad would have stuck around or even married his second wife.

When the printer finished spitting out the directions, Lance picked up the sheets and studied them. He lived and worked in a north-west suburb of Birmingham, Alabama, his dad's bank was north-central Georgia, hundreds of miles apart. Most banks were open until five o'clock most days, but tomorrow was the day before a holiday, would his bank close early? Would Derek leave the bank early or even come in the day before a holiday? If he went tomorrow he'd have to leave near dawn. Linda would be home today, they'd talk it over tonight.

When he left work that afternoon and sat down in his overheated car, he was satisfied he'd caught up with everything from his week away. He would take another vacation day to tack on to the holiday on Friday. He hoped that soon his life could settle down and get back to what had been normal only a few weeks ago. Actually, he had to think long and hard to know what 'normal' really was!

He pulled up in his driveway, but couldn't put up his garage door because a U-haul truck sat there. Linda must have left Baton Rouge very early this morning and Brenda had to have traveled well. Maybe they'd both been anxious to get home. He knew he was anxious to see them. He abandoned his car and rushed inside.

From the front door, Lance called, "Sweetheart, I'm home!"

Fast moving little feet and slower moving bigger feet sounded the instant Lance spoke. Brenda had her arms spread as she dashed through the kitchen archway. "Daddy! Daddy! We come home! You be home!" Lance scooped up his little girl in one arm.

Lance held out his other arm toward his wife hurrying toward him. "Yes! We're all home!" After kissing both his wife and daughter, he exclaimed, "Wow! I'm glad to see you!"

"Daddy, we don't gotta go back there in a long time."

"Really? Wow! I guess that's good."

"Oh, yeah. Aunt Alli come see us next time."

"Ah, that's good."

Brenda squirmed, so Lance set her down, then put that arm around his wife and pulled her close, as the child ran off. After a long, breath-taking kiss, he said, "Man, I missed you! You made it in good time, Love. I guess you left early?"

Linda chuckled. "Yes, Brenda was anxious to get home to her dollies. She woke me up before sunrise and there was no going back to sleep! We woke Alli up with our noise, but she wanted to see us off. I know you had to play catch-up, but did you find out anything?"

"I did. Dad's in way north Georgia. It's a long ways from Atlanta, but of course, closer than here. There wasn't a phone number listed and as far as the map search is concerned, there is no place listed where he lives. I'll have to find him at his bank first."

"Tomorrow? You'll go find him tomorrow?"

Lance sighed. "I'm afraid that's the option. Would you want to go with me?"

"Honey…" she chided, "I was never on the 'outs' with him. Don't you think he'd like to know he has a granddaughter?"

"Yes, he probably would."

Once they decided to go the next day, Lance and Linda worked feverishly to empty out the U-haul truck. Rather than take every piece into the house to find a place for it in an already furnished home, they filled up Lance's parking place in the garage. They could do the much slower job of placing each piece at another time. Linda had already been home long enough to empty hers and Brenda's luggage, so by bedtime, the suitcases were repacked and the truck ready to return to the rental store. Fortunately, they could do that on their way out of town and not get a very late start for Blairsville, Georgia.

# Fifteen

Another good thing, when Lance pulled the front door closed in the morning, birds twittered in the trees and the sun was shining in a clear blue sky. Lance loaded their luggage into the trunk, while Linda buckled Brenda into her seat in the back, then Linda drove Lance's car ahead of the U-haul truck into Birmingham to the rental store, where they dropped it off. It was only a few minutes after eight o'clock when Lance sat down in the driver's seat of his car and Linda punched the information into the GPS that hopefully would guide them to the city in north Georgia. Lance was very glad that it was interstate driving most of the way to Blairsville. They should arrive before the bank closed today. He could only hope his dad would be there.

The dash clock told them it was four-thirty. He wheeled into the parking lot to the nearest empty space and jammed the stick into park. He kissed his wife, but left her and Brenda and sprinted for the front door. Mentally he had rehearsed several scathing speeches that would spew out of his mouth the minute he saw the man. However, he decided to hold off on saying anything until he saw him with his own eyes after all these years.

The front door of the bank was unlocked. That caused him to breathe a sigh of relief. He had no idea how else to find Derek Casbah. As he went inside tellers were behind the counter, in fact, there were quite a few people doing business. Off to one side in the back was a desk, a lady sat at it working at her computer and behind the lady was a half open door. He couldn't see the person at the desk in the room, but he wondered if that was the president's office. Perhaps he was there, since the door was open.

He walked resolutely to the desk and asked, "Is the president in?"

Marlene looked up with a smile, nodded at the door and said, "Yes, Mr. Casbah is in his office. Could I tell him whose asking for him?"

"No, no! Don't announce me! I'll introduce myself, thanks."

Marlene continued to smile and said, "As you wish, sir."

Lance stepped around Marlene's desk, but instead of angry steps, his progress seemed a bit hesitant. He took another step, turned sideways and without touching the door took one step into the room, his back against the wall. He saw the white-haired man working on a short stack of papers and just gazed at him. Expecting all the hatred of the years since his teen years to well up and flood him, he was amazed when the overwhelming feeling that consumed him was love.

He stood silently for several minutes, but when he realized that the man didn't seem to be aware that someone else was in the room, he spoke, barely above a whisper, "Dad?"

Derek was unaware of anyone until that moment. He'd been concentrating on reading and signing his name, intent on getting finished with his work so he could take the next two days off. He was happy to spend it with Carolyn. The one word greeting registered, he glanced up, his pen flew from his hand and he was on his feet. Unaware of it, his rolling chair crashed into the wall, but his feet were on the move.

His arms out, his smile encompassed his face and three words flew from his mouth, "Lance, my son!" His feet never stopped until his arms circled the younger man. Without asking, Derek gave the man a bear hug.

Hesitantly, Lance brought his arms up and hugged his dad, but not nearly with as much enthusiasm. "Dad?" he asked, after several silent minutes, "Do you know where Carolyn is?"

"Oh..." the situation finally registering, Derek dropped his arms and took a step back from his son. All those years of silent war came crashing down around him. Of course, Lance would be more concerned about his sister than anything to do with his dad. After another quiet moment, Derek nodded. "Yes, she is at my home."

Lance scowled, but before he could speak, Derek led him to a sitting area in front of the windows. When they were seated, Lance was still scowling and had his mouth open to speak, but Derek held up his hand and said, "Before you say anything or make a judgment, let me tell you the circumstances."

Lance nodded, closed his mouth and both men sat looking at each other across the small space. The fierce scowl never left Lance's face, but he waited. Finally, Derek said, "Back the first of May a lady from the town where I live contacted me and told me there was a young woman who was being discharged from the hospital to a rehab center the next day who looked very much like me, but had no idea who she was. They were calling her 'Jane Doe'."

Lance's scowl had deepened to a very fierce expression, but Derek kept on, "I went to see her the next day at the rehab center. I knew immediately she was Carolyn, but she didn't recognize me. Her face still had some puffiness and there was puffiness in what I could see of her arms, but what I noticed immediately were the dark bruises everywhere. I mean *everywhere!* Some of her hair had been shaved so that a three inch gash could be sutured and her left arm was in a large cast, starting well above her elbow, actually right below her shoulder." Derek pulled in a deep breath and continued, "When I asked what had happened to her the nurse told me she had been brutally beaten and dumped in the woods near Vansville. She was unconscious and remained so for four days. We are sure her assailant meant for her to die from her wounds and exposure. She was also bound and gagged when she was discovered. Only because a young man was sitting on his porch and saw the car race from the woods was she discovered."

"Wow!" Lance murmured.

Derek took a deep breath he was talking about his beloved Carolyn after all. "She spent four days in a coma in the hospital then was in excruciating pain when she finally woke up, but she never knew who she was or what had happened to her. She still has no recollection of her life before she woke up in the hospital. I have told her what I could up to her graduation night, but nothing has triggered her memory, except one day last week she saw a poster picture of a criminal and identified him as the man who had done the atrocity. She has seen a doctor periodically and even he is wondering how long her amnesia will last."

"Oh, my, God!" Lance said, breathlessly. "How… what…" he shook his head. "I can't wrap my mind around this!"

Derek nodded. "Since coming to my home, she has had a nightmare, obviously about what happened, but remembered nothing when she woke up. Last week she spent some time back in the hospital because she had a miscarriage. Since she identified that criminal, he has been apprehended in Atlanta and is facing murder and attempted murder charges there. Since she came to live with me another young woman was discovered with the exact same injuries but who wasn't as fortunate as Carolyn, thus the murder charges against the criminal. Since she remembers nothing, she pretty much stays at my home in the house. She has had misgivings about men in general, but is very charming. Will you come home with me to see her? Perhaps seeing you would open her mind."

"My wife and daughter are in the car, but yes, I'll come see her."

A smile spread across Derek's face. "Your wife and daughter?"

An answering smile came to Lance's mouth, but deep affection lit his eyes, as he nodded and said, "Yes, Linda and our daughter, Brenda."

"Oh, my! Oh, my!" Derek's hand touched Lance's arm and he said, "Please! Come home with me and spend the weekend. We have lots of room and I certainly need to get to know my daughter-in-law and granddaughter." Derek's eyes took on a far away look and he asked, "Wasn't it a girl named Linda you were going with when…?"

"Yes, that's who became my wife."

"Lance, it's truly wonderful to see you! Do you not hate me any more?"

"Dad, I've harbored hatred all these years. Linda will verify that quickly enough. I have been very reluctant to search for you because of my strong feelings." Hesitantly, he continued, "Just the other night I found you on the internet and determined to barge into your office and scathingly demand to know what you'd done with my sister, but when I entered the bank all of that melted away." He pulled in a deep breath and added, "And when I saw you, the only emotion I felt was love for my dad."

Derek's arms went around his son and Lance hugged his dad. "Oh, Son, you can't know how wonderful that sounds!"

For several quiet moments they hugged each other and tears soaked both men's shirts. Marlene came to the door to tell her boss that she'd locked up for the night and to wish him a happy holiday, but instead she stood silently in the doorway watching the reconciliation that had taken years to happen. Tears blurred her eyes she turned silently and pulled the door closed behind her. Derek had shared with her about his children being estranged from him. She had noticed that the young man resembled Derek when he'd stopped at her desk.

"*Oh, God, thank You!*" she murmured, as she grabbed her purse.

A few minutes after five, Derek led Lance out the back door. They passed his car, but went to the parking lot that now only had one car parked in a customer parking space. It was running and two people were sitting in it. Lance stepped ahead of his dad, but Derek eagerly followed his son to the car. Lance opened the door and smiled at his pretty wife.

"Sweetheart, meet my dad after so many years!"

Recognizing her immediately, Derek exclaimed, "Linda! Oh, my!" She jumped out and while they embraced, Lance opened the back door and unbuckled Brenda from her seat. Derek's eyes followed Lance's movements and saw the little girl get out. Taking one arm from Linda, he turned and grinned at the little girl. "You must be Brenda!"

Shyly, the little girl nodded. "Uh huh."

He voice so choked he finally was able to croak, "Oh! My heart can hardly take anything more! This is beyond spectacular!"

Derek kissed Linda's cheek, then bent down and put his arms around the little girl. His face was wreathed in a broad smile. He kissed the child on the cheek and said, "Brenda, I'm your grandpa! Your daddy said you can come to my house! Your auntie Carolyn is there. I know you'll be glad to see her."

"She is? Mommy and Daddy said we lost her."

Derek nodded. "Yes, she's there. She may not know you, but she's there."

Nodding enthusiastically, Brenda said, "Come on, Daddy! I wanna see Aunt Carolyn!"

"Okay, Sweetheart, your grandpa will lead us there."

Derek left for his car, the little family hurried to get in theirs and as Lance pulled behind his dad's car, Linda asked, incredulously, "What happened?"

Lance shook his head. "I don't know, but as I walked in the bank all that hatred just drained away! When I stood in his doorway all I could feel was love for Dad."

Linda placed her hand on Lance's leg, her face wreathed in a smile. "Oh, Honey, I'm so glad! You even look like a different man!"

"I feel different, too," he whispered. Lance had to swallow, but he added, "Dad gave me a bear hug the minute I walked in!"

"Oh, Lance, I'm *so* glad! So Carolyn is here?"

"Yes, she was abducted and left for dead. She was in a coma in the hospital for four days. When she woke up she had amnesia and still does. She remembers nothing before her attack. Dad said she was horribly abused!"

"Oh, my! No wonder she's been missing! I'm glad I thought to search for your dad."

"Yes, I am too, in more ways than one."

Carolyn sat on her chaise on the deck and watched Sam and Ernest work all day at putting the finishing touches on the pool. Sam had originally forgotten that Friday was the holiday, so the tanker driver was coming at three o'clock to fill the pool and the men had several last minute things they needed to do to be ready when he came.

It took quite a while to fill the pool. Sam made careful inspections at different levels as the man let the water run into the large hole. Carolyn still stayed on the deck, twenty feet away, but she sat up, her feet on the floor and watched carefully as the water worked its way up the sides until she could see it. When it reached the proper level a ways from the top, right below the overflow ledge, where Sam instructed the man to shut off the water, Carolyn couldn't help the grin that spread across her face.

After a few words, the man got back in his tanker and pulled out of the back yard. However, Sam and Ernest became like busy beavers, taking different things from the back of their truck to test the water and add other things to it. Finally, Carolyn heard the chime clock inside start its full chime for five o'clock when Ernest got in their truck and Sam walked toward the deck. Carolyn could only smile.

Sam also grinned. "Got 'er all done for the holiday, Ms Carolyn!"

Enthusiastically, she exclaimed, "Oh, I see that! It looks great and so inviting!"

"Should your dad be home soon?"

"I expect him any minute, yes."

"Great! I'll wait in the truck with Ernest."

"I'll tell him you want to see him!"

"Thanks."

More than a half hour later she heard the garage door go up so she put on her wrap and went inside. Mrs. Beecham was in the kitchen, but Carolyn heard her dad say, "Carolyn! Did they finish the pool today?"

"Yes, Dad, Sam's waiting in his truck, wanting to talk with you," she said, as she crossed the dining room toward the kitchen.

At that moment she saw a man who was not a stranger. She opened her arms a grin covered her face as she ran to her brother. "Lance! How did you find me?"

"I didn't. I found Dad on the internet." He couldn't contain his own happiness. He hugged his sister and swung her up off the floor. As he set her down, he asked skeptically, "So you remember me?"

Nodding enthusiastically, she said, "Your face opened the door!"

"Wow!"

"You found Dad on the internet?"

"Yes, over the last while I discovered that your phone didn't work, then I got Email's from your work and finally letters from your apartment manager and your work saying you no longer had a job and your rent was past due. When I found Dad on the internet I decided that was the only option I had to try to find you."

Tears came to her eyes, but before she could say anything, Brenda burst through the garage door with Linda on her heals. "Aunt Carolyn! Aunt Carolyn!"

Carolyn scooped the child up. "Brenda! I'm so glad to see you!"

"How come you be here?"

"Believe me, it's a long, complicated story. I'm not even sure I know all about it."

"Huh? How come?"

Carolyn gave the child a tiny smile. "I'll try to tell you some time."

Derek came back from talking to Sam, saw the family reunion and said, "Carolyn?"

Still holding Brenda, but her eyes shining, she spun around and said, "Dad! Lance walked through the door and that strong castle fell down! I remember!"

"Oh, Sweetheart, I'm so glad!"

Looking at Linda, whom she hadn't acknowledged, Carolyn said, "Hi, Linda, good to see you! Umm, Dad, could we call Ramon and Sandy maybe to come over?"

"Of course, my dear! I can smell Mrs. Beecham's roast in the oven, I'm sure there will be plenty for us all to have dinner together."

Tears leaked slowly down Carolyn's cheeks. "Oh, Dad, thank you; thank you for everything. You've been terrific all these weeks."

"My dear, I have been delighted to have you here!"

Derek made the call then came to the living room where the sister, her brother and his family had migrated. "Ramon's not home from the trail yet, but Sandy said she and Jon would come over. I'd better go move my car so she can park and come in." He grinned at his family. "Be back in a jiffy!"

As they heard the door close in the kitchen, Lance scowled and looked at his sister. "Why does he have to move his car?"

"Sandy's in a wheelchair."

His scowl deepened. "So?"

"It's better for the lift to be on the level. The driveway isn't level enough." Both Lance and Linda looked at each other and shook their heads.

They heard the garage door go up and an engine start. Only a few minutes later they heard another vehicle outside and soon there were other noises that Carolyn knew as the lift operating. Both Linda and Lance had totally perplexed expressions on their faces, but Brenda said, "Aunt Carolyn, what's that noise?"

"Honey, that's the lift in Sandy's van working so she can get to the ground and come in."

"Oh." Obviously, Carolyn's explanation didn't help any of the three to understand.

Sandy was barely inside the kitchen when she called, "Carolyn! You remembered?"

Beaming, Carolyn jumped up and headed for the kitchen. "Yes! Come meet my brother, sister-in-law and my niece!"

However, the minute he saw her, Jon squealed, "AnTEECar!"

The child's voice brought Brenda off her seat and she raced to Carolyn's side. "What?" She looked at the lady in the strange thing with wheels and the little boy on her lap. Still perplexed, Brenda said again, "What?"

Sandy, of course, was crossing the kitchen and had one arm out, so she and Carolyn hugged each other fiercely. Jon was between them on Sandy's lap and wouldn't be ignored. Carolyn, of course, had to let Jon kiss her, then give him a kiss, then he wanted down, since he saw the other child. The two children stared at each other silently, as children often do when they first meet, but the adults ignored them.

Only minutes later, Sandy and Carolyn appeared in the archway into the dining room. They could see into the huge living room where the others were. At the archway, Carolyn exclaimed, "Sandy! This is Brenda, my niece. That's Lance, my brother and Linda, his wife. Folks, meet a terrific friend and might as well say, sister, Sandy DeLord and her little boy, Jon."

At a loss for words, Lance stood up and came to Sandy. He held out his hand and Sandy took it. "I... I'm pleased to meet you," he said, hesitantly.

"And I you," Sandy said.

Lance discretely looked around and saw only an adult Sandy and a toddler, little boy. "Umm, you drive yourself?"

"Yes, I have my own handicapped van. I'm sure everyone is pleased that you arrived. You've been the trigger for Carolyn's amnesia."

"Yes, I'm honored in that capacity."

Derek moved up behind Sandy, put his hand on her shoulder, but before he could say anything, from beside Sandy's chair, Jon saw him and squealed, "Japa!"

Derek leaned over and scooped up the little boy who immediately gave him a slobbery kiss. Derek kissed Jon's cheek then the little boy wanted down. After he was on the floor he continued to inspect Brenda, who continued to watch the little boy. Derek said, "By the looks on your faces I think I need to explain."

Lance nodded, but went back to sit by his wife. "Yeah, we are really in the dark, Dad. This is definitely a strange development."

"My second wife, Millie, had a son, Ramon. Millie ran off several weeks ago and left no forwarding address, so I have no idea where she is. However, she left without telling her son, daughter-in-law or grandson where she went either. Since all three of them have become a treasure to me, I've adopted them all, so as you heard, I'm Japa."

While Derek took a breath, Sandy smiled at Carolyn's family and said, "My husband Ramon and I run a hiking service here in Vansville. Since it's the holiday weekend, he and all our guides are busy leading hikes in the foothills around the area. He and Eric will be back with their hikers on Saturday."

Before anyone else could speak, Derek said, "And you will persuade both of them to come have steak on the grill that evening, won't you?"

Sandy grinned up at the man beside her. "If you insist, Dad. I'll be sure to pass that command along as soon as they hit the parking lot."

"Good! I think Mrs. Beecham has dinner ready. Let's gather around the table and enjoy her good meal. Lance and his family will be staying the weekend. They'll probably have to leave sometime on Sunday, so we'll do our steak dinner on Saturday instead. Mrs. Beecham will have the next three days off, anyway. She's going on a short vacation herself."

Everyone gathered around the table, the smells drew them quickly. It was a rowdy meal with everyone catching up on the events of the last few months. Finally, when everyone finished the delicious dinner, Sandy was quick to say, "Well, Dad, you tell Mrs. Beecham that she fixed a delicious meal! Even Jon has cleaned his plate."

Derek smiled, he was too happy to remember all the wasted years. "My dear Sandy, I'll be sure to pass that on to her. It will make her happy."

As they sat around the table, Derek looked at Carolyn and asked, "By the way, my dear, what is it you do?"

"Dad, the job I had was head physical therapist at the Med Center in Atlanta. I had just started there, in fact, I only worked a week. The board had just opened an aquatic section in the physical therapy department and I was head of it."

"Oh, my! Will it be waiting for you?"

"No, Dad, I received a letter just the other day saying she has been replaced."

"Oh, Carolyn, I'm sorry! You had your heart set on that, didn't you?"

"Yes, Dad, I did, but I'm not as disappointed as I could have been. I've found you that's way better, believe me!"

Tears came to Derek's eyes. His voice nearly choked in his throat, he murmured, "Oh, Carolyn, thank you for saying that."

"I meant every word, Dad."

After an enjoyable evening of getting to know everything about each other, Sandy took Jon home and Linda put Brenda to bed in a lovely room upstairs. They had visited until well after dark. Friday was the holiday and Derek was glad the pool was finished so his family could relax and enjoy some time together with him. After everyone was behind bedroom doors, he spent some time in his room having a praise session with his Lord. His only regret was that Carolyn would probably leave him, since she now knew where she had worked and what her job had been. However, he had had some wonderful time with her.

Mrs. Beecham always made way too many pastries each morning, so the extras were stored in freezer bags in the freezer. After Carolyn thawed some and made coffee in the morning, the family sat around the kitchen table and Carolyn said, "Dad, I was sorry to hear that Lance got a letter telling him I lost the job, but of course I understand. They were more than generous holding it for so long, but not hearing from me put them in a bind, I know. I think I'd better leave with Lance and Linda and go back to Atlanta to see what I need to do."

Derek couldn't help the catch in his voice, as he said, "Sweetheart, I'm sorry about the job. It sounds like it was a great job. However, I was sure that's what you'd decide to do. Remember, however, you will always have a place in my heart and a room in my home whenever you want it."

A tear trickled down her cheek as Carolyn whispered, "Thanks, Dad. But Dad, I'm not as disappointed as I might have been because I've found you and that's way better."

Derek couldn't keep his eyes from misting over. "Oh, Carolyn, thank you; thank you! That does my heart good."

Derek also looked at his handsome son. "The same goes for you, Son and your family. You have always had a place in my heart that only a son can fill, but there will also be a room in my home whenever you can get away to visit."

"Thanks, Dad. That's terrific!" He chuckled and looked out the big patio doors toward the back yard. "That pool out there will be a great incentive to come."

Derek also chuckled. "Great! I'll look forward to that."

"Lance has paid the rent for this month on the apartment I rented, so I must go back to decide what to do about that. I furnished it with things from our home."

Derek left his chair and came to Carolyn. When she knew his intent, she scooted back from the table and they hugged. Still keeping her in his arms, he said, "My darling daughter, I would like nothing better than for you to come back here to live. Surely we could be creative. Of course, we couldn't build a med center in Blairsville to rival the one in Atlanta, but something could turn up." He shrugged. "And the furniture…"

"That's really super of you, Dad, but I do need to go back, at least to find out what I can. My apartment is furnished with my things, I won't leave them there!"

His eyes twinkling, Derek asked, "What about Eric?"

Carolyn's face instantly turned red and felt like it was on fire. "Dad! You're being mischievous! What about him?"

Lance saw the color blossom in Carolyn's cheeks and immediately his guard went up. Eric… what about Eric? What was he, who was he? Had some man taken advantage of his sister while she was in such a state? He looked from her to his dad. That dreadful scowl appeared on his face again. "Dad?"

Her face still flaming, Carolyn looked away from her dad and said, "Dad's only teasing, Lance. Eric is one of Ramon's hiking guides. He had just come home for a day off and was on his porch when he saw a car race out of the woods. He went to investigate and found me in the woods when the man left me to die. We've spent some time together, but really, we haven't started any kind of relationship, since I had amnesia and he's so busy with leading hikes this time of year." *Liar, liar…*

"He's a hiking guide?" Lance couldn't help the skepticism in his voice. If all the man was was a hiking guide… he didn't finish the thought.

Derek answered, "Yes, for now. Before he came here he was a Marine and did some crucial work in Afghanistan, but starting next month he'll be a deputy sheriff for the county. By the way, remember, he's coming for our steak dinner tomorrow."

The red in Carolyn's face didn't fade before she said, "Dad, you are no help!"

Derek chuckled. "I'm not sure I meant to be, Sweetheart."

Sometime after breakfast cleanup the family went out to the deck to enjoy the beautiful weather the holiday supplied for them. Of course, Carolyn dove into the pool and showed her family just how much of a mermaid she was. Derek also swam, but of course, Lance and Linda hadn't planned to do any swimming in their search for Carolyn, but they enjoyed the day relaxing and Linda let Brenda use some play clothes so that Carolyn could teach the child to swim. They had a terrific day!

At dinner time, Carolyn and Linda dug into Mrs. Beecham's supplies and fixed a meal fit for a king. Knowing that Sandy would also add her kitchen expertise on Saturday, Derek had no worries that another delicious feast would be their fare the next day. The only thing that clouded his day was to know that Carolyn would be leaving him on Sunday. His big house would be a vast wasteland with just himself and Mrs. Beecham, since that lady kept to herself whenever she wasn't working in Derek's house.

Saturday at two o'clock, two groups of hikers straggled onto DeLord's parking lot. Ramon's group had come by way of the high plateau and the cold pool. Eric's group had only been out since Wednesday and couldn't use that trail. However, they'd all had a great time and neither group had encountered any wild animals. After all the hikers' cars had left the parking lot, both guides and Jerry walked toward the office where Sandy and Jon waited for them.

"So. We're back at the same time," Ramon said. "You haven't met our guide-in-training, Jerry Monahan, have you, Eric?"

Eric grinned and held out his hand to shake Jerry's. "No, but it's good to meet you, Jerry. Eric Thomas. So you'll be taking over my spot."

"Oh, really? Are you leaving?"

"Well, not leaving the area, but I've been approached by the sheriff who's employed me to become a deputy in the Vansville area, come August first."

"Wow! Sounds sort of prestigious!"

"Well, I hope I can do the job he's expecting of me," Eric answered modestly.

"Jerry, I guess you can get on home for the rest of the weekend. You need to be here at seven again, you'll be going out with Eric on Monday."

"Thanks, Ramon. I'll see you then, Eric."

"Yes, have a good weekend, Jerry."

"Don't forget it's breakfast at seven," Ramon called after him.

"Oh, I wouldn't miss Sandy's great breakfast!"

Jerry headed for his car, but Ramon and Eric turned toward the office. "So, you'll come in for your next assignment, man?"

"Yup, looks that way. You'll get to spend time with your wife and son. I'll go to my cabin and splurge on a TV dinner."

"Ah, surely you have somewhere to go for the holiday?"

"Nope. My brother should be there today sometime. I know there'll be some catching up with him. Of course, there're services on Sunday."

Sandy was in the office holding out some papers in Eric's direction when the two men walked in. Before either of them said anything, Sandy said, "Eric, here's your next hike going out on Monday. It's one of our regular youth groups we've had for several years. However, I had this all ready so we wouldn't waste time. We're all supposed to be at Derek's house within minutes. Ramon's going in to take his shower, you're to go take your shower and be ready so we can get you on our way there right away."

"Oh, really?" both men said together.

"Absolutely! I was given strict instructions with no other options, so hop to it!"

Eric snapped his boot heels together, stood to his impressive military height, gave Sandy a Marine salute and exclaimed, "Yes, Ma'am!"

Since no one in her family or Ramon had been in the military, Sandy wasn't expecting what Eric did, but she cleared her throat and said, "Since we must go by Isabel's to get to Derek's, we'll stop by for you. Will twenty minutes be long enough?"

"Sure, that's fine." He took the papers and left on the run for his cabin.

Matt sat on Eric's porch when he wheeled into his parking spot moments later. Glad to see his twin, he slammed his car door and raced for his cabin. "Bro! So good to see you! You arrived safe and sound, I see."

When Eric reached his porch, the brothers embraced. "Yep! As of now, I'm to get all my earthly possessions into cabin three. So what's on?"

"I'm to be showered and dressed for an evening with Ramon and Sandy at Derek Casbah's place as soon as I can be ready."

"I won't hold you up, then. I'm ready for some R & R after a hectic week. Trying to remember all the things I had to do and make sure I got it all done before life as we know it stopped for the holiday is exhausting. Say 'hi' to them all for me, would you?"

"Sure! Not a problem."

The brothers split, Matt went to his cabin and Eric hurried inside his. He only had time to shower, shave, start his washer and dress before he heard a vehicle on Isabel's parking lot and knew it was the DeLord's coming for him. He grabbed up his keys, not that he would lock his door, but just because of habit, he shoved the small handful in his pocket and ran out the door. The lift was just settling on the gravel when Eric stopped beside the van. He quickly stepped on the lift and worked the control in the handle beside him.

Ramon was in the driver's seat, as Eric pressed the buttons to close the lift and the big door. Of course, his only option to sit was the bench seat where Jon sat in his car seat. After they were underway, Sandy said, "I forgot to tell you when you were at the house that Carolyn's memory came back on Thursday. Her brother showed up and he was the trigger."

"Oh, wow!"

Giving the young man a grin, Sandy said, "Eric, you must work fast! Carolyn intends to go back to Atlanta. Her brother's taking her on Sunday, but she really needs an incentive to come back. You… um, can't live… oh, I mean, Derek can't live in that big house without her!"

With Eric sitting beside him, Jon wouldn't be ignored, so he said, "Ick!"

Torn between paying attention to Jon and answering Sandy, Eric said, absently, "Hi, Jon, how's it going? Sandy, will you give me a break! I'm in shock."

From his car seat, Jon whacked Eric's leg and exclaimed, "Ick!"

Eric grinned at the little boy and said, "How's my friend, Jon?"

The toddler nodded. "Ja good, Ick good?"

"Sure am. Got a kiss?"

"Uh huh."

Eric only had a few minutes to process Sandy's words. Moments after leaving Isabel's parking lot, Ramon pulled up on Derek's driveway. The garage door was up and there was an empty space inside. Of course, Ramon knew to pull into it they had done this several times during the summer since Millie had left. It was an oversized garage with plenty of room for Sandy's lift to go down.

Eric saw the unknown car and asked, "So her brother's still here?"

"Yes, he brought his family. He found his dad on the internet, but it was a long shot. He didn't know how else to find Carolyn. He had no clues about her. All he knew was that she was somehow missing, since he couldn't reach her on her cell phone and he got Emails and letters saying her rent was past due and she hadn't shown up for work."

Sandy unlocked her chair and turned around, but Eric was releasing Jon from his car seat. The little boy was happy enough to let Eric pick him up and take him off the van. He loved his mama and dada, but 'Ick' was a special buddy. Even before they reached the opening, while they waited for the lift to come back for them, he gave Eric a slobbery kiss.

Before Eric gave the child a kiss, Jon rubbed his tiny hand over the place he'd kissed on Eric's cheek and said, "Wuv Ick!"

Eric chuckled and kissed the little boy. "I love you, too, Jon."

Inside, in the kitchen, Linda and Carolyn were busy fixing the meal, but that made no difference with Jon. Instantly, he wanted out of Eric's arms, as he held out his arms toward Carolyn and called, "AnTEECar!"

Carolyn moved toward the little boy, but also was very aware of the silent Eric holding him. Their eyes met over the child's head. The man was devastatingly handsome. She could see he'd recently shaved and smelled like some masculine aftershave, of course, he'd only just returned from a hike. His hair had grown a bit, which allowed the soft curls to show in his sandy hair. He was several inches taller than she was, but very much in shape. She knew he wasn't trying to draw attention to himself, but his clothes fit him well. She couldn't look away from his arresting blue eyes, but it seemed he couldn't look away from her either. Carolyn couldn't help the tiny gasp that was loud enough for Eric to hear, since he was so close.

To cover her discomfort, she took Jon and said, "Hi, Jon!"

"Wuv AnTEECar!" he said and gave her his slobbery kiss. She kissed him, but he said, "Down, AnTEECar!" When Jon was on the floor, he left intent on finding Brenda. "Bena," he called. "Bena?" The sound faded as he toddled off.

However, that left Carolyn facing Eric. For those brief minutes, he'd watched the beautiful woman. She was a lovely creature, personifying everything beautiful about a woman. He swallowed as she stood back up and whispered, "You remembered?"

"Yes, my brother, Lance opened the door when I saw him. My memory came back, all except what that man did to me."

Eric raised his hands and tentatively put them on her arms, but his eyes told the true story about his feelings for the beautiful woman. "I hope that part never comes, Carolyn. Let's let God keep that in His bank," he said for her ears alone.

Carolyn nodded. "I'll be glad to do that."

At that very moment, even though there were two other women in the room, one Eric didn't even know, he wanted very much to pull the woman he was holding with his hands into his arms and kiss her. In fact, he looked down at her lips, they looked moist and very kissable, but he hadn't kissed her before, with an audience, he shouldn't now. Even so, he felt the object inside his chest was tearing in two.

Carolyn couldn't take her eyes off Eric. The man was everything she could imagine a man could be. After several heartbeats, she cleared her throat and said, "Oh, you must come see! The pool is finished, come out and see!" She quickly stepped out of his arms, but took his hand and took a step toward the dining room.

Trying to get his mind wrapped around the drastic change in subject, Eric cleared his throat and said, "Sure! Sam finished it before the holiday?"

"Yes, Thursday afternoon and we swam in it yesterday, it's perfect!" Before they left the kitchen, Carolyn giggled behind her hand. "Oh, I forgot, Eric, that's my sister-in-law, Linda Casbah. Linda, the man who found me in the woods, Eric Thomas."

"It's good to meet you, Mrs. Casbah. Welcome."

"Thanks, thanks for finding Carolyn! Dad's told us that criminal did the same thing to another woman, but she died."

Eric nodded. "The Lord had me in the right place at the right time."

Carolyn still held Eric's hand as they made their way through the dining room. On the way to the patio door, she introduced Eric to her brother and pointed out her niece who was busy playing with Jon. They made a cute pair on the living room floor. However, Carolyn only slowed down momentarily she pulled open the sliding door and took Eric out onto the deck, then across the deck and down the steps to the patio below.

When Eric knew they were alone and no one could see them, he said, "Carolyn, you have always been lovely, but now with your memory back, you seem to have an inner glow."

"Eric, I have my family; I have my memory; I even remember that I'm a Christian!"

"Ah, Carolyn, how wonderful!"

A tear glistened in her eye, as she said, "The only bad thing about it all is, I must go back to Atlanta when Lance and Linda leave tomorrow. I know I don't have a job or even any prospects, but Atlanta has more opportunities I'm sure. I really would love to stay here, now that I've found Dad, but what is there in Vansville?"

"There isn't anything that I know of, but God has a plan." Eric took a deep breath, turned Carolyn to face him and whispered, "Carolyn, may I kiss you? Would you think I'm being too... ah, forward?"

Looking at the handsome ex-marine, Carolyn gazed into his eyes then her eyes dropped to his lips. He realized she was looking at his lips just as he wet them with the tip of his tongue. "Yes, Eric," she whispered, "I'd like one of your kisses." Of course, Eric wasted no time accepting her invitation. His arms circled the lady before him and drew her close. He lowered his head and placed his lips on her, intending to give her a chaste kiss. However, several minutes later when they finally came up for air, they both knew that fire had passed between them.

Monday morning, Eric wasn't quite as enthusiastic about the hike he was to lead as he left DeLord's parking lot at eight o'clock with his next group of hikers. He would be back on Saturday they were another youth group that wanted to be home for church on Sunday. This never made Eric upset, he could go to church anytime he was home on Sunday. He had even gotten his twin to reluctantly go with him yesterday. He didn't do much of a job of persuasion, but at least he was someone to take Carolyn's place beside him. He missed the beautiful young woman immensely. He hoped and prayed she could come back. At this point in time that seemed to be an impossible happening, but God was in control – all the time!

Lance and his family had taken Carolyn to Atlanta. They'd left Sunday morning right after breakfast, as Lance had to be back to work on Monday. After just finding her, all of them were reluctant to leave her, but Carolyn had lots to do in Atlanta. She really had no idea what to expect once she arrived, other than to know her apartment waited for her.

She must see her former boss at the Med Center and explain what had happened, but she had no idea what would be waiting for her, if anything. Several things she knew for sure, she had many cards to replace, including a driver's license and a bank account card, a new cell phone to acquire and a car to buy. Derek had given her easy access to his account so that those things which cost money she could buy. She had a little savings, because most of her extra money had been used in her recent move. She only had one week's pay coming.

After a mug of Mrs. Beecham's good coffee and two Danish which he didn't taste, a solemn Derek arrived at the bank at his usual time on Monday morning. He sat at his desk and gave Marlene a ghost of a smile when she brought him his usual mug of coffee. "Mr. Casbah," she asked, "who was the young man who came just before quitting time on Thursday? Was that your son, by chance?"

"Yes, that was my son, Lance. We had been estranged for a dozen years. Not knowing what else to do, he'd found me on the internet and came to see if I knew where Carolyn was. He was the trigger, Carolyn knew him. Everything before her ordeal clicked in when she saw him." He breathed in a long sigh. On the exhale, he said, "She returned to Atlanta with him yesterday."

"Oh, my! So you're alone at home now?"

"Yes, only Mrs. Beecham is there," he said, dejectedly. "Except that she needs a home and a job, I'd gladly let her go and move from that huge place. Certainly without Carolyn that place holds no appeal."

Looking down at the newspaper in her hand, she said, "The paper came early today, so here it is, Mr. Casbah."

"Thanks, Marlene." Again he gave her only a raising of one side of his mouth, as he held out his hand for the paper. "I'll read the headlines maybe they'll boost my spirits."

"Yes, we can hope, Derek."

Instead of the Atlanta paper, this was the Blairsville Gazette, but the top headline caught Derek's eye immediately:

## HEAD OF HOSPITAL PHYSICAL THERAPY DEPARTMENT FOUND DEAD IN HIS HOME. BELIEVED TO BE FROM A MASSIVE HEART ATTACK SUFFERED SOMETIME ON SATURDAY

Derek read the entire article, then lifted the receiver and dialed a local number. When a woman answered, he said, "Is anyone in the physical therapy department this morning?"

"Ah, no, not this morning, I'm afraid, given the circumstances, but I could put you through to the hospital administrator, sir. Who could I tell is calling, please?"

"This is Derek Casbah."

Derek had been the president of the bank for a decade, so his name was well known around town, so she said, "I'll put you through immediately, Mr. Casbah."

When a man answered, Derek said, "Mr. Hartmann, Derek Casbah. I'm sorry for your loss. I read about it in this morning's paper."

Derek heard the man clear his throat before he said, "Thank you, Mr. Casbah. He'll be a hard man to replace, believe me."

"I'm not for sure, but there's a possibility I could help you out with another physical therapist, if you're interested."

Again the man cleared his throat and drew in a long breath. "Well, we usually hire within, but let me hear what you have to say."

Anxious to get his request on the table, Derek didn't hesitate. "Perhaps you recall the Jane Doe that was there in the hospital for a week back in May?"

"She was the young woman who had been beaten and left for dead?"

"Yes, that's right. It turned out she is my daughter, Carolyn Casbah. Her memory came back on Thursday when she saw her brother, but not before she lost a job as head physical therapist at the Atlanta Medical Center."

"Oh, my! Do you know, I had heard of her! She's into aquatic therapy, isn't she?"

"Yes, her double major in college was swimming and physical therapy."

"Mr. Casbah, if she could be persuaded… I know we are a much smaller entity than the med center in Atlanta… but I'd be more than delighted to employ her! That is, if she is at all interested. I'm sure I couldn't pay her near what she was getting there or what she's worth. But…" he chuckled a bit, "… she sure would be a feather in our cap!"

"Mr. Hartmann, at the moment I have no way of reaching her, but she promised me that as soon as she acquires a new cell phone she will contact me with the number and I'll give her your message. That's the best I can do."

"Fair enough! Be sure to pass on my desire with much enthusiasm!"

Derek chuckled, the first since Carolyn left. "I'll be sure to do that, Mr. Hartmann."

With much more enthusiasm, Mr. Hartmann said, "Thank you, thank you!"

It was nearly three o'clock when Derek's phone rang on his desk. When he answered, a dear voice said, "Dad, I've seen the head of the department at the med center. I went to see him first thing this morning. He's sorry, but all his positions are taken now. I've been to the license branch and they'll order me a new license. Of course, I went to the phone company and they've replaced my phone and reworked my account, since my phone was destroyed in May, well, probably April. I guess tomorrow I'll see about buying a car."

"After that what'll you do, my dear?"

"I don't know. Why should I stay here if there's no position at the med center? But if I didn't, what would I do with four rooms of furniture?"

Derek tried to mask his excitement, as he said, "There was a headline in today's hometown paper about the head of the physical therapy department at the local hospital. He died on Saturday from a massive heart attack. Umm, I called the hospital to give my condolences, but I also told the hospital administrator about you. Carolyn, he's heard about you! Your expertise has given you a name! He said he'd be glad to offer you the position of head of his physical therapy department. He wanted me to pass that word along with much enthusiasm."

A smile on her face and in her voice, she said, "Dad! Give me his number and I'll give him a call tomorrow. That sounds great!"

There was a catch in Derek's voice as he exclaimed, "Oh, Carolyn, it sounds out of this world to me! You can't imagine how silent and massive that house is without you! I felt like Mrs. Beecham and I were just rattling around there yesterday. Don't worry about your furniture! We can store it or give it away or… something! But Sweetheart, I miss you so much!"

"I miss you, too, Dad." She giggled. "And my pool…! Thanks for finding that out and I'll call first thing in the morning."

"That, my dear, is music to my ears!"

"And Dad, I have a feeling I'll be home this weekend!"

On August first Carolyn Casbah left Derek's house to start her new position as head of the Physical Therapy Department of Blairsville Hospital. She was extremely excited to fill the position. Mr. Hartmann had been most excited to hire Carolyn to fill the spot his former head had left so suddenly. He hadn't even consulted anyone in the department about filling the position, but everyone in the department was excited with his choice and they were all looking forward to Carolyn's coming.

Also on that same day, Eric Thomas put on a brand new deputy sheriff's uniform and much to Isabel's surprise, because he'd found another place for the brand new sheriff's car that was now finding its home in Vansville, walked away from his cabin. Of course, during the day, most days the new deputy was expected to make his presence felt throughout the rural acres and the country roads of the county so Isabel wouldn't have to see the car except during the evening. Eric had chuckled several times since she'd let him know how she felt about that car.

At five minutes after five that afternoon, Carolyn pulled the door to the physical therapy department closed. She had seen all of her staff leave for the day and she was pleased with how things had gone. Glad for the day to be over, she headed for her car. She'd looked outside several times during the day to see that the sun was bright it was a typical summer day. At noon when she'd looked out, the sun had made the parking lot shimmer, so she knew it was a very warm day. She was looking forward to a good dip in the swimming pool.

She was anticipating just that as she drove the highway toward Vansville. She slowed to make the turn onto the country road that led to Derek's house, but realized a car nearly blocked the turnoff. Cars could leave the country road, but they had to make a very awkward turn to get around the car from the highway. She scowled, but as she came closer, she realized it was a white sheriff's car. That turned her scowl into a smile. With a grin on her face, she determined to make that turn around the car and pay it no attention, unless, of course, someone in that car would stop her for some reason. In her brand new car she knew exactly where her new license and registration were, of course.

As her car approached, the sheriff's car door opened and a very handsome deputy stepped out. He looked absolutely breathtaking in his new deputy uniform. His sheriff's hat was even in proper position. Just seeing him, Carolyn heart went into over drive. She rolled down her window and tried to scowl, as if she had no idea why the deputy would be stopping her. "Deputy?" she asked, "Is something wrong?"

The deputy approached to her car without a smile. "Ma'am, I need you to leave your car, but bring your license and registration with you."

"Leave my car? Is that a new requirement?"

Still with a straight face, Eric replied, "Yes, Ma'am!"

Going along with his request, Carolyn reached for her purse and with hands that trembled just a bit pulled her license from her wallet. Without looking back at the deputy, she reached in her glove box for her registration. However, when she opened her door to step out, the young man was on one knee on the road. Instead of taking her two cards, he took her hand and said, as he looked into her eyes, "Miss Carolyn Casbah, would you do me the honor of being my bride? Would you consent to marry me?"

Giving him the widest grin of her life, she exclaimed, "Oh, yes, yes! Deputy Thomas, I'd be happy to be your wife sooner rather than later!"

He stood, but kept her hand and drew her to his chest. After a kiss, he murmured, "Oh, Carolyn, you honor me. I love you so very much."

"I love you, Eric, more than my life!"

Another car came toward the intersection, but when the driver realized what was happening, he pulled behind Carolyn's car and slammed on his brakes so hard the car stalled. Oblivious to that, a grin split his face, as he exited his car. "Is this what I think it is? Has Eric asked you to marry him, Carolyn?"

"Yes, Dad!" she exclaimed. "Yes, just this minute and of course, I said yes!"

"Ah, good! We'll remodel that mansion and eventually get it filled up. Soon?"

"Yes, Dad, soon."

Derek grinned, pulled both Eric and Carolyn in to a group hug and said, "This has been a time to remember."

Both Eric and Carolyn put an arm around the man and Carolyn said, "Yes, Dad it has. God has done awesome things!"

www.ingramcontent.com/pod-product-compliance
Lightning Source LLC
Chambersburg PA
CBHW021439070526
44577CB00002B/216